HUNGARIAN STUDENTS IN EXILE

HUNGARIAN STUDENTS IN EXILE

Jews, Leftists, and Women, 1920–1938

ÁGNES KATALIN KELEMEN

INDIANA UNIVERSITY PRESS

This book is a publication of

Indiana University Press
Herman B Wells Library
1320 East 10th Street
Bloomington, Indiana 47405 USA

http://iupress.org

Parts of chapter 3 were originally published as Ágnes Katalin Kelemen, "Next Year in Brno?: Brno's Significance for Hungarian Jews in the Age of the Numerus Clausus and Beyond," in *Quotas: The "Jewish Question" and Higher Education in Central Europe, 1880–1945*, ed. Michael L. Miller and Judith Szapor (New York and Oxford: Berghahn, 2024), 359–384.

For customers in the European Union with safety or GPSR concerns, please contact Mare Nostrum Group B.V., Doelen 72, 4831 GR Breda, The Netherlands. Email: gpsr@mare-nostrum.co.uk

First printing 2026

Cataloging information is available from the Library of Congress.
ISBN 978-0-253-07661-8 (hdbk.)
ISBN 978-0-253-07662-5 (pbk.)
ISBN 978-0-253-07663-2 (ebook)

In loving memory of my grandfather Zoltán Bárdos

CONTENTS

ACKNOWLEDGMENTS

AS I SAT DOWN TO write the acknowledgments to formally express my gratitude to those who made it possible for me to write this book, I thought it was among the harder parts to write. I was anxious that I would unintentionally omit someone and then regret it. (In fact, I still am worried I may have done this.) However, I realized that it is the most rewarding part of writing. While I thought through the genesis of this book and how much I was helped and supported in this process, countless warm memories arose, although sorrowful ones did as well because some people involved in my journey passed away during these years: my father, János (Jimmy) Kelemen; Mária M. Kovács and Robin Bellers; and two of my interviewees, Tamás Zoltán and Ivan Ivanji. In addition, my alma mater, the Central European University, was pushed out of Budapest and relocated to Vienna, a trajectory similar to that of many of the subjects in the story I tell.

I wish to start by thanking many descendants of numerus clausus exiles who trusted me enough to share sensitive family stories, photos, and documents. This kind of guidance for research is the hardest to give since it involves recalling traumatic events. First, Anna Maria Habermann inspired me to dive into the story of Hungarian Jews who studied in Fascist Italy and write my master's thesis about them. As I expanded the scope as well as the depth of my research during my doctoral studies, I received invaluable help from János Almai, Esther Bánki, Ivan Ivanji, Ádám Kis, Alan Mandl, and Ines Fenyves Sadalla. I thank Péter Merényi Lengyel for sharing the photographs taken by his father, Endre Merényi, in Brno in the early 1930s. I likewise appreciate the support of László Elek, Éva Forintos,Esther Bánki, Alan Mandl, and András Meller, in providing photographs for the book.

During my PhD studies, I was still afraid to get involved with the history of Communists, especially Communists of Jewish origin. Nevertheless, András Kovács sparked my interest in the Brno group, and I am grateful for that. I dove into their story during the interwar period and beyond only after my doctoral studies. I will never forget the openness with which numerous Brno children—Emma Cole, László Elek, Éva Karádi, György Seres, György Spiró, Annamária Szőke, András Talyigás, Katalin Talyigás, and Tamás Zoltán—talked to me about their parents' relationship with Communism and Jewishness. In addition to enriching my research, interviewing them triggered me to reflect on the parent-child relationship, which is likely to influence my relationship with my own children for decades to come.

I am fortunate to have had Victor Karády, Mária M. Kovács, and Michael L. Miller as supervisors during my master's and PhD studies; they not only supported my professional development as a historian but also engaged in great conversations about life with me. I could not have wished for better academic writing mentors than Robin Bellers and Eszter Timár. Martina Steer helped me grow up from academic childhood. Regina Fritz was tireless in commenting on my dissertation so that I could later base my present monograph on it. Judith Szapor offered invaluable support in developing the content as well as the style of my publications and in navigating the North American academic world.

Michael Brenner and David Rechter made comments that led to "lightbulb moments" as I was writing my dissertation. I am grateful for the Central European University's full doctoral fellowship and to the German Studienstiftung, through the Leo Baeck Fellowship, for making my archival research trips to Berlin, Bologna, Prague, and Vienna possible. This program also made me part of a cohort where I received valuable insights and feedback from fellow graduate students and mentors. I am equally grateful to the Leonid Nevzlin Research Center for Russian and East European Jewry for supporting the International Forum of Young Scholars on East European Jewry, of which I was part. The forum enabled me to present and discuss my research with yet another cohort of fellow PhD students, who offered insight from new perspectives, and also with Israeli historians whose works I had read but with whom I never thought I would one day speak in person.

As a postdoctoral research fellow, I was part of a wonderful team at the Masaryk Institute and Archives of the Czech Academy of Sciences working on the European Research Council Consolidator project "Unlikely Refuge? Refugees and Citizens in East-Central Europe in the 20th Century." Our principal investigator, Michal Frankl, and my colleagues Doina Anca Cretu, Maximilian

Graf, Karla Koutková, Julia Reinke, Francesca Rolandi, Nikola Tohma, and Lidia Zessin-Jurek were always willing to discuss my draft articles and book chapters. Their feedback was indispensable for an earlier version of this book's third chapter. Being part of this project also gave me occasion to learn Czech and travel to Brno several times to research the documents of this city's former Deutsche Technische Hochschule (German Technical College). In addition, I greatly appreciate the detailed commentary on my book proposal by Laura Almagor and on my book's structure by Alexandra Kardos and Tetiana Zemliakova. I am equally thankful to my current academic community, Budapest's Jewish Theological Seminary where I receive ardent support from Professors Szonja Komoróczy, Gábor Balázs, and András Zima.

As an undergraduate student of history, I was told by a professor, half jokingly, that archivists' main aim is to keep sources away from historians. My own experience was usually the opposite. This book benefited from the work of helpful archivists who got excited about my topic and wanted me to make the most of their institutions' collections, especially Paulus Ebner at the Viennese Technical University's archives.

I thank the editorial and production teams at Indiana University Press for bringing this book to publication, particularly Julia Turner and Maria Rita for their patience and conscientious and meticulous work on my manuscript. The multiplicity of those who helped me along the way notwithstanding, the ultimate responsibility for this work, and any shortcomings, rests solely with me.

I want to emphatically thank my parents, Judit Bárdos and the late Jimmy Kelemen, for always supporting my studies and academic endeavors morally and financially. I wish my father was alive and could see the publication of this book. I am likewise immensely grateful to my husband, Tibor Kiszely, for taking care of our children—Máté and Róza—in my absence so that I could focus on writing the book. In addition, he keeps reassuring me that I am not failing as a mother for taking some time to focus only on research and writing.

I dedicate this book to the memory of my grandfather Zoltán Bárdos, who dreamed about studying English and German literature at a faculty of humanities. However, he was Jewish and graduated from high school in Budapest in 1942. He was fortunate enough to survive the Shoah and to study at a university later, but then he opted for a field deemed more practical. His story always reminds me of what a privilege it is to study, especially at the university of one's choice.

HUNGARIAN STUDENTS IN EXILE

INTRODUCTION

LILI FENYŐ, ONE OF THOUSANDS of Hungarian Jews who studied abroad in the interwar period, noted of her and her classmates' professional outlooks, "Sad and great is our destiny. Yet it is fascinating. . . . We cannot just pass the exams, we cannot *only* become doctors, engineers, teachers—we have to become the best doctor, the best engineer, the best teacher. . . . We must prove that the sacrifices were not in vain."[1] Fenyő's ambition to study at university was frustrated in Hungary by the restrictive Jewish quota established by the infamous numerus clausus law of 1920,[2] yet she did not give up her aspirations; instead, she moved to Italy and graduated in Florence. Her choice of emigration for the sake of her studies was not unique but rather typical for Hungarian Jewish youth during the time. Those migrant students who were pushed out of Hungarian higher education by antisemitism in the interwar period are often called "exiles" or "refugees of the numerus clausus."

This book tells the story of students' emigration from interwar Hungary; it is both a chapter of Jewish history and a narrative of how political dissenters and women were marginalized through exclusion from higher learning. It contributes to scholarly literature on discrimination, social exclusion, and intersectionality, approaching these themes from the history of universities. The university as an institution is necessarily a combat zone between social groups because it provides not only knowledge but also a certificate that one possesses knowledge, thereby enabling its graduates to be(come) members of the elite. Consequently, it really matters who is allowed to study at a university, regardless of the portion of society that has the prerequisites for higher education in any given temporal and spatial context. To demonstrate that conflicts over whom to include (and exclude) in higher education is an inherent part of this history, I have embedded case studies of overlapping types of exiles—Jews, leftists, women—of interwar Hungarian academia within a concise history of European universities. This history is examined through the changing reasons and manifestations of academic migration (peregrination) and exclusion of subaltern groups, respectively.

Although studying abroad is much more common now, the protagonists in the following story of student migration studied at foreign universities against all odds. The 1920s was a decade of anxiety over university graduates' "overproduction" and unemployment; many Hungarian students and policymakers were eager to reserve the universities and the diminished labor market for the sons of the "Christian middle class." Therefore, the numerus clausus law was implemented to push out Jews and Communists, and quotas were set up to restrict women's access to universities. Pressure from the Christian middle class, among other factors, compelled the political elite to put these policies on the agenda. Following the historian Béla Bodó, we can see the numerus clausus law as an achievement of bottom-up initiative by the radical rightist student movement rather than of senior politicians.[3] Thus, even if Jews made it to university, they faced hostility and violence from fellow students. Meanwhile, studying abroad was also difficult; after the First World War, new states created visa regulations and surveilled foreigners, creating barriers to migration. Yet, five to ten thousand young Hungarians—the majority Jewish but also non-Jewish leftists and women—chose to take on the challenges of emigration, with its material and psychological costs, for the sake of studying.[4]

The numerus clausus law continues to be a controversial topic in historiography and public discourse even a century after its promulgation. By introducing a restrictive Jewish quota, it set in motion a process of de-emancipating Jews.[5] In this way, Hungary preceded the Nazi Third Reich by nearly a decade and a half. While the numerus clausus law was the first piece of antisemitic legislation in twentieth-century Europe and contributed to massive brain drain from Hungary, there is a tendency to belittle its significance. On the one hand, it is seen as a starting point of the tragic path leading to the genocide of two-thirds of the Hungarian Jewry in the Shoah; on the other hand, mainstream historiography and public memory upheld for nine decades what the historian Mária M. Kovács called the "myth of repeal."[6] The 1928 amendment of the numerus clausus law in fact merely changed the method of singling out Jews: Instead of targeting Jews as a "racial group," the protocol was to discriminate based on a student's father's profession.[7] Due to the occupational structure of Hungarian society, it was predictable which occupations would be advantaged (civil servants) for the sake of admitting preferably non-Jewish students, and the law, keeping the professional statistics in mind, indicated the professions.

In this book, chapter 1 elaborates on the historicity of peregrination and the exclusion of religious minorities and women. It is intended as not a mere overture to the story I tell in chapters 2, 3, and 4 but as evidence for the inherent importance of whom to admit to universities, revealing much about the stages of minorities' emancipation and de-emancipation and about secularization. Up until the nineteenth century, in addition to their intellectual merits, prospective students were judged by their religious affiliation as came to be done in the aftermath of the First World War. Although religious affiliation remained the predominant method for defining Jews at this time, anti-Jewish movements began targeting Jews as an ethnicity in the 1880s. In the eyes of antisemites, baptism no longer turned Jews into Gentiles (as it had in most premodern contexts).

Chapter 2 provides a historical sociology of Hungarian students exiled by the Jewish quota, grounded in my own sample of over a thousand Hungarian emigrant students of the interwar period. I also analyze less statistical sources, most notably memoirs and autobiographies by students. Based on this research, I argue that although the numerus clausus law is rightly known as an anti-Jewish law, it also functioned as a tool to push out leftists from Hungarian academia and that the antisemitism behind it was heavily intertwined with misogyny.

Chapters 3 and 4 go into detail about the exile of the aforementioned two groups of students: leftists and women. The former zooms on the case study of the so called Brno group, a community of Hungarian Communist engineering students. A part of them was pushed to study in Brno, Czechoslovakia by Hungary's Jewish quota (in fact, the city's German Technical College trained the highest number of Hungarian engineers between the two world wars just after Budapest's Technical University) and radicalized during their studies abroad. Another part of them were Communist already before their emigration and in fact were exiled by the numerus clausus law in their capacity of not being "loyal to the Hungarian nation." The latter shows the mechanisms of women's de-emancipation that took place parallelly to Jews' de-emancipation in post-First World War Hungary and peregrination as one possible reaction by women to resist Hungarian academia's misogyny.[8]

Thus far, the two main bones of contention in historiography have been the duration of the age of the numerus clausus (1920–28 or 1920–45) and the question of continuity between the numerus clausus law and the Shoah in Hungary. I make the case that beyond these questions, we should also pay attention to who the targets of the numerus clausus law were and how the admission system based on it affected university populations.

Although those who downplay the numerus clausus law's significance—including Holocaust relativizers—usually emphasize the fact that the word *Jew* is not mentioned in the law's text, we, historians who maintain that there is a continuity between the numerus clausus and the Shoah in particular and between minorities' exclusion and genocide in general, should also keep in mind that discrimination against Jews was not the legislators' sole aim. We must take the law's text seriously while pointing out that the enacting clause as well as the proponents of the law stated clearly enough that the established quota system was directed against Jews. The law stipulated that the proportion of every nationality in the student body should reflect that in the general population, and the enacting clause referred to the citizens of "Israelite faith" as if they were a national minority, quoting the number of Israelite citizens as the number of citizens of a distinct nationality (*nemzetiség*), even though in the Hungarian legal system Jews existed only as members of a religious denomination.[9]

Indeed, before the passing of this legislation, Jews were the only minority present in the student body in numbers greater than they should have been according to the new quota. Since legislators aimed to limit Jews' access to higher education, faculties were required to make sure that different groups' proportion in the student body should correspond to their demographic weight in the country's general population. This meant that Jewish enrollment as first-year students could not exceed 6 percent of the first-year cohort. Since the second, third and older cohorts still being present at the university had started before the introduction of the quota, in the whole student body there were more than 6 percent Jews. Given that in the last academic year during the Great War (when all secondary school graduates were entitled to university enrollment), Jews constituted over one-third (34%) of university students, the quota meant a grave limitation of the formerly free, large-scale educational mobility of the Hungarian Jewry.[10]

If we reflect on the terms of the numerus clausus law, we see that it targeted revolutionaries more than it did Jews. The law stipulated "loyalty to the nation" and, thus, noninvolvement in the 1918 Aster Revolution and the 1919 Hungarian Republic of Councils as prerequisites for enrollment in the universities. Jews could at least fill up 6 percent of the student body, whereas all revolutionaries were excluded. Universities set up committees to examine applicants' behavior in 1918 and 1919. Even previously enrolled students of the older cohorts were excluded on these grounds. However, the Jewish quota affected more youth who wished to study than the exclusion of revolutionaries. Within a few years, the revolutionaries disappeared from the cohorts of applicants to universities, yet "loyalty to the nation" remained a requirement for admission. Students considered revolutionary became either political emigrants or were excluded from universities and had to keep a low profile if remaining in Hungary. Younger cohorts of subversive students in the interwar period tended to belong to the underground Communist movement, and if their activism was discovered, exclusion from all universities and colleges in Hungary was part of their punishment. During this period, in addition to students who migrated to study due to their Jewish origin or their politics, women, too, continued to migrate because numerous faculties in Hungary still excluded female students or admitted very few of them.

In order to direct attention to the thus far less visible targets of the numerus clausus law and the exclusionary admission system that grew out of it, separate chapters are dedicated to political dissidents (chapter 3) and to women (chapter 4). Such separation of the target groups is necessarily somewhat artificial, since in fact the three groups overlapped—an excluded person could have been a Jew, a Communist, and a woman. Yet, this narrative choice enables the examination of different factors that prohibited minorities from studying in Hungary. The reader of this book may get the impression that almost all Communist and female students leaving interwar Hungary were also Jewish and that by demonstrating this, the narrative underpins theories upheld by antisemites. In fact, however, the significant overlap between Jewish, Communist, and female emigrants was itself a result of antisemitism permeating Hungarian legislation, society, and academia. The leading politicians of interwar Hungary saw what they called the "Jewish question" as the most pressing social problem of their era.[11] This was reflected in the execution of many discriminatory laws, not only those that were purposefully anti-Jewish. Hence, Jewish background was an aggravating circumstance for culprits of political crimes. Jewish youth was surveilled with greater suspicion to begin with, and Jews had a higher chance than non-Jews of being punished immediately and thus being forbidden from all Hungarian universities and ending up abroad. In addition, I emphasize the intertwining of antisemitism and antifeminism examined by numerous historians before me and the high rate of Jews among the female graduates of secondary schooling, out of whom applicants to universities were recruited. It was therefore practical for antisemites to attack feminism as well.

By choosing to call interwar Hungarian migrant students "exiles" of antisemitism, right-wing authoritarianism, and misogyny, I intend to embrace the concept of exile in general without taking sides in the interwar assimilationist versus Zionist debate, which hinges on whether it was ultimately good or bad for Jewish youth to leave Hungary. *Exile* is a good term for these students' emigration because it contains the idea of a person either choosing or being forced to live abroad. The students concerned here indeed *chose* to study abroad rather than giving in to the legislators' will and abandoning their intellectual ambitions or were *forced* to leave if they were leftist activists. Furthermore, *exile* is a key term in the historiography of Jewish intellectual escape from antisemitic and Nazi persecution, used by several historians before me.[12] Nevertheless, it must be noted that Hungarian Jewish students were allowed to return to Hungary—albeit usually not allowed to work in the fields they had graduated in. Moreover, after 1938, most of them had no other choice than to return.

My empirical research concerned twentieth-century youth who left Hungary for Austria, Czechoslovakia, Weimar Germany, and Fascist Italy. Yet I did not want to lose sight of the longer historical trends of the interplay between minority existence and peregrination. Peregrination is migration originally with a religious and then with an intellectual aim. Hence, section 1.1 puts students' peregrination in a European historical perspective, and sections 1.2 and 1.3 focus on religious dissenters' and women's situations at universities, which often motivated peregrination.

With regard to Jews, in the age of emancipation, higher education became an important channel of upward social mobility and integration. This is the exact reason why universities were central to antisemites ever since the birth of modern antisemitism as a movement in 1879–80. Simultaneously, once higher learning became available to Jews, the eventual restriction of their access to it (first in the Russian Empire in 1887) meant a great loss and triggered emigration to western Europe. In Hungary in 1919–20, previously marginal antisemites came to dominate politics and immediately started the process of de-emancipating Jews by introducing the numerus clausus law. As a result, thousands of Hungarian Jews became part of the broader story of east-central European Jews' westward student migration.

In the sociological analysis given in chapter 2, special attention is given to those students who were Jewish by religion, representing over 80 percent of the sample, and who are thus identifiable as victims of the Jewish quota of Hungarian universities established by the numerus clausus law. Comparing their social background with that of Jews who were able to enroll in Hungarian universities shows that—contrary to prior assumptions—studying abroad was a way for lower-middle-class Jews to achieve upward social mobility rather than an escape route reserved for the privileged.

The phenomenon of political student exile is exemplified by the stories given in chapter 3 of Communist students expelled in 1932 from Hungarian universities. The politicization of Jewish emigrant students is presented through the stories of well-known future engineers who engaged in rebuilding Hungary and in "building socialism" after the Second World War. Yet during the Stalinist dictatorship, they were put on trial, imprisoned, and some even executed as members of presumed dissident groups, which the state named after places the members had studied after being excluded from Hungarian universities: for example, the "Swiss group" and the "Brno group."

How the de-emancipation of women went hand in hand with that of Jews in post–World War I Hungary is shown in chapter 4 alongside the bumpy road few women could take toward the medical and engineering professions. The focus, however, is on to what extent female emigrant students' social profiles differed from those of their male counterparts and on what we learn from the specificity of women's experiences of peregrination from their ego documents.

The epilogue highlights the impact emigration had on the minds and lives of Hungarian students who left because of antisemitism, political persecution, and sexist exclusion during the interwar period. They then faced the expansion of the Nazi Third Reich, which left less and less space for Jewish, especially if foreign, students across Europe.

PART I

THE UNIVERSITY AS A SITE OF EMANCIPATION AND DE-EMANCIPATION

ONE

PEREGRINATION, RELIGIOUS OTHERS, AND WOMEN IN THE LONG HISTORY OF UNIVERSITIES

THE AUSTRIAN WRITER (and a doctor philosophiae who spent almost no time attending classes) Stefan Zweig was convinced "one can become an excellent philosopher, historian, philologist, lawyer, or what you will, without having attended a university or even a Gymnasium."[1] Indeed, there were and always will be alternative sources of knowledge. However, the university provides not only scientific knowledge but also certification that its graduates possess mastery of that knowledge, and it further instructs students in the protocols for practicing that knowledge in the professional communities in which they aim to participate. Through this process, the university enables its graduates to be(come) part of the elite. Therefore, it is always significant who is allowed to enter this institution, no matter how few people can become students in any given time or place. Arguably, as the number of students, academics, and universities grew throughout history, the university increasingly became a setting through which hierarchies between social groups (and the subversion of such hierarchies) formed and through which historians could study the inclusion and exclusion of marginalized people. To embed in history the stories of this book's protagonists—three overlapping yet distinguishable groups who were excluded from intellectual professions in interwar Hungary: Jews, political dissidents, and women—this first chapter presents a European history of peregrination (migration for the sake of academic studies) and religious outsiders' and women's inclusion in or exclusion from academia.

PEREGRINATION: A NECESSITY FOR WHOM?

In the early history of universities in Europe (the twelfth through thirteenth centuries), institutions were few and far between, meaning that for many would-be students, long-distance migration was required to attend them. While the list of universities that emerged within the two centuries after the foundation of the first one in Bologna (1088) is long, including notably Oxford (1096), Paris (1150), Cambridge (1209), Salamanca (1218), Padua (1222), Naples (1224), and Siena (1240), large portions of the continent remained without a nearby institution of higher learning. Yet even before the emergence of the university as such, there had been academic pilgrimage (in Latin, *peregrinatio academica*), or migration for the sake of studying and teaching. Masters and scholars set out for renowned learning centers, including monastic or episcopal schools and those teaching specialized trades, such as the school of medicine in Salerno or the translators' school in Toledo.[2] As the term *peregrination* indicates, these migrant students and teachers were considered pilgrims (*peregrini* in Latin), even though their pilgrimage was to a university town rather than a saint's tomb.[3]

As few had the chance to study at any level at all, only a very thin layer of society was able to engage in higher studies (going beyond basic writing and reading), even in those areas where the earliest universities existed. As a result, these institutions sought to attract students from not only their immediate surroundings but farther-flung places as well, and they were able to solicit students and instructors from across the continent because those few individuals who were in the position to aspire to higher studies shared a common language: Latin. The lingua franca function of Latin greatly facilitated the spread of the university.

During the early days of the university, a major cause of conflict for university founders was the power struggle between the papacy and secular monarchs. Importantly, the early history of universities in the late eleventh and twelfth centuries unfolded during the Investiture Controversy, where the primacy of power between the church and the kingdoms in the Western Christian world was at stake. In the twelfth century, the papal as well as the imperial power was encouraging peregrination. The Authentica Habita, a constitution issued by Emperor Frederick I Barbarossa in 1155 declared those who, in pursuit of knowledge, traveled far from their own countries praiseworthy and deserving of protection and granted professors and students the privilege of freedom of movement and safe residence in all seats of learning. Although the emperor himself violated the Authentica Habita just a few years later when he expelled from Bologna students who had come from Milan, Brescia, and Crema,[4] the decree is memorable as an early recognition of and encouragement for student migration.

Pope Alexander III, the great enemy of Frederick I Barbarossa, also played a significant role in the early history of universities. At the Third Lateran Council of 1179, the pope declared that education should be free of charge and that masters should be paid by benefices. Thus, in the early days of universities, becoming a student or a teacher depended on the individual's intellectual merits rather than wealth. By the late Middle Ages and early modern period, however, peregrination was a type of elite (temporary) mobility. Any middle ground of less wealthy individuals undertaking migration or pilgrimage for educational purposes was no longer part of the social fabric. Peregrination as the mobility of the elite stood in stark contrast to the mobility of vagrants and itinerant beggars, which was stigmatized as "vagabondage."

A less well-known aspect of the early history of the university is that monarchs encouraged academic peregrination by less wealthy intellectuals more in the early period than later. As the number of students from the upper echelons—lay as well as clerical—grew, such encouragement of more humble students became less common. By the fifteenth century, the university had become an aristocratic institution. Due to this social selection, university graduates were likely to later hold positions of power in their native lands, and it is fair to conclude that the knowledge they gained during their studies probably influenced their home countries' political and religious milieus. Hence, the impact of peregrination was far greater than the low number of university students would suggest. With time, an increasing number of universities emerged throughout western and central Europe, making long-distance academic peregrination no longer necessary; distant travel had been, of course, more costly for scholars and often excluded students of fewer means. Peregrination to more distant universities nevertheless had remained possible for poorer scholars, usually through attending as the servant of a wealthy student.

By the end of the fifteenth century, nearly every ecclesiastical or political governing entity in (western) Christian Europe had its own center for higher learning. As a consequence, peregrination became less necessary as well as less common. It was the ambition of ecclesiastical and secular rulers to establish their own *studium* to train their subjects locally rather than encourage peregrination abroad. Hence, from this period on, it was customary to distinguish between students' external and internal migration. To ensure their institutions' survival, many sovereigns enforced penalties for local students preferring a foreign university over a local one, such as exclusion from state offices. For example, after Emperor Frederick II founded the University of Naples in 1224, he forbade his subjects to frequent any other university.

Similar protective measures were in place for the Universities of Pavia (1361, 1392, and 1412) and Padua (in 1407 and 1468).[5] As a result of a proliferation of new institutions and increased protective measures to keep scholars at home, a regionalization process took place and external academic migration came to a halt, regaining its popularity later with the help of Italian humanism. However, at the end of the Middle Ages, three-quarters of all students went to the university nearest them or at least stayed in their own region. Even the remaining quarter (especially English, Spanish, French, Italian, and, to a lesser extent, German students) who left their local regions remained within their own countries.[6]

Turning the discussion from the European history of peregrination to Hungary, first it can be established that students from the Kingdom of Hungary traveled to study at the most ancient universities as early as the late twelfth century, but migration picked up especially in the thirteenth century. Their early presence is documented in the universities of Paris, Padua, and Bologna.[8] Once universities in Prague (1348), Kraków (1364), and Vienna (1365) were established, most of the students from Hungary pursued their studies within central Europe. Historical tradition of academic pilgrimage notwithstanding, according to the medievalist historian András Kubinyi, the demand for university graduates was low in the Hungarian kings' chancellery and the ecclesiastical structure, so there was little incentive for individuals with the means to do so to obtain a degree. Instead, for Hungarian students, university training served more general purposes: acquiring erudition and making contacts abroad. With fewer scholars in need of higher education, the earliest universities founded in Hungary did not survive for long.[9] The University of Buda, founded by King Sigismund, functioned from 1389 to approximately 1450; the University of Pécs, founded by Louis I the Great, from 1367 to approximately 1400; and the University of Bratislava,[10] founded by King Matthias in 1465, only until 1492.[11] In turn, due to the lack of a permanent university in the country until the mid-seventeenth century, peregrination remained an important phenomenon of Hungarian intellectual-cultural life.

Educational peregrination increased further in Hungary in the aftermath of the Protestant Reformation, when the churches of all denominations throughout Europe took the education of their ecclesiastic and secular intelligentsia into their own hands. In the territories that had become Protestant, the rulers tended to take over existing medieval universities and—possibly with some intermission—relaunch education with new curricula that was compatible with the ruling religious affiliation.

On the whole, Catholic students typically studied at Catholic universities and Protestants at Protestant ones. This was important not only for transmitting religiously "appropriate" knowledge but also for the sake of forging, maintaining, and strengthening transnational connections and, thereby, alliances within denominations. However, there remained exceptions; the University of Padua, for example, was exceptional for accepting students of various faiths, including Protestants and Jews.[12] The interest of Hungarian would-be scholars in enrolling at Padua was remarkably high from the time of the Protestant Reformation in the 1520s. This had to do with the religious division of the country following the Ottoman victory in the battle of Mohács (1526), partitioned among the Habsburg-ruled Royal Hungary, the central territories annexed to the Ottoman Empire, and the principality of Transylvania. The Habsburg dynasty promoted the Counter-Reformation and successfully established the dominance of the Catholic faith in Royal Hungary, but a number of Transylvanian princes were ardent advocates of Calvinism. Over the centuries, Calvinism became an identity marker for anti-Habsburg Hungarian gentry, while many of the wealthiest aristocratic families were Catholic by the end of the Counter-Reformation.

Following the Reformation, Catholic scholars from Hungary enrolled mostly in the universities of Vienna, Graz, Prague, and Kraków and occasionally in Rome, while Protestants peregrinated to German, Dutch, and English universities. The Calvinist Church of Hungary was led by priests who had studied at foreign universities. After Hungary in its entirety became Catholic Habsburg–ruled by the end of the seventeenth century, Calvinists felt their positions were endangered and were eager to network with fellow Calvinists abroad, which made peregrination particularly valued and supported by their church. László Szögi, a leading historian of Hungarian peregrination, argues that the wide geographical scope of Hungarian peregrination was exceptional for the region, with most of the similarly peripheral countries having academic ties to the universities of only one foreign region.[13]

Education and the peregrination that enabled it were considered important for the status of a denomination. This can be demonstrated by the efforts taken by the Unitarian Church. Its leaders were eager to send youth to study abroad from the days (in the 1560s) of the foundation of this denomination in the Principality of Transylvania. They aimed to catch up with the level of education in more established churches (i.e., the Calvinist and the Catholic).[14] With competition and deep conflicts between the different denominations, Protestants certainly did not represent a united front against Catholics. Calvinists marginalized and pushed competing Protestant denominations out of the

Kingdom of Hungary. The principality of Transylvania was more religiously diverse: for instance, even Sabbatarianism emerged there with a rich cultural and intellectual life in the second half of the sixteenth century. After 1638, however, Sabbatarians were persecuted (essentially until 1868) and found refuge in the Unitarian Church, eventually formally converting to it.

Importantly, nearly all peregrini returned after completing their studies and applying their knowledge to the service of their community. This was considered a moral obligation, one sometimes even enforced. For example, the Calvinist collegium of Debrecen had a budget called Bursa Nigra dedicated to covering stipends for its alumni to study abroad, and these migrant students were obliged to return and join the Calvinist clergy or otherwise pay the money back.[15] The same collegium did not even hire *domidoctus* teachers (those trained only in their home country) until the twentieth century.

From the sixteenth century, more Hungarian migrant students enrolled in Protestant than in Catholic universities abroad. The volume of the peregrination of Catholics caught up to that of the Protestants only in the middle of the eighteenth century, and most of these were enrollments at the University of Vienna. For a while, it was assumed that the Habsburgs purposefully and successfully impeded Protestants' peregrination from Hungary in the eighteenth century, but this is no longer the consensus.[16]

A voluminous database of migrant students from historical Hungary from its medieval beginnings to 1919 was constructed under the leadership of László Szögi, the aforementioned historian of universities.[17] This database contains the data of immatriculations of all those born in the territory of historical Hungary in universities in twenty-seven European countries.[18] In its references from the nineteenth century, the intensive growth in Hungarian students' interest in the universities and colleges of Vienna between 1850 and 1880 is conspicuous. However, due to the expansion of higher education within Hungary by the end of the 1870s, Vienna had lost much of its attraction. External peregrination in general declined as most students pursued higher education within the country. Peregrination for the sake of postgraduate training, however, was still popular, particularly to Germany, which became the internationally recognized center of science and scholarship. Hungarians also discovered the famous Technical College of Zurich (today it is called the Swiss Federal Institute of Technology), the Eidgenössische Technische Hochschule.[19] Other institutions of higher education in Switzerland, pioneers in the admission of women into universities in Europe, attracted Hungarian female students in an era when Hungarian women could receive a secondary school education but were still excluded from Hungarian academia.

For the purposes of the research presented here, the high proportion of Jews among Hungarian migrant students is the most important aspect of modern Hungarian peregrination. In the migrant student population, the proportion of Jewish students was much higher than the share of Jews in the general Hungarian population. Antisemites called this seeming imbalance "overrepresentation," although they mostly talked about this in the context of universities within the country. The expression *Jewish overschooling* in social history indicates a situation when Jewish families invest more in the children's education than non-Jewish families of the same socioeconomic standing and as a consequence the Jewish minority becomes disproportionately educated in comparison with the majority society.[20] It is justifiably criticized due to its implication that there is a normal level of schooling for minorities.

It is noteworthy that because the bulk of the Jewry of Hungary originated in Moravia and Galicia, with their massive immigration (particularly from Moravia) beginning in the late eighteenth century, many Jewish families had strong ties to Czech lands. Therefore, Jewish scholars were more likely to pursue studies there, particularly in Prague, than were other students from Hungary. Before 1848, over half (52%) of Hungarian migrant students in Prague were Jewish.[21] Between 1851 and 1919, the percentage of Jews (25.21%) among students from Hungary who studied in Prague, compared to the percentage of Jews in the general population of Hungary was five times higher than the percentage in the country's population (5%). Although not every migrant student's religious affiliation is known, there was certainly a great "overrepresentation."[22] In this period, Jewish students were still as likely to pursue higher education in Hungary as abroad. In German-speaking areas—the main targets of Hungarian peregrination—before 1919, Szögi estimates the proportion of Jews at 20 percent.[23] Migrant students from the Russian Empire at western European universities were much more likely to be Jewish than were students from Hungary. The peregrination of the former was a reaction to the Russian numerus clausus of 1887—detailed in chapter 2—and its context was a large-scale migration of Jews, not only students, fleeing antisemitism between the 1880s and the First World War. Although few (merely thousands) compared to the 2.5 million Jews who left eastern Europe between 1880 and 1914,[24] the Russian Jewish students constituted a large group when examined against the background of general (i.e., not only Jewish) student migration.

The emigration of Jewish students from the Russian Empire from the 1880s to the First World War was so significant that they became protagonists (the typical migrant student in a European university was someone from the Russian Empire) of peregrination from eastern Europe to the West. Among Russian students enrolling in western European universities, Jews surely represented the majority, although the scale of this majority is debated.[25] Jack Wertheimer estimates their proportion at three-quarters among all the Russian subjects studying in higher education between 1900 and 1914 in Germany, which was one of the major target countries of peregrination.[26] At that time, Russian students peregrinating mainly because of exclusion in their home country was specific to Jewish students.

In the meantime, the expansion of higher education in the second half of the nineteenth century affected all of Europe, including the south and eastern European states emerging or refounded after centuries of Ottoman rule, because training professionals was a prerequisite of modernization and economic success. So long as countries lacked institutions that could train students in specialized fields, states supported their talented youth studying at prestigious foreign universities, with the expectation that they would return and use their knowledge in the service of their home countries. Hence, for a while, studies abroad functioned as a vehicle to succeed in one's native country, and professors of newly institutionalized study fields were necessarily trained abroad.

The First World War and its consequences dramatically changed the patterns of peregrination in general. Unlike in the nineteenth and early twentieth centuries, the typical peregrini of the interwar period were not intellectuals who were voluntarily mobile but members of ethnic, national, and political minorities pushed out from their native countries by nationalism, antisemitism, and political persecution. Hungary was the most notable case, as it was the first state to legislatively introduce an anti-Jewish law in the twentieth century, and it was no coincidence that the numerus clausus concerned admission to universities.[27] Due to this limitation on their study possibilities in Hungary, thousands of Hungarian Jews became part of the broader story of eastern and central European Jews' westward student migration. Although the idea of establishing a university in Hungary for Jewish youth was raised,[28] emigration to existing foreign universities and fundraising for that aim became incomparably more popular.

At the same time, in the aftermath of the First World War, Jews were also pushed out from Romanian and Polish universities by academic antisemitism that was manifested there in unofficial quotas and repeated violence and humiliation (e.g., ghetto benches) against Jewish students.[29] Similar to their fellow Hungarian Jews, many of them studied abroad as a result. In fact, due to the larger size of Poland and Romania and their respective Jewish populations,

Romanian and Polish Jewish emigrant students most likely outnumbered their Hungarian Jewish peers in all the popular central and western European university cities (in Austria, Czechoslovakia, Germany, Italy, France, and Switzerland), and they certainly did in Italy.[30]

In the meantime, the Hungarian state did support the peregrination of other types of students as part of the cultural politics of Kunó Klebelsberg, minister for religion and public education (1922–31). He organized a network of Collegia Hungarica and institutionalized stipends for Hungarian students and scholars to go on study and research trips to Vienna, Berlin, Rome, and Paris. Klebelsberg was remarkably successful in fundraising and lobbying, efforts that culminated in the stipulations of Law 1927: XIII on Hungarian cultural institutes abroad and stipends for study and research trips.[31]

Occasionally, intellectuals of Jewish origin benefited from such stipends. However, the intellectuals who obtained them were typically non-Jews and students of humanities who spent a few months or at most two years abroad to polish their linguistic skills in preparation for careers as high school language teachers in Hungary.[32] In fact, contemporaries suspected that the Jewish quota of the Hungarian numerus clausus law creeped into the Berlin Collegium Hungaricum too. When this institute welcomed its first cohort of state-funded scholars in the spring of 1927, German as well as Hungarian public opinion was most interested in the religious affiliation of the thirty scholarship recipients, 6 percent of whom were Jewish. Although, in the case of such small numbers, this distribution could have happened by chance, contemporaries saw it as proof that the numerus clausus was in place in Hungary's cultural institutions abroad too, not only at the country's universities. And as a matter of fact, the number of Jews receiving scholarship from the state later converged to zero. As the historian Michael L. Miller puts it, "the system of state-funded scholarships created two classes of Hungarian scholars abroad, those funded by the state, and those funded by the Hungarian Jewish community."[33]

Because of these events, the typical Hungarian peregrini of the interwar period were Jews, mostly students of medicine and engineering who pursued their higher education abroad entirely at their own or at Jewish communities' and organizations' expense. This book tells the story of these thousands of people, most of whom struggled to make ends meet in order to study abroad after being pushed out from Hungarian universities by antisemitism, political exclusion, and misogyny. It is deliberately not a story of the most famous emigrant intellectuals, such as those who became Nobel laureates or contributors to the Manhattan Project, but one of the rank-and-file exiled students.[34] The number of Hungarian Jewish emigrant students in the age of the numerus clausus (1920–1945) can be estimated in the thousands, more than 5,000 during the 1920s alone, if we count 1,450 new enrollments each academic year, which is the number of Hungarian Jews who graduated abroad with the financial support of the Central Jewish Student Aid Committee (Központi Zsidó Diáksegítő Bizottság, henceforth KZSDB) until 1928.[35] The phenomenon continued on a similarly large scale up until the late 1930s. Hence, altogether the number of the emigrant students in this period approached 10,000.

RELIGIOUS OUTSIDERS AND ETHNIC MINORITIES AT UNIVERSITIES

The origin of the university as an institution of higher education was embedded in Western Christianity and in the power relations of medieval Europe, and as a result, non-Christians, including Jews, were not heavily involved in this history. Although we know of Jewish university students and instructors long before their emancipation making Jews equal to Christians in front of the law. (This included the right to enroll in a university under the same conditions as a Christian.) Their roles can be seen as the exception that proves the rule and were the outcome of contradictions inherent in medieval and early modern scholarly culture.

Abraham Avigdor of Arles (born in 1350), a Provençal Jewish physician, philosopher, and translator from Latin to Hebrew, was among the earliest documented Jewish university students in general and the very first one we know of at the University of Montpellier, an institution famed for its tolerance. In the preface of his translation of *Introduction to the Practice* by Bernard Gordon, Abraham recalled that "I went up on the mountain therefore, that is to say, the city of Montpellier, in order to study the science of medicine from the mouth of the Christian scientists and erudites."[36] Abraham is known from his writings as a pious Jew, but his writing also demonstrates he took pride in the fact that he studied with Christians. Thus, his Jewish readers appreciated Christian scholarship enough for him to reference his background at Montpellier for credibility.

The University of Montpellier counts Jews even among its founders and medieval professors preceding Abraham Avigdor's life. Isaac ben Abraham and Meschulam and Shem Tov ben Isaac had their names engraved in marble at the entry of the institution. However, neither Hebrew nor Latin sources confirm that they ever taught or even studied there. According to Joseph Shatzmiller, a historian of medieval Jewry, Montpellier's myth of tolerance is exaggerated and was based on a misinterpretation of a charter that Count Guillem gave to the city's scholars in 1181. The most that can be said is that around 1300 and afterward, some Jewish scholars had intellectual exchanges with scholars of this university.

Among those scholars was Leon Joseph of Carcassonne, physician and devoted translator of Latin medical literature into Hebrew. He studied in Montpellier sometime between 1384 and 1394. Similarly to Abraham Avigdor, Leon Joseph also provides a source about Jewish students' presence in Montpellier in a translation of a medical work. He described the University of Montpellier with admiration in his introduction to the translation of Gerard de Solo's commentary on *Kitāb al-Manṣūrī* (Manṣūr's Book) by Razes and mentioned that he had not been the only Jewish student.[37] After his studies, Leon Joseph practiced medicine in nearby Perpignan where the notarial documents referred to him as *medicus* and *phisicus,* not as *magister* (the title of university graduates). However, after his conversion sometime between 1414 and 1418, he came to be referred to as magister.[38] This case suggests that Jews, although allowed to study there, were discriminated against even in Montpellier. Being able or unable to use the magister title made a big difference in professionals' lives not only because it conferred prestige but also because magisters could charge higher fees.

Granting university titles, particularly doctorates, to Jews was problematic under Roman law; when the title was interpreted as a *dignitas* (dignity), as was generally done, the Theodosian Code, which excluded Jews from all dignities, prohibited them from receiving the title.[39] Importantly, at the Council of Basel in September 1434, the church reinforced this interpretation by banning universities from conferring degrees on Jews. Even in Bologna where a significant number of Jewish students studied in the mid-fourteenth century, they were denied titles at the completions of their programs. At the same time, we know about Jews who were referred to by their university titles in fourteenth- and fifteenth-century Italy despite the general prohibition. In 1396–97, a certain master Isaac was mentioned as a *licentiatus* (graduate) of the University of Padua. In 1406, three Jewish men, Elia di Sabbato da Fermo, Moses of Tivoli, and Moses of Spain, attained the *laurea* (degree) with the support of the papacy as a token for their services rendered to the Holy See.[40] Similarly in Italy, in 1426 another Jewish doctor, Guillelmo, son of Isaiah of Urbino, received the laurea.[41] Luckily for historians, an extraordinary document survived that explains what this doctorate meant in practice. According to this source, Guillelmo was entitled to teach, dispute, and interpret at an institution of higher learning where he had studied. On receiving the laurea, he received as well all the usual insignia: a closed book, a ring, and a *biretus* (the appropriate hat). Such celebrations were usually held in a church, but for the sake of Guillelmo, the Jewish graduate, this was circumvented. His degree was conferred on him in one of the halls of the university instead of the cathedral.

Although in the first half of the fourteenth century some of the most esteemed medical professors of the period taught in Montpellier, during the second half of the century its popularity declined so much that in 1378 it was abandoned by most of its students. This may have been the main motivation for accepting the elsewhere unwanted Jewish students.[42] Nearby Perpignan's university apparently also accepted Jewish students, which we can conclude because in 1390 the university council attempted to revive an exclusionary regulation. At the same time, the presence of Jewish students in the successful universities of Bologna and Padua suggests that lack of students was not the only motivation for accepting Jews. Especially considering that fourteenth- and fifteenth-century Jewish presence in the student body of Italian universities laid a solid precedent for centuries to come, we can see that Jewish students were admitted on their merit as scholars. With regard to France, the expulsion of Jews from the whole kingdom put an end toward French universities welcoming Jewish students.

It is perhaps not a coincidence that several of the previous examples are of Jewish students pursuing medical studies, for medicine was one of the first fields of study where accepting non-Christians was conceivable, mainly due to a lack of doctors at a time when they were direly needed. Medicine's openness may seem counterintuitive from a post–twentieth century perspective of modern antisemitism, which creates anxieties about Jews treating Gentile bodies,[43] and even at the time, similar concerns surfaced, albeit for distinct reasons. For example, from 1227 onward a number of medieval synods prohibited Jews from prescribing medicaments to Christians and Christians from turning to Jewish physicians. Provençal legislation of 1306 and a *licentia practicandi* (license to practice) conferred on a Jewish doctor, David of Arles, in the same year provides an explanation. It was feared that Jewish doctors would prevent dying Christians from taking the last sacraments. David of Arles was forbidden to go near the sickbed of a Christian unless that person had confessed and received the Corpus Christi already.[44] Nevertheless, the early dates of such prohibitions suggest that there were Jewish medical practitioners who treated Christian patients before there were Jewish university students of medicine (or before we know of them).

Medicine as a discipline greatly expanded in the first half of the thirteenth century thanks to the phenomenon called the medicalization of society, referring to the growing interest in and appreciation for this science. As a result, the services of medical professionals ceased to be limited to the ruling elite and proliferated somewhat to people of more modest origin. Later, after the disastrous black death epidemic (1348–52), municipal councils were even expected to hire professionals at public expense and to at least some extent take care of the health of the poor to stem the transmission of the disease.[45]

In the meantime, even the structure of the healing profession changed. From the realm of charity—where it was largely practiced by enthusiastic volunteers, such as the members of religious orders—it left for the realm of professional service. Physicians were increasingly expected to go through formalized professional training (at a university, thus the title of magister) and held responsible for their successes as well as their failures in healing sick people. These practitioners were secular, and they charged fees for their services. Their activity was no longer charity but wage labor.

The Catholic Church had a hard time accepting the transformation of medicine from Christian charity into secular wage labor. Church authorities repeatedly passed bans prohibiting clerics from practicing medicine. Of course, the repetition of bans suggests that these policies were not respected, so it is hard to establish to what extent the official ecclesiastical standpoint contributed to the lack of physicians in a period when demand for them was growing. Simultaneously, another factor affecting the turnout of a sufficient number of university-trained medical doctors was the cost of a university education and living expenses during it.

As a result of these phenomena, the medical profession was an underpopulated sphere and hence even Jews could enter. It is also noteworthy that Jewish communities tended to live in urban centers, where medical doctors were most highly sought. The opening up of the medical field is similar to that of professions that emerged in the nineteenth and twentieth centuries (e.g., photography and psychoanalysis); Jews again could enter in "disproportionately" high numbers compared to their demographic weight because new professions do not have the same kind of rigid written or unwritten exclusionary rules as long-established professions and are not yet dominated by the societal majority. Although medicine in the Middle Ages was not entirely new, like photography was new in the fin de siècle, the way of practicing it was renewed through the medicalization of society.

In the High and late Middle Ages (from the mid-thirteenth century onward), there was hardly a Jewish community in the Mediterranean that had no medical doctor among its members, according to Joseph Shatzmiller. While Jews constituted at maximum 5–8 percent of the population even in the largest cities, at times as much as 50 percent of medical practitioners were Jewish.[46] This does not mean that this many Jews were trained at the medical faculties of universities, but there certainly were Jewish medical experts in many university towns with whom Christian scholars could exchange ideas. There were also Jews who were ready to enter university if the possibility presented itself, as was the case in Italy from the mid-fourteenth century and in France in the late fourteenth century.

Thus, a confidential enough relationship between Jews and Christians was possible in terms of medical practice. It was nevertheless far from evident from a medieval Christian or Jewish perspective that Jews and Christians should study together at a university. The university as an institution, as well as the body of knowledge transmitted there (in which the Christian theology of western Europe played a central role), was intimately related to (Western) Christianity. Hence, in principle it was problematic to have Jewish university students and instructors for Christian and Jewish communities. And yet it was not an anomaly that some Jews made it to medieval universities to study medicine without converting.

It is also noteworthy that while the university as we know it today is rooted in medieval Christian culture, other cultures, such as Islam and Judaism, had their own institutions of higher education to train intellectuals. In the fourteenth and fifteenth centuries, a quasi-public Jewish higher education system came into existence in German-speaking territories, in which communities contributed to the livelihood of students who came to study at their academies.[47] In the sixteenth and seventeenth centuries, east European Jewish communities even fully supported incoming students.[48]

Allowing Jews to join universities' scholarly communities, which by default were Christian, was possibly motivated by their role in transmitting medical knowledge from the Islamic world, where Jews were active in the profession and where medicine was more developed. Some Sephardim who migrated between the two worlds translated medical works from Arabic into Hebrew.[49] These Jews had access to ancient Greek medical literature translated into Arabic much earlier than to Latin and Sephardic Jews had a more active exchange with Ashkenazic Jews than Muslim and Christian scholars had with each other (except for on the Iberian Peninsula), European Jews had access to a body of literature for a while unknown to Christian scholars. An increase in the number of Jewish physicians may have taken place one or two centuries earlier in the Islamic world than it did in the Christian one.

The question then arises: Why were Jews motivated to enter the sphere of universities? On the one hand, medical science and education improved a lot during the thirteenth and fourteenth centuries, notably in universities. On the other hand, although there were Jewish doctors to learn from and medical literature available in Hebrew, a university education (even if one could not ultimately use the magister title, as the case of Leon Joseph of Carcassonne shows) elevated a doctor's esteem. Most medieval and early modern Jewish medical practitioners, nevertheless, lacked formal university education and learned their profession in Jewish academies from Jewish masters.

Besides medicine, Italy provided precedents for accepting Jews as partners in intellectual exchanges in the humanities.[50] The famous "Ad fontes!" ("To the sources!") rallying cry of humanism was manifested in Italy by growing interest in reading the Hebrew Bible. Gradually, the principle that the sources of the Christian faith should be studied in their original languages proliferated. This new intellectual stream led to the opening of a possibility to not only study but also teach at universities for Jews, albeit mostly for converts.[51] Although Jewish tradition did not allow the teaching of Gentiles, evidence from fifteenth-century Italy reveals that Jewish communities did not adhere to this prohibition. Additionally, many of the first humanists had Hebrew instructors who had abandoned the Jewish community and converted.

During the sixteenth century, the habit of hiring Jews to teach Hebrew at universities spread. Moreover, it came to be regarded as essential for theology students, opening a new career prospect for coverts. The Reformation gave an additional impetus for the spread of Hebrew instruction begun by humanism. Nevertheless, many examples reveal that Christians' interest in the Hebrew language was often not accompanied with the acceptance of Jewish people. For instance, the grammarian Elijah Levita was invited by the French King Francis I to teach Hebrew at the university in Paris; however, Levita declined because he did not wish to live in a city where his coreligionists were not allowed to reside.[52] Moreover, the practice appears more insidious when we consider that papal encouragement for studying the sacred language of Judaism was originally motivated by an intention to convert Jews to Christianity (e.g., in the 1311 Vienne and 1434 Basel councils).

There are documents suggesting that Jews who achieved the right to use their university titles (thus to be regarded as laureati) despite the prohibitive norm taught at Italian universities as early as the fifteenth century. According to the interpretation by Ariel Toaff, Stanislao Majarelli, and Ugolino Nicolini, this was the case in Perugia and Bologna.[53] Ladislao Münster and Joseph Shatzmiller disagree, however.[54]

Similar to Jewish language university instructors, Jewish students, once they converted, were also allowed to reside in territories forbidden to Jews or nonlocal Jews. (It was often the case that a Jewish community was granted the privilege of residing in a city but could not permit new members to the community thereafter.) For instance, Paul Tobias Levith studied with Melanchthon in the 1550s in Saxony. In 1557, Elector Augustus, who forbade foreign Jews to remain on Saxon soil for even one night,[55] offered a stipend to Levith to study in Wittenberg (with the understanding that he would also teach Hebrew).[56]

Anthonius Margaritha, possibly the best-known Jew of his generation in German lands to convert to Christianity (in 1521), earned his living as a Hebrew instructor in several places.[57] After being a private teacher in Leipzig and Meissen, he received a position at the University of Vienna. It is noteworthy that sixteenth-century Vienna banned new settlement of (unconverted) Jews, similar to Saxon cities.[58] The sixteenth-century proliferation of Hebrew instruction at universities significantly impacted the lives of Jewish intellectuals, though only those willing to convert. While in the Middle Ages converts characteristically found employment in the ranks of the church, in the early modern period they were likely to find their place at a university.[59]

The idea (mostly disconnected with practice) of accepting Jews as Jews to study at a university together with Christians as a matter of course rather than as an exception is tied to the Enlightenment. Austrian Empress Maria Theresa's regulation Systematica gentis Judaicae enabled her Jewish subjects to attend public schools and encouraged the opening of Jewish schools where pupils could learn the local languages. This, of course, encouraged acculturation and met resistance among Jewish religious leaders, but it also contributed to more Jews being able to become qualified for university studies. Even promoters of the Jewish Enlightenment (Haskalah), called maskilim, offered different evaluations of this regulation. Naphtali Hirz Wessely was supportive, while Moses Mendelssohn remained rather skeptical.[60]

Maria Theresa's heir, Emperor Joseph II, issued the famous Patent of Tolerance (1781), which also entitled Jews to enroll their children at public schools and moreover enabled Jewish men to enroll in universities. Prussian educational reforms by Karl von Hardenburg, Prussian minister of state, and by Wilhelm von Humboldt, minister of education, also opened universities to Jews. In practice, however, it took until several decades into the nineteenth century for Jews to appear in great numbers in (general) higher education.

The labor markets opened to Jews significantly slower than the university faculties of the Habsburg Empire. Jewish youths themselves were first and foremost open to faculties where a tradition of Jewish presence existed, such as those for commerce and medicine. For instance, although Jews enrolled at the Polytechnic University of Vienna from 1815 onward, for decades they preferred commercial studies over engineering and architecture.[61] In the Hungarian part of the empire, Jews made up 42 percent of all medical students in 1845–46 and 1846–47, when only 2 percent of the general population was Jewish. This piece of data is very worthy of attention in light of the fact that the secondary schools of the era were run and staffed by the Christian (mainly the Roman Catholic, Calvinist, and Lutheran) churches,[62] which shows on the one hand that Christian denominational schools started to accept Jewish youth without converting them and on the other hand that a critical mass of Jewish parents allowed their children to be educated in a Christian environment.

Such attitude of institutions and members of marginal faith communities toward each other could not be taken for granted, however, when we look at a larger geographical perspective. In fact, it was not the case that Western institutions were more open than their counterparts in eastern Europe. In addition, development from exclusion to inclusion is not a linear process. As elaborated earlier in this chapter, early modern universities belonged to different Christian denominations and discriminated not only against Jews but also against Christians of denominations other than their own, a practice that was characteristic of prestigious universities, such as Oxford and Cambridge, even in the nineteenth century. Frustration over this led to a movement for a secular university in England and resulted in the establishment in 1827 of University College in London, where Catholics as well as Jews were admitted. Meanwhile, in Cambridge, Oxford, and Durham, religious tests for applicants' adherence to the Anglican Church were still in practice as late as 1871.

While in western Europe the university's early modern confessional legacy lingered on with the exclusion of religious Christian dissenters as well as Jews, in the Russian Empire universities emerged late in the age of Enlightenment (the first one in Moscow in 1755), and this timing had important consequences for Jews. Russian universities were the results of a state initiative that aimed to reduce the czar's dependence on the hereditary nobility, and thus, these institutions were relatively open to commoners. Unlike contemporary English universities, Russian institutions allowed students to take enrollment and graduation oaths in a way that conformed to the student's religion. Jews' eligibility for elementary school, gymnasium (secondary school), and university enrollment was spelled out as early as 1804 in the opening paragraph of the Statute on the Jews.[63]

In addition, for the larger part of the nineteenth century, czarist policy in the Russian Empire used state education as one of the means to push Jews toward assimilation. For eight decades, the czarist government strove to attract Jewish children to Russian schools. For a long time, many Jewish families opposed it out of fear that Russian education would be a first step of their children's alienation from the Jewish way of life and community. However, after the government of Alexander II in 1861 decided to grant Jewish university graduates the rights and privileges of their Gentile counterparts—including unrestricted residence and choice of occupation[64]—Jewish participation in higher education expanded. The year 1861 was the beginning of the reform era and the year serfdom was abolished. The two events were only connected because both stemmed from the reformism of Czar Alexander II; however, Jewish as well as Russian contemporaries attributed great symbolic value to the liberation of millions of Russian serfs and the liberation of university graduate Jews from the restriction of residence taking place in the same year.[65]

The extent of Jewish presence in secondary and higher education became a much-discussed topic in the 1870s because the growth of Jews' participation in higher education had been very visible since 1861.[66] This was also connected to a growing acceptance of secular studies among Jews thanks to the spreading of Haskalah in east-central Europe during the nineteenth century. Between 1878 and 1886, for instance, 42 of 268 students at St. Petersburg University were Jewish, 33 of 298 at Moscow University, and 76 of 237 at the University of Kyiv.[67] In the empire as a whole, a mere 0.6% of university students were Jewish in 1840, 3.2% in the mid-1860s, 5% in 1876, and 14.5% by 1886.[68] By some, this was considered too high a proportion.

Earlier, the proportion of Catholics was deemed too high, and so the access of Poles to Russian universities was limited in the 1860s with a quota that, until 1872, also applied to Lithuanians.[69] In the case of Jews, the idea of limiting the access of citizens of certain faiths was accompanied with racial hatred.

Importantly, the era of reforms ended when Alexander II was assassinated in 1881 and his son Alexander III acceded to the throne. The new czar was not interested in Jewish integration, and as a result the legal and economic conditions of Jews worsened. His reign started with the infamous wave of pogroms that lasted from April 1881 to the spring of 1882. Notwithstanding the powerful narrative established by the great historian of Russian Jewry Simon Dubnow,[70] in which he argues that the czarist authorities instigated the pogroms, according to current historiography this was not the case.[71] Nonetheless, Jews did not expect any benevolence from Alexander III. The new czar's aim was to hinder Jews' entrance in the Russian intelligentsia, and he therefore embraced limiting Jewish presence in secondary and higher education. Numerous secondary schools started to restrict the number of admitted Jews at their own initiative during the 1880s; the government only needed to confirm such practice. The official decision was formulated in July 1887 by the Ministry of Education as a quota system restricting Jewish access to the secondary schools of the state. Enrollment in universities was in addition rendered difficult by the rule that Jews could do so only if graduating from secondary school as excellent pupils with a "gold medal."

For the Jews concerned, it was disappointing not to get into higher education and liberal professions after being enrolled in Russian secondary schools. Moreover, there was no real way back to traditional Jewish life. What Jewish parents throughout the century had feared indeed happened: Many secondary school graduates were alienated from their parents. They had a hard time being enclosed in the Pale of Settlement and having to be engaged in trade and petty commerce, as so many of their parents had done. Jewish parents had every reason to be disappointed with the results of czarist policies: They promised a bright future for educated Jews and led to bitter disillusion and disintegration of Jewish families instead.[72]

Importantly, the possibility of Jews studying in higher education and entering intellectual professions that facilitated their integration into society met resistance in western and central Europe, not only in the Russian Empire. Modern antisemitism, as opposed to anti-Judaism (religiously motivated anti-Jewish hostility going back to antiquity), as an ideology emerged in the German context in the 1870s and 1880s. The term *antisemitism* was popularized as a neologism by agitator Wilhelm Marr from 1879 on. The antisemitic movement opposed the very legitimacy of emancipation and aimed to revert it. Universities were hotbeds of antisemitism from the inception of this political stream. From the early 1880s, some *Burschenschaften* (student fraternities) excluded Jewish members,[73] and later more fraternities introduced an "Aryan paragraph" in their regulations that made Aryan (i.e., not Jewish) descent a prerequisite of admission.

At the University of Vienna, racial hatred toward Jewish students and professors, often expressed in violence, was a dominant factor of everyday academic life from the discussion and publication of *Über das Lehren und Lernen der medicinischen [sic] Wissenschaften an den Universitäten der Deutschen Nation* (About the teaching and studying of the medical sciences at the universities of the German nation), a pamphlet by medical professor Theodor Billroth in 1875–76.[74] Vienna continued to draw Jewish migrant students from the other parts of the Habsburg Empire on a mass scale; meanwhile, antisemitic student associations flourished and encountered active and sometimes violent resistance from Jewish students.[75] They later founded Zionist sport and fencing clubs preparing Jewish students for self-defense. Both phenomena continued into the interwar period's Red Vienna, when

Galician and Hungarian Jews became foreign students even in terms of citizenship. (They had already been labeled "aliens" by antisemites during the Austro-Hungarian period.)[76]

Universities played an important role in Jewish acculturation, integration, and assimilation and enabled Jewish students to achieve upward social mobility through careers in liberal professions, all of which antisemites intended to stop. Following the momentum that the antisemitic movement gained internationally in 1879–80 due to publications by Wilhelm Marr, anti-Jewish student riots broke out also in Budapest in early 1881. The rioters protested the high proportion of Jewish students, which was 36 percent and 26 percent in the medical and legal faculties, respectively.[77]

Unlike the Austrian government, the Hungarian government decisively condemned antisemitic campus attacks. However, despite the Hungarian government's commitment to Jewish emancipation and social inclusion, antisemitic forces opposed these efforts and strengthened over time. Although the very first radical right-wing political party of Hungary, the National Antisemitic Party, existed for less than a decade (1883–92), its anti-Jewish ideology and politicians found their way into the much more successful Catholic People's Party, established in early 1895.[78] The party's official program did not refer to Jews, but many speeches by its MPs in the Lower House and especially its press organs were marked by antisemtisim, which grew in intensity as years went by.[79]

As Miklós Szabó, the renowned historian of radical right-wing politics in Europe, explains, in Hungary new conservativism appeared as a movement in the 1890s, because landowners became increasingly aware of traditional conservativism being no longer sufficient to reconquer their social position from the ascending bourgeoisie. Before the turn of the century, the new conservative movement radicalized only in the university sphere, especially at the Hungarian Royal University in Budapest.[80] Such radicalization was the context for the following case of antisemitic mobilization among university students, known as the "cross jape."

On the night of May 25, 1900, crosses were removed from the decorations of the walls in the new main building of the Hungarian Royal University in Budapest. The National Party, a right-wing student group leading the student union at the time, accused unknown Jewish students. They submitted a document known as the "cross memorandum" to the university council requesting that the perpetrators be excluded from all the universities of Hungary and that in addition to the missing crosses from the corridors being replaced, crosses be placed in all the university lecture halls of the country. Another edition of the memorandum requested that crosses be placed in "representative spaces" only, meaning aulas and council halls. The university council rejected both versions and, moreover, suspended the student union for three months, demonstrating that the university leadership wished to prevent the new conservative movement from gaining more ground in student life. Indeed, the cross movement of radical right-wing students did not achieve the attention in public opinion they and their supporters in the Catholic People's Party had hoped for.[81]

Nevertheless, the struggle for keeping up the "Christian nature" of Péter Pázmány University (which had been established by the Catholic bishop Péter Pázmány in 1635) went on. "Christian nature" originally referred to the rejection of liberalism, atheism, and bourgeois democracy's religious indifference. However, within a few years "Christian" was used by the radical right wing to mean "not Jewish."[82] As Miklós Szabó points out, in the long run the cross movement can be evaluated as successful because it influenced the political generation that instigated the 1919 counterrevolution and built up the counterrevolutionary political system of interwar Hungary.[83]

If looking on the 1900s only, the next two instances of antisemitic mobilization, the "Pikler japes," were more consequential since they mobilized the other side—progressive, anticlerical students who self-identified as freethinkers—to launch the Galilei Circle in 1908.[84] The japes targeted Gyula Pikler, professor of legal studies at the university, who taught that legal systems have to change with ever-changing historical circumstances and human needs. As a consequence, he heavily criticized the remnants of feudalism in Hungary, which went against landowners' interests. He also happened to be Jewish, so his "godless," "unpatriotic" teachings were easily tied to his Jewishness by antisemites. In April 1901, he was accused of trying to wipe out national values and vilifying religion. Pikler refuted the accusations, and over two hundred students signed a petition in support of the professor. Clashes between supporting and protesting students during his lectures led to physical altercations. The university's council as well as the Ministry for Religion and Public Education stood up for Pikler. In 1907, the same conflict broke out again and escalated beyond the legal faculty of the university.

From the students supporting Pikler, the Galilei Circle emerged.[85] While the antisemitic students were supported by the new conservative and agrarian right-wing political forces, the Galileists were backed by "bourgeois radical" (*polgári radikális* originally, in English better called "radical democrat") intellectuals and the radical-oriented Free Masonic Lodges. Their main activities were scientific self-education and disseminating science among workers. Famous Galileists include such internationally acclaimed scientists as Karl Polányi, Mihály Polányi, and Karl Mannheim as well as some protagonists of the Hungarian Republic of Councils in 1919, including a number of Communist commissars (e.g., the philosopher Georg Lukács). At the same time, Oszkár Jászi, an opponent of the Republic of Councils, was also a central figure. Many of the political leaders of the postwar revolution(s) and counterrevolution were student activists from both sides of the political spectrum in the 1900s who struggled for right-wing and left-wing ideals first at the legal faculty in Budapest and then beyond.[86]

Returning to Jews' integration in universities and in society, in both the Austrian and the Hungarian parts of the Habsburg Dual Monarchy Jewish assimilation continued up until the First World War. Within the Dual Monarchy, the Hungarian unit favored Jewish integration more than the Austrian one because doing so aligned with its broader interests. The Hungarian political elite working on nation-building in a country where less than half of the population belonged to the politically dominant Hungarian nation needed Jews, who constituted around 5 percent of the population, to appear as Hungarians in the censuses.[87]

Therefore, according to some historians, an (unwritten) assimilationist social contract came into being after the Jewish emancipation. This term refers to the mechanism by which most channels of integration were opened for Jews in exchange for their linguistic and cultural assimilation. This contract theory is not unique to Hungarian nineteenth-century discourses about emancipation and assimilation. For instance, according to David Sorkin, a "contract" involving Jews was part of a broader political abstraction when German Jews struggled for emancipation: a gentlemen's agreement (inasmuch as not being written down) between the emerging nation-state and all its citizens. Sorkin emphasizes the unspoken nature of it.[88] For a transnational historiography of the term, one should turn to the valuable overview by the historian Kati Vörös.[89]

Regarding Hungarian history, the contract theory was introduced into scholarly discourse by Victor Karády.[90] He uses it to frame the dynamic process of assimilation rather than the legal event of emancipation. It was not a deal for two onetime services but a continuous welcoming attitude from political leaders and a continuous performance of patriotic attitude by Jews. To put it simply, Jews were ready to take on the Hungarian language, culture, and identity in exchange for equality. The contract had two basic clauses: loyalty to the nation-state and a (discriminatory) division of labor where Jews were free to enter the liberal professions and were free as economic entrepreneurs. However, they were basically excluded from state administration.[91] With the signing of the Peace Treaty of Trianon (1920), when Hungary lost all the territories where most non-Hungarian citizens lived, the country was left with an almost homogeneous Hungarian population, and Jews were no longer needed as a demographic element to raise the proportion of Hungarians. However, the division of labor clause of the contract survived because the Hungarian economy continued to need Jewish entrepreneurs.

One can find many arguments and supporting data in favor of and against the contract theory. As another major historian of the Habsburg monarchy and of Jewish assimilation, Péter Hanák, demonstrates (not in debate with Karády, but earlier), Jewish assimilation was not at all unique in Hungary. Approximately 1.7 million people were assimilated to the Hungarian nation between 1850 and 1910, out of whom only 600,000 were Jewish. An equal number of Germans became Hungarians and 400,000 Slovaks in the same period.[92] I believe this is the most important argument against Karády's claim of the uniqueness of Jewish assimilation.

The most outspoken criticizer of Karády, Gábor Gyáni, emphasizes that the assimilation of Jews in Hungary was not unique in the transnational arena either. It followed similar patterns in numerous European countries, and therefore, it was unnecessary to introduce a new conceptual tool for it, especially such a counterintuitive one as Karády's social contract.[93] In addition, according to Gyáni, Karády insists too much on Ferenc Erdei's problematic, if pervasive, theory of dual society: the tense division of labor between a capitalistic and a feudal elite in interwar Hungary.[94]

To my mind, Karády's social contract theory is still tenable if we remove the notion of uniqueness. *Contract* may not be the best metaphor for the phenomenon since traditionally for contracts, the signing parties and who they represent are clear: If something is unwritten, it is not a contract. Nonetheless, it is not mere fiction that there were mutual benefits for the political elite who encouraged assimilation and for minorities who performed it. With the term used by as many and as diverse scholars as Jacob Katz, János Kőbányai, Ferenc Fejtő, Vera Ránki, George L. Mosse, and David Sorkin, it deserves acknowledgment.[95]

Nevertheless, the decline in the acceptance of Jews was caused not only by a unilateral cancellation of an assimilationist social contract after Jews no longer helped make the country Hungarian after the Great War. Antisemitism also gained traction during the First World War (not only in Hungary) and was mercilessly manifested during the Red and White Terrors: The Red Terror was committed by revolutionaries against those they saw as counterrevolutionaries and the White Terror was committed by counterrevolutionaries against their enemies (revolutionaries and Jews).[96]

In the aftermath of the First World War, the Red Terror and the Treaty of Trianon, the scapegoating of Jews became popular. Jews were seen by many as responsible for the collapse of former Greater Hungary. Even though there were Jewish victims of the Red Terror and obviously there were Jews (merchants, entrepreneurs) whose interests were not served by the Republic of Councils, the myth of "Judeobolshevism" was popular. As the historian Miklós Konrád points out, prewar antisemitic mobilization at the universities and in the right-wing press should not be neglected. "Christian" middle classes (which could simply mean not Jewish or, more broadly, opponents of the liberalism and secularism of the prewar governments) experienced the Republic of Councils as a "Jewish" dictatorship because cries of alarm about Jewish domination had been voiced regularly since the 1900s.[97]

The numerus clausus law of 1920 was seen as a central measure of symbolic and practical importance by its proponents and opponents. It can be seen both as the declaration of intention of the new political establishment and as an antisemitic response to the challenge the overcrowding of universities and liberal professions represented. As described in the introduction, the numerus clausus law, the first anti-Jewish law in the twentieth century, and its enacting clause established that only 6 percent of first-year students in each faculty could be recruited from among Jews.[98] Even though not all the faculties applied the law in the strictest way and there were ambiguities around its application (such as whether to accept converted Christians), being enrolled in a Hungarian university was not the end of a Jewish student's struggles. During the 1920s, verbal and physical aggression against Jewish students in universities was regularly on the agenda.[99]

The Russian Empire's step back from assimilationist state policy in the form of a numerus clausus law in 1887 can be seen, in retrospect, as prefiguring Hungary's numerus clausus law in 1920. An important difference between Hungary and the Russian Empire is that while the first granted Jewish emancipation in 1867, the latter never did (only the revolution that swept away the empire brought about the Jewish emancipation). Nevertheless, the Russian numerus clausus law lends itself for comparison with the Hungarian one because both were antisemitic policies reacting to the phenomenon of Jewish overschooling, both reversed an earlier state policy encouraging Jews to enter state higher education, and both provoked massive Jewish student emigration. The expression *Jewish overschooling* in social history indicates a situation when Jewish families invest more in the children's education than non-Jewish families of the same socioeconomic standing and as a consequence the Jewish minority becomes disproportionately educated in comparison with the majority society.[100] It is justifiably criticized due to its implication that there is a normal level of schooling for minorities. Importantly, "the most visible proof of the shift from assimilation to exclusion was in laws regulating access to education."[101]

The Russian numerus clausus was known in Hungary and served as a direct inspiration for antisemites well before they had the chance to legislate their own version of the law. In January 1907, an MP of the Catholic People's Party, Károly Hencz, demanded in the Lower House that the minister of religion and public education "finally establish a numerus clausus" at the university in Budapest.[102] An anonymous pamphleteer in 1911 praised Russia for limiting the access of Jews to the graduate professions and recommended that Hungary also limit the percentage of Jews in these professions to their proportion in the general population.[103] This pamphlet was recommended to the attention of the readers in a prestigious Catholic literary and scientific journal, *Katholikus Szemle*.[104] Thus, the information reached a broader Catholic intellectual audience, not only committed antisemites.

In July 1920, Pál Teleki, an internationally acclaimed scholar of geography and convinced antiliberal and antisemitic politician was nominated as prime minister by the governor Miklós Horthy.[105] Teleki's government ended the White Terror for the sake of consolidation, but satisfying antisemitic students by restricting Jews' access to universities was also part of consolidation in their view. This government also had to ratify the Treaty of Trianon, which diminished Hungary's territory by two-thirds and led to the arrival from across the new state borders of 426,000 Hungarian refugees,[106] many of whom were intellectuals whose children aspired to enter higher education. In addition, many men who had been required to suspend or postpone their studies because of fighting in the First World War demanded the ability to complete their educations. Consequently, in the intermediate aftermath of the war and of Trianon, universities were overcrowded and the Ministry out of necessity limited admissions. Because of the counter-revolutionary and antisemitic fervor of the time, however, decision makers did not simply define a limited number of admissible students, but excluded youth implicated in the revolutionary events of 1918–19 and set up a Jewish quota. Nevertheless, of course, the exclusion of both groups was also highly motivated by ideology. As we see later, the very first idea of the numerus clausus was directed also against women's presence in the student body, but this did not materialize in the written version of the law. Most university faculties rather applied a numerus nullus toward women in the following two and a half decades.

During the 1920s Hungarian politicians often declared that the Jewish quota was a temporary measure to cope with postwar social tensions. Not everyone took this argument seriously. Some conservative politicians apparently did think that there was temporary need for a Jewish quota but not a permanent one, while their more right-wing, antisemitic allies had always regarded it as a first step in a longer process of marginalizing Jews. Opinions on whether politicians' declarations on the temporality should be believed differed among Jews. Perhaps understandably, when István Bethlen—a conservative liberal, not an antisemitic politician—succeeded Teleki as prime minister in 1921, many Jews hoped that Hungary was going in the right direction and, consequently, the Jewish quota would not last forever.

The hope of temporariness of the numerus clausus was mirrored from the beginning in the functioning of fundraising and philanthropy for the exiles of the law. Lajos Szabolcsi, the editor in chief of *Egyenlőség*, found a new vocation in saving Jewish youth from the numerus clausus. As he put it two decades later: "The youth took the wandering staff. The biggest task of my life stood ahead of me . . . to use the huge publicity of the magazine [*Egyenlőség*] so that I can save the youth of Hungarian Jewry from the catastrophe of the numerus clausus. I envisioned a previously unseen mass movement, so that we can support the Jewish youth who wished to study and we can send them abroad from donations to foreign friendly universities."[107]

Beyond fundraising, Szabolcsi's weekly newspaper collected and published useful information about foreign universities. Szabolcsi visited numerous German university towns in 1921 with this aim, and his paper connected the "wandering students" living abroad with prospective ones still in Hungary. By 1922, this coordinating activity outgrew the framework of an editorial board. Hence, the support was institutionalized in the form of the Central Jewish Student Aid Committee (Központi Zsidó Diáksegítő Bizottság, henceforth KZSDB) set up by the Pest Israelite Community (Pesti Izraelita Hitközség, henceforth PIH). Importantly, KZSDB was called "Central" because there were a number of local student aid committees across the country.

The central committee worked in the framework of the presidential department of PIH; thus, it was directly controlled by the president of the country's largest and most affluent Jewish community.[108] KZSDB simply distributed as much money as it managed to raise in a given academic year among all the students who applied for support without applying meritocratic or social criteria. Serious discussions about how to make the committee functional in the long run emerged only after the 1928 amendment of the numerus clausus, when it was established that anti-Jewish discrimination was there to stay in Hungarian universities and Jewish students' emigration would continue.

In the new quota system set up by the amended numerus clausus law, students had to be selected on the basis of their fathers' professions rather than their "race."[109] Those applicants whose fathers had professions in which, for historical reasons, hardly any Jews worked were to be admitted in higher proportion. Gyula Gömbös, a radical right-wing politician and future prime minister (1932–36), was not too greatly exaggerating when he claimed that "the Jews will long to have the current form of the numerus clausus back."[110] Although the Jewish quota was less strict between 1928 and 1932 than between 1920 and 1928,[111] the new and hypocritical discrimination made clear that the law would not be abolished (whereas, until 1928 there was space for hope that the Jewish quota at universities would be temporary); furthermore, the superficial alleviation instigated antisemitic violence on campuses. The historian Róbert Kerepeszki demonstrated these dynamics using the case study of the antisemitic student riots in Debrecen. The most intense period in this regard was the second semester of the academic year 1927–28, when the amendment of the numerus clausus law was being debated in parliament.[112]

Antisemitic students did not necessarily need to be provoked to turn violent. "Jew beatings" and "Jew-free days" organized by radical right-wing student fraternities (whose main organization was the Turul fraternity) were a regular occurrence every November and around Easter.[113] Jewish students were prevented from attending classes by threats and physical abuse so that they would be failed for excessive absence.[114] The autumn of 1929 was especially tough for Jewish students; even those who studied abroad witnessed antisemitic demonstrations by students in several of their places of study: Vienna, Prague, Brno, and Bratislava. In Bratislava, students of the Comenius University explicitly demanded the introduction of a numerus clausus law. In Vienna, the rioting resulted in serious injuries for Jewish and socialist students, and the furnishings of the Anatomical Institute of the university was also damaged.[115] In Prague, medical students of Charles University were the first to demonstrate on November 14 and 15, complaining about the lack of space in lecture halls and dissecting rooms, allegedly from overcrowding by foreign Jews. In the meantime, the medical faculties of German universities in Czechoslovakia and of German technical colleges had more foreign students—most of whom were Jewish, including hundreds from Hungary—each year. Yet, they were not as many and apparently not as visible as Jewish students from Poland. The discourse on "troublesome foreigners" in Czechoslovakia revolved around Polish Jews, as the historian Miloslav Szabó demonstrates.[116]

WOMEN AT UNIVERSITIES: SLOW ACCESS AND QUICK EXCLUSION

The exclusion of women from universities was longer and more comprehensive than that of Christian religious dissenters and of Jews, the latter being discriminated against also on racist grounds. We know of fewer female than Jewish students at medieval universities. The coeducation of women and men was harder to imagine and accept than that of Christian and non-Christian men. Women lecturers are better remembered than women students. David de la Croix and Mara Vitale have identified twenty-three women who taught at European universities prior to 1800.[117] Not all of them held professorships; some temporarily replaced their fathers in teaching or simply gave lectures. This does not necessarily mean that they were also university students before teaching; for example, the daughters of professors were presumably home-schooled, and their fathers vouched for their competence. The first woman remembered as a university professor, however, the jurist Bettisia Gozzadini, is known to have graduated in 1237 from the university in Bologna, where she later taught.[118]

Nevertheless, in terms of practicing an intellectual profession, women had an easier time with medicine than with law. Some women, even a few Jewish ones, acted as physicians without university education and also without being persecuted for unlicensed practice in the Middle Ages. Similarly to the case of Jewish men, Jewish and Christian women got to practice medicine because of dire need. Such dire need presented itself (for reasons of sexual mores and confidentiality) when female patients or children needed treatment. More surprisingly, ophthalmology was also a field where women got to work as medical doctors. All the medieval female doctors we know of stemmed from medical dynasties.

During the Enlightenment, similar to the marginalization, segregation, and oppression of religious outsiders, the inequality between women and men was questioned, and the idea that it was not right started to regularly arise. Yet, even during the nineteenth century, after girls' secondary schooling had further developed and more universities admitted women, many universities admitted women only in faculties of medicine and arts or teachers' training institutes, preparing them for professions seen as suitable for women.

In the second half of the nineteenth century, Hungary was not particularly backward in the field of women's rights. Women's higher education had been discussed in the press since the 1870s. The first Hungarian woman to earn a university degree, Vilma Hugonnai, read in the Hungarian journal

Hon—edited by the famous author Mór Jókai—that in Switzerland women could study medicine, which put her on the path to move to Zurich to attain a medical degree.[119] She wanted to practice in Hungary but doing so was a two-decades-long struggle. Her foreign degree was not accredited on the grounds that women in Hungary could not get a university degree because girls were not permitted to attain the "matura" (*érettségi*)—the secondary school leaving exam—required for university enrollment.

The University of Zurich did not require a matura to enroll,[120] so many foreign women, most notably from the Russian Empire, studied there. Zurich came to play a pioneering role. When Nadeschda Suslova in 1864 asked the university's council to permit her to visit lectures, the council nominated a committee to examine whether women should be allowed to study at the university, and it judged in favor of women's education. The presence of open-minded professors was not a mere chance. Numerous liberal German academics had found refuge in Switzerland after 1848. In addition, this small country's universities could not draw enough students from the local population and heavily relied on foreign students. Since the universities of Bern, Neuchâtel, Zurich, and Lausanne were also quite new, they could not yet rely on centuries of fame and needed to draw students with something else. Hence, it was a useful market gap for them to accept students who were unwelcome elsewhere, such as (foreign) women.

As we have seen, medieval women were mostly unable to attend a university, but if they came from a medical family, they had a chance to practice. In the nineteenth century, the situation was the opposite: Medical faculties slowly opened up for them, but they had a very hard time setting up practices. Similar to Hugonnai, the Austrian Gabriele Possanner studied medicine in Switzerland, and was not immediately allowed to work as a doctor in her home country.

In fact, Hugonnai struggled for a long time to have her Swiss degree naturalized in Hungary and this happened as late as 1897. Until then, she taught in the school of the Országos Nőképző Egyesület (Association for Girls' Education) and published articles on birth and midwives' education. She also became a leading figure of the women's movement and her as yet unnaturalized foreign degree was a subject for debates.

An 1895 ministerial decree opened a few faculties—humanities, pharmacy, and medicine—for women in the Hungarian part of the Habsburg monarchy before such a thing happened in Austria. The same decree allowed the foundation of girls' gymnasia in Hungary as a result of a three-decade-long struggle by the Hungarian Association for the Education of Women.[121] The 1896 opening of the first such institution in Hungary followed its German counterpart by three years.[122] In fact, Hungary's governing liberal party intended to make a point with introducing emancipatory reforms around the festivities for the millennium celebration of the state's foundation in 896.[123]

Even Austrian debates about women's access to universities were galvanized by the events in Hungary.[124] Yet, the Hungarian reforms were also strongly opposed by many politicians as well as medical and pharmacist organizations. The country's feminist movement was not populous. The Feminists' Association (Feministák Egyesülete, henceforth FE) nevertheless had a leadership of internationally significant and well-connected women, some of whom—Rosika Schwimmer and Vilma Glücklich—were among the founders of the currently functioning Women's International League for Peace and Freedom. Shortly before the First World War, FE hosted the seventh conference of the International Suffrage Alliance in Budapest, demonstrating Schwimmer's international network.[125] Schwimmer and her colleagues tried to keep feminism out of (or above) party politics; however, during the Great War, they got close to the Social Democrats, and in 1918, their cause became intertwined with that of the Aster Revolution. Schwimmer became the world's first female ambassador as the Károlyi government's diplomat in Switzerland. This was one of several reasons for feminists' ostracization in post-1919 counterrevolutionary Hungary.

Antifeminism crystallized as a movement in central Europe before the Great War, as the 1912 foundation of Germany's antifeminist alliance (Deutscher Bunde gegen die Frauenemancipation) shows.[126] However, it gained additional momentum in the war's aftermath as a backlash against developments in women's employment, education, and suffrage, processes that had been accelerated by the war. The antifeminists identified their alliance as national and Christian from the beginning; they accused feminism of weakening the nations' military force and its potential to win its potential to acquire all the resources (most notably territories) it needs and deserves.

In the aftermath of the conflict, women were even accused of taking away space from men in the labor market and in the universities within their own nation. It was indeed very visible that while masses of young men were forced to go to the front instead of university, women replaced them in faculties where they were admitted. During the fin de siècle, fewer than 10 women enrolled in Budapest's medical faculty per year; however, in the first semester of 1914–15, 220 women enrolled, and in 1917–18, women represented over a quarter of the students (28.4%) with 576 individuals.[127]

In 1918 the Károlyi government abolished gender-based discrimination, granting women access to all faculties; however, this reform was annulled in

1919 as an immediate backlash against liberal developments. Law and engineering faculties were again closed to women until after the Second World War, with a few exceptions.

The counterrevolutionary right-wing Hungarian political structure built from 1919 onward favored an illiberal, patriarchal model of family and gender advocated by right-wing nationalist and antisemitic women. They founded the National Alliance of Hungarian Women (Magyar Asszonyok Nemzeti Szövetsége, henceforth MANSZ) in 1919, in opposition to the liberal and the Communist revolutions. This remained the largest Hungarian women's organization throughout the interwar period. The intellectuals of MANSZ managed to tie their ideology with mainstream counterrevolutionary politicians' official national project: the revision of the Trianon Treaty. According to Judith Szapor's analysis, MANSZ was even a close precursor to the Spanish Falangist women's movement.[128]

Although MANSZ did partially stand up for women's right to education and intellectual jobs, straightforward feminist values, its members were opposed to feminism and considered it an alien international ideology threatening the Hungarian nation. Only Christian women could enter MANSZ and after 1941 only women "of Aryan descent."[129] Its leader, Cécile Tormay, was an (in)famously antisemitic writer. For instance, in her welcoming address to MANSZ's almanac for 1920, she referred to Jews as a threatening alien race and with abusive words five times within one page. She did so without mentioning the word *Jew*, yet it was very easy to decode her meaning, especially her statement that Károlyi "threw his homeland to the hatred of Szamuellys [*sic*] and Kun-Kohns."[130] Here, she identified Tibor Szamuely, deputy people's commissar during the Republic of Councils, as responsible for the Red Terror and Béla Kun, commissar of foreign affairs and war, as representatives of the entire Jewish population of Hungary.

While the course of history seemingly pointed toward the emancipation of women in the early twentieth century, the interwar period disappointed feminists in Hungary (and elsewhere). In 1918, all university faculties of Hungary had been opened to them, but only a year later, this reform was repealed. In fact, even the first idea leading to the numerus clausus law was sexist. The "racial quota" was added later, and ultimately, the exclusion of women was dropped.

Up until 1920 all men in possession of a secondary school leaving exam were entitled to university enrollment, while until the Károlyi government's reform women had access only to faculties of humanities, medicine, and pharmacy and only those who had achieved a certain level of grades. In the Great War's aftermath, universities became overcrowded as multiple cohorts of men whose studies had been interrupted by service returned to continue them, and when they did, they encountered a higher number of female students than they had before the war. As a result, they directed their ire against the women, and the first proposal to limit the number of female students arose. It was decided at the medical faculty of the Hungarian Royal University in Budapest that no more women would be admitted until the gender proportions in the student body returned to the prewar norm, and even then, the women admitted would have to be at least twenty-two years old. This faculty indeed rejected all women applicants until the academic year 1925–26. In the fall semester of that year, eleven women enrolled.[131]

Jewish women were seen as especially threatening to Christian men's privilege in studying and pursuing intellectual careers. It was hard to miss that Jewish overschooling was stronger among female than male students. Even in the prewar era, 38 percent of female while 21 percent of male university students were Jewish.[132] The historian Anna Borgos has reconstructed the discourses about and measures against female and Jewish students at the humanities faculty of the Hungarian Royal Univerity in Budapest. Since access to universities became a scarce resource, it became very important for the traditional owners of this privilege—Christian men of the upper and middle classes—to exclude the relatively newcomer minorities: Jews and women. With regard to both groups, a rhetoric of defense was used, as if they were occupiers.[133]

The higher rate of Jewish overschooling among women than men was a transnational phenomenon. One example is from Vienna, where in the winter of 1917–18, the majority of female university students were Jewish and women made up 46 percent of students due to the war. The high rate of Jews also had to do with the presence of Galician and Bukovinian Jewish refugees in the city. According to Michaela Raggam-Blesch, Jewish women in Vienna's universities before the First World War were first and foremost discriminated against as women and, after the war, as Jews, when they were also targets of violence.[134] As Harriet Pass Freidenreich notes for the situation in Austria and Germany in the first decades of the twentieth century, "Although many more Jewish men than women received a higher education, the proportion of Jewish women among female students remained roughly twice as high as the proportion of Jewish men among male students."[135]

Also within Hungary, Jews were overrepresented among female high school graduates, the only population qualified to apply to university in the first place. In the ten years following the partial admission of women to universities in 1895, at the University of Budapest, nearly half of female students were Jewish, whereas only about one-third of male students were.[136] During the First World War, as the proportion of women among (academically active) students increased due to the front service of many male students, so did the presence of Jews. As a consequence of this and of the intertwining of sexism and racism, it was practical for antisemites to restrict female access to universities.

As a summary of this historical contextualization of the case study the remainder of the book focuses on, one should remember that academic migration for the sake of studies (peregrination) was first a necessity for all students due to the large geographical distances between the first medieval universities. By the late Middle Ages, most European kingdoms had their own universities, which made internal (within a country) peregrination more common than external travel. In the early modern period, however, Reformation, Counter-Reformation, and most of all confessionalization (the process of identity formation based on religious affiliation) rendered long-distance migration a necessity for aspiring students who did not belong to the dominant religion of their birthplace. Jews necessarily belonged to such religious dissidents until the establishment of the State of Israel in 1948.

On the one hand, during the nineteenth century religious groups with a faith different from a country's mainstream, including Jews, were emancipated in most of Europe and, hence, no longer likely to be excluded from higher education (if they were men, since women's emancipation was much slower and more partial than that of religious groups). On the other hand, modern antisemitism took the place of premodern mainly religious-motivated anti-Judaism. It provided anti-Jewish hostility with a pseudoscientific and modern outlook and turned Jewishness from a religion into a race, which individuals could no longer escape by converting to Christianity. The modern antisemitic movement created a demand for the reexclusion of Jews from universities as a first step toward their general de-emancipation.

In the meantime, during the nineteenth and early twentieth centuries, peregrination was more often motivated by a quest for high-quality education in possibly better universities abroad. Then the First World War and its consequences dramatically changed the patterns of peregrination. Unlike in the previous period, the typical peregrini of the interwar period were not intellectuals who were voluntarily mobile, but members of ethnic, national, and political minorities pushed out from their native countries by nationalism, antisemitism, and political persecution.

A few similarities can be observed between the situation of women and Jews in premodern and twentieth-century academia. Medicine as a discipline was a sphere for partial (sporadic) inclusion for centuries and for intellectual emancipation in the late nineteenth and early twentieth centuries. In addition, dire need for physicians sometimes enabled Jews and women to practice medicine even if they had not graduated from university. During the nineteenth century, medicine was generally one of the few university faculties where women were allowed to enroll. However, women's emancipation in academia was much slower and less comprehensive than that of Jews, and the backlashes against it appeared promptly. Moreover, the demand to undo Jewish and female emancipation were interwoven due to the intersection between educated Jews and women across the continent. Women among Jews were even more overschooled than their male Jewish peers. This contributed to the meeting of sexism and racism, antifeminist and anti-Jewish hostility in the genesis of the Hungarian numerus clausus law of 1920.

PART II

INTERWAR HUNGARY'S UNWANTED STUDENTS ON THE MOVE

TWO

JEWS

"SUBCONSCIOUSLY SOMETHING IN THE JEW seeks to escape the morally dubious, the distasteful, the petty, the unspiritual, which is attached to all trade, and all that is purely business, and to lift himself up to the moneyless sphere of the intellectual, as if—in the Wagnerian sense—he wished to redeem himself and his entire race, from the curse of money."[1] This could be the concise and belletristic summary of this chapter's social-historical message. It is a prime example of when writers grasp social phenomena decades before academic historians do. The author, Stefan Zweig, was presumably aware that judging commerce and business so harshly was the internalization of an antisemitic trope, hence his reference to the antisemitic composer Richard Wagner. Assimilation was, among other factors, motivated by many Jews internalizing antisemitic prejudices, and the (potentially subconscious) desire for upward social mobility and assimilation described by Zweig was also characteristic of the Hungarian exiles of the interwar Jewish quota.

But who were these exiles exactly? Since the Jewish quota was introduced as a vehicle to reverse Jewish upward social mobility through limiting Jews' educational mobility, identification of the quota exiles is here to be understood in terms of their social background and looked at in quite large number. This is a social history of thousands of students, not of a few individuals whose "brains were drained" as a consequence of academic antisemitism in Hungary.[2] Because this study includes students who were pushed out of Hungary due to their political dissent and their sex in addition to those pushed out by antisemitism, I refer to those pushed out for their Jewish descent as exiles of the Jewish quota.

This chapter focuses on the largest group hit by the numerus clausus law: Jews. This group overlaps with political dissenters and with women. However, to show the threefold function of this law regulating access to Hungarian universities, we focus on the aspects of antisemitism, oppression of left-wingers, and misogyny in three different chapters.

First, I make the case for examining the social and educational mobility within Jewish families whose children circumvented Hungary's Jewish quota by studying abroad and explain my methodology. Then I present the research results and interpret the historical sociology of the Jewish quota's exiles before moving on to the impact studying abroad had on Jewish migrant students' identities. Finally, I raise students' narratives of their forced peregrination, as recorded in their ego documents.

WHY AND HOW TO EXAMINE SOCIAL MOBILITY

As I argue in chapter 1, regulating access to universities is more about regulating access to intellectual professions, and thereby to elite society, than about access to knowledge. Educational and social mobility subvert social hierarchies, and therefore, the mobility of marginal groups easily inflames conservatives, but especially radical right-wingers. Different antisemites may have different aims, but in the late nineteenth century and in the first four decades of the twentieth, those in the mainstream focused on undoing Jewish emancipation. Since antisemitism looked at Judaism as a race, unlike premodern anti-Judaists, antisemites were horrified by the possibility of Jews assimilating. Jews may have aspired for education for the sake of social integration and may have assumed Hungarian linguistic and national identity in order to become Hungarians, but in the eyes of antisemites, they remained racial aliens; if a Jewish person held an intellectual profession or any elite position, antisemites saw this role as taken from Hungarians. Jews in pre–First World War Hungary (and throughout Europe) indeed successfully and en masse utilized secondary and higher education as a means of social mobility and integration.[3] It is telling data that between 1900 and the Great War, around 24 percent of university students were Jews, while only about 6 percent of the general population was.[4] Péter Tibor Nagy, a sociologist and historian of education, has argued that due to these social-historical facts, the implementers of the discriminatory law, a coalition of different (Christian socialist, anticapitalist, and antisocialist) antisemites, identified higher education as the field in which Jewish emancipation could be the most efficiently withdrawn, and they did so on a rational basis.[5]

Thus, a concern with social and educational mobility was very much on antisemites' minds. The older cohorts of Jewish intellectuals were also very much, and painfully, aware of what was at stake for Hungarian Jewry when its youth was pushed out from higher education. For instance, Ernő Ballagi, the president of the KZSDB, argued in the following way when the numerus clausus law was amended in 1928, which in his interpretation, meant that academic antisemitism was there to stay:

> This institution, the central organization of student aid which thus far has been an ad hoc organization of charity, has to be properly built up and established, it has to be put on stable, unshakeable grounds. Such an organization of Hungarian Jewry needs to be created, which will be able to send a proper number of Jewish students to foreign universities for decades to come and to enable them to study. Hungarian Jewry cannot renounce of the resupply of a sufficient number of intellectuals. Hungarian Jewry cannot allow to be pushed back intellectually and morally, cannot allow its historical development to be turned back by decades, its occupational freedom to be limited. . . . Let us restart fundraising for the Central Jewish Student Aid Committee, for saving Hungarian Jewish students and our intelligentsia![6]

Along these lines, relevant questions are to what extent were the Jewish quota and Jewish pushback against it successful, to what extent could Jewish youth escape the quota by peregrination, and what happened to Jewish educational mobility? Here, the main concern is from what social background did the Jews who were able to study abroad or make it through the antisemitic quota system in Hungary come from? The contemporary and historical assumption that student migration was the escape route for the wealthy is challenged by empirically examining the "ideal type" of the Jewish emigrant student.

I compare the exiles' social profiles with those of Jewish youth who filled the 6 percent Jewish quota and thus studied in Hungarian higher education. It is possible to hypothesize that Jewish families who possessed economic and social capital were able to mobilize their influence for the sake of getting their children into a Hungarian university. Autobiographic sources reveal the importance of nepotism, independent of grades, in securing one of the quota spots, despite the fact that since so few Jews were admitted to Hungarian universities, in theory only those with excellent grades should have had a chance.[7]

Possibly, the emigrants were those who lacked such means. According to an earlier interpretation, the statistical data on the families of Jewish students enrolled in Hungarian higher education in 1932–33 suggest that Jewish students who studied in Hungary came from rather well-to-do families.[8] A smaller-scale study of Hungarian Jewish numerus clausus refugees at the University of Bologna hinted at the possibility that Jewish migrant students who studied in Italy were not predestined for higher education. Their birth and residence certificates showed that the majority did not come from urban middle-class intellectual families. On the contrary, they characteristically hailed from the provincial lower middle class and tended to represent the first generation in their family to study at a university.[9]

The hypothesis I present here is grounded in an extrapolation from this small study. I assume that a significant part of the Jewish exiles pursued university studies in spite of, not because of, their social background and not as a means of maintaining their families' social status but as a means of moving upward. Thus, besides the hypothesis that most Hungarian migrant students were Jewish, it is assumed that Jewish students' emigration in the age of the numerus clausus law helped Jewish upward social mobility, despite the law's intentions. If this is so, the majority should have come from small towns and villages rather than from urban centers and from less educated rather than high school or university graduate fathers. (The available sources only identify the fathers' occupations; mothers are only mentioned if widows.)

In order to test the hypotheses, I constructed a sample of Hungarian students enrolled in every fifth academic year after 1921–22 in medicine and engineering in Vienna, Prague, Berlin, and Bologna.[10] Austria, Germany, and Italy were the three most popular target countries of Hungarian student migration in the interwar period, but in the very beginning of the 1920s, Czechoslovakia also had a huge popularity. Medicine and engineering were the fields most often chosen by migrant students, due to these degrees' easy international transferability. The sample includes every Hungarian student, not only Jews, to test the hypothesis of a Jewish majority among them. Since most universities did not register citizenship, "Hungarian" does not necessarily mean a Hungarian citizen in this context. Instead, I used a broad definition when I selected which students to include in my data set. I chose to include those who were born in the territory of post-Trianon Hungary, were resident there, or had studied there before enrolling in a university abroad because they were likely to have been influenced by the numerus clausus law introduced in 1920 when making a decision about their studies. Nevertheless, some became citizens of neighboring countries that gained formerly Hungarian territories due to the Treaty of Trianon (June 4, 1920), which was signed less than four months before the numerus clausus law was accepted in Parliament.

Based on the accessibility of the sources, I must point out some limitations of the sample. Not all universities' relevant documents survived the Second World War, and slightly different types of data were collected about students in different countries. The sources are the enrollment forms and students' documents preserved in the archives of the University of Vienna, the Technical

Fig. 2.1 Lívia Fleischmann, who immigrated to Italy to study and stayed there until her death in 1959. She became a teacher of mathematics and chemistry and founded a school for poor children. Courtesy of Éva Forintos.

University (former Technical College) of Vienna, Charles University in Prague (which inherited the documents of the German University of Prague, closed down in 1945), the Czech Technical University (which preserves the archive of the German Technical College of Prague, closed down in 1945), Humboldt University (former Friedrich-Wilhelm University) in Berlin, the Technical University (former Technical College) of Berlin, and the University of Bologna.

These sources do not provide insight into the financial background of students' families, except for a few special cases when students submitted certificates of poverty to reduce their tuition fee.[11] However, in the case of Vienna, Prague, and Berlin, the enrollment forms almost always include fathers' occupations, and in Bologna, fathers' occupations are revealed by birth certificates. Hence, the focus is on educational mobility, whether or not the students, who by virtue of being university students were necessarily graduates of gymnasia or equivalent schooling, stemmed from fathers with a lower level of education. In the end, the data set came to contain information on 1,131 Hungarian medical or engineering students enrolled in the University of Vienna, the German

University of Prague, the University of Bologna, the German Technical College of Prague, and the Technical College of Berlin. We know the place of birth, the gender, and the field of study for all of them, but about the majority we know more: religion, date of birth, place of residence, father's name, and father's occupation. In some faculties in some academic years, even more data were required by the enrollment form—namely, citizenship, mother tongue, nationality, previous place of study, and father's residence. Importantly, we do not know to which denomination of Judaism—Orthodox, Neolog, or status quo ante were the three in Hungary—the students belonged. When Christians filled university enrollment forms (or dictated their data to clerks), they identified themselves according to their denomination, such as Roman Catholic, Calvinist, and so on. Contrastingly, Jews indicated only that they were Jewish; although there were three different terms students used to signify this (jüdisch, mosaisch, or israelitisch), they all mean Jewish in general. Thus, the denomination within the Jewish faith was not as central as Judaism itself or Jewish descent to either university administrators or Jewish students.

I include in the data set all students of Jewish religion or descent who studied abroad in the age of the numerus clausus law (1920–45). Thus, converts are included because they were counted as Jewish in Hungary when universities applied the numerus clausus law, and this law and other manifestations of antisemitism were push factors for conversion. Jewish religious affiliation is nevertheless the best proxy for identifying most of the quota exiles. Yet since there were converts among them, I first separated the issue of religion and being pushed out by antisemitism, handling them as two different variables in my data set.

When analyzing the data of Hungarian students found in university documents abroad, I regarded everyone who claimed Jewish religion or nationality as a Jew as well as an exile of the Jewish quota.[12] I encountered a dilemma in cases where students claimed a religion other than Jewish but whose biographies revealed Jewish origin. On the one hand, historians have to respect the self-identification of their subjects; on the other hand, it is only possible to examine the consequences of antisemitism if we take into account that certain people were regarded as Jewish by antisemites even if this was against their will. In addition, since conversion was one of the strategies to evade the Jewish quota and also a possible reaction to the 1919–20 White Terror pogroms in Hungary, Jews who converted and enrolled in a foreign university as Christians are not regarded as Jewish, but they were still pushed out by antisemitism. It is noteworthy, nonetheless, that the large majority of students of self-reported Jewish religion in my data set suggests that the emigrant students typically kept their Jewish religious affiliation and were not eager to hide it when enrolling in a university abroad. This would have been hard wherever the secondary school leaving exam had to be presented, anyway, as it included religion. Because of this, if someone converted as an adult, they were still identifiable as Jewish when documents from their childhood were looked into.

With regard to the fewer than a dozen students who did not fill anything in the row for religion in their enrollment forms, I was able to find out they were Jewish from the database of university students of interwar Hungary, since they also enrolled in Hungary at some point after their emigration. Knowing that, I regard them as quota exiles. One example of this type of case is the famous Nobel laureate Leo Szilard and his brother, Bela Silard. Their religion was Calvinist by the time they enrolled in the Technical College of Berlin. However, their biographies show they were originally Jewish and converted shortly before they left for Berlin after a humiliating antisemitic attack they suffered at the József Technical University in Budapest.[13] When they went to register for the academic year 1919–20, they were stopped at the entrance and were told that Jews could not study there. In vain Leo argued that they were not Jewish but Calvinists; they were beaten up.[14]

In short, Jewish religion is not a perfect proxy to identify Jews among Hungarian migrant students, but it is a quite good one and the best we have. In addition, Jews are such a majority in the sample even without those who did not self-identify as Jews that it confirms the hypothesis that an overwhelming majority of Hungarian students abroad were Jewish in the 1920s and 1930s.

A HISTORICAL SOCIOLOGY OF JEWISH QUOTA EXILES

After taking into account all the aforementioned considerations, 919 out of the 1,131 students, thus 81 percent of my sample, were Jewish by religion. When counting those exiled by the Jewish quota in the sample, it was necessary to take into consideration external information aside from the university documents. However, in the end the number of quota exiles (921) is almost identical to the number of those who were Jewish by religion. Such proportion strikingly reaffirms the estimation of Alajos Kovács (an antisemitic statistician of the interwar era), who assumed that, after 1920, 80 percent of Hungarian students abroad were Jewish (not counting the 5–7 percent who went to study abroad with a stipend provided by the state).[15]

Yet, quota exiles did not constitute the same majority in all the examined faculties. Their proportion among Hungarians was highest in Bologna (95%) and lowest in Berlin (70%) (see table 2.1). This contrast is exaggerated by the

Table 2.1 Migrant students by study location

Study location	Berlin	Bologna	Prague	Vienna
Jewish exiles	82 (70%)	73 (95%)	445 (87%)	321 (85%)
Whole sample	137	86	530	378
Valid cases	117 (100%)	77 (100%)	509 (100%)	376 (100%)
Missing data	20	9	21	2

Table 2.2 Migrant students by field of study

Field of study	Engineering	Medicine
Jewish exiles	246 (72%)	675 (85%)
Whole sample	341	790
Valid cases	316 (100%)	763 (100%)
Missing data	25	27

fact that in Bologna the information on religion comes from official documents, while in Berlin it was self-reported. Examining all four cities, the field of study made more difference than the study location. Less than three-quarters (72%) of engineering students while more than four-fifths (85%) of medical students were quota exiles (see table 2.2).

After investigating the social background and social mobility of the students, with particular regard to quota exiles among them (their majority), I compared them to the social background and mobility of Jewish students who in the age of the numerus clausus law were studying in Hungarian universities—that is, those who were admitted in the framework of the restrictive Jewish quota. The latter group's data were extracted with the help of Victor Karády, Péter Tibor Nagy, and Csaba Bendzsák from the historical sociological survey on university students in Hungary, conducted in the research project "Culturally Composite Elites, Regime Changes and Social Crises in Multi-Ethnic and Multi-Confessional Eastern Europe."[16]

The most important information available in university documents about the social background of students is fathers' occupations. I used a categorization applied by Victor Karády and Péter Tibor Nagy in the aforementioned research where occupations were divided into thirteen categories.[17] In this system, one considers both educational level and social class; for example, secondary school teachers and elementary school teachers are separated. This enabled me to look at the émigré students' educational mobility. My special interest was to see to what extent these students with so much intellectual ambition came from intellectual families. For being secondary school graduates (a prerequisite for university enrollment), they could already regard themselves as intellectuals according to the social norms of the period; however, those who intended to work in the prestigious liberal professions of medicine and engineering would reach even higher educational status.

Regrettably, fathers' occupations are known in only about two-thirds of the cases (66%). However, these confirm the hypothesis that the typical Jewish migrant student was not of intellectual and privileged origin. The proportion of lower-class merchants, such as retailer and shopkeeper families, is especially striking (42%). Since four in five (921 out of 1,131) students are quota exiles, their characteristics are to a large extent the features of the whole group. Yet, having a retailer father is remarkably more frequent among them (42%) than the whole sample (37%) (see table 2.3). The only other category where there is a visible difference between the whole sample and the Jewish exiles is the proportion of fathers of unknown profession, where only 33 percent of Jewish students, while 38 percent of all students did not provide information. This means that students of unknown religion usually provided very little information about anything in enrollment forms. Thus, Jewishness was not something migrant students were especially eager to hide.

Considering that medical and engineering students are under examination—that is, youth who aimed to enter classical liberal professions—we can speak of keeping an already achieved social status by the family if the father is to be found among the "specialized public employees," the "clergy, teachers, and employed intellectuals in humanities"; "doctors and medicine-related intellectuals"; and "other professional intellectuals." In the interwar period people employed in these fields were high school graduates and normally also pursued some kind of professional training after the secondary school leaving exam (érettségi), although it was not necessarily a university education.

Of course, there could have been university graduates in the previous generation of a family even if a student's father had not been one. Intellectual uncles, aunts, or other relatives may have in fact served as inspiring examples for would-be intellectual youth. In addition, as Judith Szapor historian highlights, "the extended family often served as a network that financially supported the children's education. Better-off relations routinely contributed to the expense of children's education, especially when the children studied abroad."[18]

Table 2.3 Fathers' occupations among migrant students

Father's occupation	**Whole sample**	**Jewish exiles**	**Class background**
Farmer (*földműves*)	13 (2%)	11 (2%)	
Unskilled and skilled worker (*munkás, szakmunkás*)	27 (4%)	26 (4%)	Lower than middle class
Artisan (*kisiparos*)	49 (7%)	40 (7%)	
Retailer (*kiskereskedő*)	264 (37%)	257 (42%)	
Private clerk (*magánhivatalnok*)	58 (8%)	49 (8%)	
Public clerk (*közhivatalnok*)	97 (14%)	78 (13%)	Lower middle class
Specialized public employee (*szakosított közalkalmazott*)	11 (2%)	6 (1%)	
Clergy, teacher, employed intellectual in humanities (*pap, tanár, alkalmazott humánértelmiségi*)	23 (3%)	20 (2%)	
Elementary school teacher and director (*tanító, elemi iskolai igazgató*)	6 (1%)	5 (1%)	Middle class proper
Doctor, medicine-related intellectual (*orvos, egészségügyi értelmiségi*)	44 (4%)	33 (5%)	
Other professional intellectual (*más szakértelmiségi*)	48 (7%)	37 (4%)	
High bourgeois, entrepreneur (*nagypolgár, önálló vállalkozó*)	38 (5%)	28 (5%)	Upper middle class
Living from revenues, retired (*magánzó, nyugdíjas*)	27 (4%)	23 (4%)	
Whole sample	1,131	921	
Valid cases	705 (100%)	613 (100%)	
Missing data	426	308	

Nevertheless, when looking at over a thousand students, and through the lens of university documents, we can only rely on the father's profession as a piece of data to gain insight into the family. In addition, since this is information we know about many of those Hungarian Jews who studied abroad, as well as their peers who studied in Hungary during the Jewish quota, we can use it to compare the families' circumstances.

In terms of social stratification generally, out of the thirteen professional categories applied in this study, the first three (farmers, workers, and artisans) can be considered lower than middle class; the next four (retailers, private clerks, public clerks, and specialized public employees), lower middle class or petty bourgeoisie; the next four (clergy and teachers and employed intelligentsia in the humanities, elementary school teachers and directors, doctors and medicine-related intellectuals, and other professional intellectuals), middle class proper; and the penultimate category (entrepreneurs), upper middle class or high bourgeoisie. Living from revenues is left out from the stratification because it basically functioned to account for unidentifiable or miscellaneous professions.

In this sense, 13 percent of Jewish exiles came from lower-than-middle-class backgrounds, 64 percent from the lower middle class, 12 percent from the middle class proper, and 5 percent from the upper middle class. Thus, for over three-quarters of the sample, participating in higher education meant upward social mobility, a means to achieve middle-class status (see table 2.3).

This conclusion becomes especially important when compared to the background of Jewish students in Hungarian higher education in the age of the numerus clausus law.[19] Importantly, the following comparisons are made between medical students only because, regrettably, we lack information on fathers' occupations in almost half of the cases (49%) of engineering students abroad (see table 2.4). The comparison leads to the striking result that the proportion of middle-class Jews was, as expected, higher among those who studied in Hungary than among those who emigrated. However, somewhat surprisingly, Jewish students under the numerus clausus law in Hungary also tended to come from the lower middle class, even if to a less extent than emigrants. When examining all the Hungarian medical faculties together, the social recruitment of Jewish medical students abroad and in Hungary seems to be very similar (see table 2.5). However, when separating the medical faculty of Budapest, where the Jewish quota was more severely implemented than in the provincial institutions,[20] we see that the share of middle-class Jews was especially high (see table 2.6).

This examination reveals two other important details. On the one hand, the share of medical students whose father worked in medicine as well was significantly lower among the emigrants (6%) than among those enrolled in Budapest (21%) or one of the provincial Hungarian universities (10%). This suggests that the offspring of medical dynasties had a higher chance of being admitted in the Jewish quota than others.

Yet another noteworthy circumstance to take into account is that some Jewish exiles succeeded in continuing their studies in Hungary. Thus, there are overlaps between Jewish students abroad and in Hungary during the 1920s and

Table 2.4 Fathers' occupations among Jewish medical students abroad and in Hungary

Father's occupation	Abroad (Vienna, Prague, Bologna, Berlin, 1921, 1926, 1931, and 1936)	In Hungary (first-year enrollments, 1919–38)		Class background
		Budapest	Pécs, Szeged, and Debrecen	
Farmer	7 (1%)	13 (2%)	32 (2%)	Lower than middle class
Unskilled and skilled worker	24 (5%)	22 (4%)	59 (4%)	
Artisan	35 (7%)	27 (5%)	132 (8%)	
Retailer	210 (43%)	102 (19%)	550 (35%)	Lower middle class
Private clerk	33 (7%)	83 (15%)	172 (11%)	
Public clerk	55 (11%)	40 (7%)	67 (4%)	
Specialized public employee	4 (1%)	24 (4%)	25 (2%)	
Clergy, teacher, employed intellectual in humanities	17 (3%)	25 (5%)	47 (3%)	Middle class proper
Elementary school teacher and director	5 (1%)	12 (2%)	26 (2%)	
Doctor, medicine-related intellectual	31 (6%)	114 (21%)	161 (10%)	
Other professional intellectual	24 (5%)	35 (6%)	78 (5%)	
High bourgeois, entrepreneur	24 (5%)	28 (5%)	121 (8%)	Upper middle class
Living from revenues, retired	19 (4%)	14 (3%)	95 (6%)	
Subtotal	488 (100%)	539 (100%)	1,565 (100%)	
Missing data	187	0	0	
Total	675	539	1,565	

Table 2.5 Class background of Jewish medical students abroad and in Hungary

Class background	**Vienna, Prague, Bologna, Berlin (1921, 1926, 1931, and 1936)**	**In Hungary (1919–38)**
Lower than middle class	14%	14%
Lower middle class	62%	51%
Middle class proper	16%	24%
Upper middle class	5%	7%
Living from revenues, retired	4%	5%
Whole sample	675 (100%)	2,104 (100%)
Missing data	187	0

Table 2.6 Class background of Jewish medical students abroad, in Budapest and in the provinces

Class background	**Vienna, Prague, Bologna, Berlin (1921, 1926, 1931, and 1936)**	**In Hungary (1919–38)**	
		Budapest	**Pécs, Szeged, and Debrecen**
Lower than middle class	14%	11%	14%
Lower middle class	62%	45%	52%
Middle class proper	16%	34%	20%
Upper middle class	5%	5%	8%
Living from revenues, retired	4%	3%	6%
Valid cases	675 (100%)	539 (100%)	1,565 (100%)
Missing data	187	0	0
Whole sample	675	539	1,565
		2,104	

1930s, making the difference in the social recruitment of the two groups all the more remarkable and reinforcing the hypothesis that social capital played an important role in securing a quota spot within Hungary.

Even if someone started studying abroad, it was a good strategy to look for professional connections within Hungary for the sake of getting into a

Table 2.7 The share of Hungarian family names among Jewish medical students abroad and in Hungary

University location	Field of study	Time period	Hungarian family names
Vienna	Medicine	1921, 1926, 1931, and 1936	27.3%
Prague	Medicine	1921, 1926, 1931, and 1936	32.6%
Prague	Medicine and engineering	1921, 1926, 1931, and 1936	33.5%
Budapest	Medicine	1920–29	42.9%
Szeged	Medicine	1919–46	42.7%
Pécs	Medicine	1918–51	37.3%
Debrecen	Medicine	1919–53	39.4%

Hungarian university later. For example, László Farádi enrolled in the Viennese medical school in 1926, while he continued to apply to the universities of Pécs and Budapest each year until 1930, when he succeeded at enrolling in Pécs thanks to a fortunate encounter with Sándor Gorka, a biology professor there.[21]

The share of Jews with Hungarian last names was also examined because the Hungarianization of Jewish family names was historically an important marker of assimilation (see table 2.7). Unsurprisingly, Jews who emigrated were significantly more likely to have a non-Hungarian last name than those who studied in Hungary. Thus, Jews of less assimilated background may have more easily chosen emigration. In addition, they were presumably more familiar with non-Hungarian parts of the former Habsburg monarchy (Vienna and Prague) and may have had a better knowledge of German than their more assimilated peers, possibly thanks to less exclusively Hungarian language use in their families.

A case in point is Arthur Linksz, the bilingual son of a Hungarian Modern Orthodox rabbi and a native-German-speaking Moravian mother, who went to study medicine in Prague. Last names hinting at *ostjüdisch* (east European Jewish) family roots—for instance, several versions of Abramowitz and Moskowitz—suggest a less assimilated background than traditionally Hungarian last names but also imply less social capital. Students of such background experienced fewer pull factors for Vienna, Prague, and Berlin than their peers

Table 2.8 Types of birth place among migrant students

Type of place of birth	Whole sample	Jewish exiles
Budapest	393 (35%)	311 (34%)
Towns with county rights	160 (14%)	129 (14%)
Towns with settled councils	189 (17%)	175 (19%)
Other localities (villages and small towns)	350 (31%)	288 (32%)
Abroad (outside of pre–First World War Hungary)	22 (2%)	7 (1%)
Whole sample	1,131	921
Valid cases	1,114 (100%)	910 (100%)
Missing data	17	11

with German last names but more push factors in Hungary than their peers with Hungarian last names.

My data set is more exhaustive in terms of geographic information than it is for fathers' professions. More than one-third of the students (35%) was born in Budapest (see table 2.8). This figure is more noteworthy considering that interwar Budapest was significantly smaller than the city we know now, with such large districts as Újpest, Rákospalota, Csepel, Kispest, and Pesterzsébet not incorporated until 1950. Thus, more than 35 percent of the students lived in proximity to the capital, even having the opportunity to get their secondary education there. Therefore, I used "Budapest and its suburbs" as a region, as was customary before the Second World War.

When looking at the provenance of Jewish exiles within the sample, we see that they were basically as likely to be born in Budapest as anyone. More than one-third of them (39%) hailed from Budapest and less than one-third (32%), from small towns and villages. They similarly determined the whole sample's characteristics in terms of regional selection (see table 2.9). After Budapest and its surroundings, the western and central (Transdanubia and the region between the Danube and the Tisza Rivers) and the northeastern part of pre-Trianon Hungary (the right bank of the Tisza River in regional terms, which is now the eastern part of Slovakia) sent the most students; however, significantly smaller groups came from here than from the capital's surroundings.

Table 2.9 Regional selection of migrant students

Region of birth	Whole sample	Jewish exiles
Budapest and suburbs	433 (39%)	346 (38%)
Left bank of the Danube	43 (4%)	34 (4%)
Right bank of the Danube (Transdanubia)	154 (14%)	122 (13%)
Between the Danube and the Tisza	150 (13%)	132 (15%)
Fiume and surroundings	2 (0.18%)	2 (0.22%)
Croatia and Slavonia	4 (0.33%)	3 (0.33%)
Transylvania	15 (1%)	11 (1%)
Left bank of the Tisza	123 (11%)	107 (12%)
Right bank of the Tisza	159 (14%)	141 (15%)
Crossing of Tisza and Maros	9 (1%)	5 (1%)
Abroad (outside of pre–First World War Hungary)	22 (2%)	7 (1%)
Whole sample	1,131	921
Valid cases	1,114 (100%)	910 (100%)
Missing data	17	11

THE IMPACT OF EMIGRATION ON STUDENTS' IDENTITIES

Fortunately, the university archive sources as well as emigrant students' ego documents, provide an insight into the complex matrix of their Hungarian as well as Jewish self-identifications and into a lot more. *Ego document* is a term coined by historian and writer Jacques Presser to refer to letters, diaries, memoirs, and autobiographies—that is, to texts where the author and the narrator coincide: They are continuously present in the text as the writer and the subject.[22]

Even the bureaucratic act of filling an enrollment form provided an opportunity for students (and for the historian who studies them) to position themselves in a matrix of self-identification. Depending on the location of the university and the time of enrollment, they could claim to be Hungarian in terms of mother tongue, nationality, or citizenship and Jewish in terms of religion or nationality.

In Vienna and Prague, there was a possibility to self-identify as Jewish in terms of religion *and* nationality as well, although in Vienna the category was labeled with the more racial term *Volkszugehörigkeit* (ethnic belonging). This section was introduced by the Academic Senate of the University of Vienna (without the approval of the Ministry of Education) in December 1923 in a context of ongoing anti-Jewish student riots.[23] Ironically, thanks to this presumably hostile measure, we know the self-reported nationality of 60 percent of the sample. Since the possibility of reporting one's nationality when enrolling only existed in the two countries—Austria and Czechoslovakia—where Jews were perceived as members of both a national and a religious group, it is significant that 102 students declared Jewish as their ethnicity or nationality. At the same time, it is important to note that students of Jewish nationality who turn up in more than one academic year I examined often switched between Jewish and Hungarian nationality. Thus, their Jewish national self-identification was not necessarily an expression of Zionist commitment, yet it means that they did not reject the idea that Jews were possibly a nation(ality), contrary to the mainstream Jewish public opinion in Hungary.

In Hungary, Jewish nationality, or more often Jewish *népfaj* (race, *Volksstamm*), was mostly evoked in an antisemitic context, in the enacting clause of the numerus clausus law most notably. Although this text implied that Jews were a nationality, there was no room for a Jew to officially identify with this nationality in a census—or in an enrollment form for that matter. The Jewish quota was endorsed on the basis of religion, even though antisemites of course regarded converts as Jewish. A positive claim to Jewish nationality was rare in Hungary, unlike in neighboring Czechoslovakia and Romania.[24] The Jewish communities' institutional structure—on which fundraising activity for the sake of emigrants relied—was dominated by assimilationists who thought of Jews as "Hungarians of the Israelite faith" who were also conservative and had been terrified enough by Bolshevism in 1919 to be in several aspects supportive of the antisemitic new "Christian Course"—the right-wing counter-revolutionary policy in interwar Hungary under Admiral Miklós Horthy between 1919 and 1944—for its anti-Communism.

By contrast, Zionists in Vienna and Prague were an influential current within the Jewish scene and these cities gave place to important Zionist congresses during the interwar period. Zionism was also important in university life in Vienna. Zionist was one of the three main categories of student Burschenschaften in addition to Pan-Germanists and Liberals. Importantly, the Burschenschaft scene was a central part of student life, as half of the students "wore colors," or belonged to a Burschenschaft.[25]

This visibly had an impact on the Hungarian migrant students since almost every fifth Hungarian Jewish student (18%) declared they were ethnically Jewish, and in Prague, every tenth Hungarian Jew reported to be of Jewish nationality. Moreover, we must remember that in Prague, engineering students are also part of the sample, among whom the proportion of Jews was lower than among medical students. Vienna offered a variety of student associations. Among others there were student clubs for Jewish students organized by field of study, such as the Jüdisch-akademischer Techniker Verband (Jewish-Academic Engineer Association) and the Akademischer Verein Jüdischer Mediziner (Academic Association of Jewish Medics). The latter had twelve members who also belonged to the Bécsi Magyarnyelvű Főiskolai Hallgatók Egyesülete/Verein Ungarisch Sprechender Wiener Hochschüler (Association of Hungarian Speaking Viennese College Students).[26]

In addition, among the ninety-two medical student members of the Bécsi Magyarnyelvű Főiskolai Hallgatók Egyesülete, eighty-one were Jewish, including the president and the first secretary.[27] Seven of the medical student members were not Hungarian citizens, and six of these seven were Jewish. Thus, this club also attracted Jews who came from territories lost to Hungary in 1920. This suggests calling the club an association for Hungarian speakers, rather than just Hungarians, was an inclusive choice. Apparently, those students who were interested in joining groups based on their origin were enthusiastic both about their Jewish and Hungarian identities.

STUDENTS NARRATING THEIR EMIGRATION

As a matter of fact, enough students emigrated for the Hungarian public to notice that peregrination was tied to numerus clausus enforcement. Different Jewish and general media wrote about Hungarian peregrination as a phenomenon almost exclusively characteristic of Jews who were pushed out by the numerus clausus law. The contemporary discourse was dominated by the negative version of the exile narrative, but the Zionist press promoted a positive version of it in which the exile gave an opportunity to escape the false consciousness of assimilation.[28] Since the experience of forced peregrination was a generational experience of Hungarian Jewish intellectual youth, it created a new community of fate. Importantly, within this community some displayed Hungarian patriotism and others Jewish national consciousness, although we do not know how the majority felt. As we see in chapters 3 and 4, the Jewish quota was not the only reason to leave Hungary.

We know more details about a few dozen students who wrote ego documents. Individual perceptions of living and studying abroad naturally varied; however, most of the related ego documents begin with descriptions of feeling lost. Lili Fenyő, who went to Italy without previous knowledge of Italian and with little information on the specifics of different universities there, depicts her feeling of disorientation upon arrival as a communal experience:

> One goes to Padua, because a famous medical professor lectures there. The other goes to Florence, because if being forced to go abroad, they prefer Florence, the city of arts. The third chooses Rome. Catania is the choice of the fourth, because it's cheaper there. The fifth rolls the dice on a map. Where does it fall? They will go there. After all, it does not matter. Nobody is expected by anyone, nobody has a destination. We can go anywhere, if there is a university, where it is possible to study. . . . We are not going anywhere. We are only coming from somewhere, where we are banned from studying.[29]

Feeling lost and homesick especially characterized those who had no routine with living abroad and far away from their families, as Miklós Kun remembered over seven decades later: "I was far away from home for the first time, I did not know anybody [in Prague], I was lonely." However, he soon began to feel at home when he joined a German-speaking company in the central Wenceslas Square and joined them for a concert of Judah Maccabi by a Viennese orchestra. This episode is illustrative of numerus clauses exiles' complex identities: homesickness for Budapest in Prague overcome by joining a German company and listening to an opera with a Jewish subject performed by Austrian musicians.[30]

Kun, similar to Fenyő's adventure in Italy, ended up in Prague as a result of random choices. Or so he told his story. After leaving Hungary for the sake of studying, he felt compelled to give up his attempt to study in Graz because he had found that antisemitism was rampant there. All landladies of potential rooms to rent asked about his religion and were unhappy to rent a room to a Jew. Hence, Kun returned to Budapest, where he bumped into a former (Jewish) schoolmate who was preparing to move to Brno for his studies. Kun followed suit; however, he found out during the train ride that in Brno medicine was only taught in Czech, and he was looking for a German-language medical faculty. A fellow traveler told him the closest German medical faculties were in Dresden and Prague. Kun opted for Prague because it was closer to Budapest.[31]

This narration must be taken with a large grain of salt, since the German University of Prague had the second best medical school in central Europe right after the prominent Viennese school, which was the single most important

Fig. 2.2 Portrait of György/Giorgio/George Mandl, Parma, Italy, 1937. After medical studies in Italy, Mandl established a successful dentistry practice in Parma in 1935. Due to the passage of Italian racial laws in 1938, he left for France in early 1939, and in March of that year he left from Bordeaux to Cuba, where he lived until he gained entry to the United States in 1941. There he became a family doctor and lived until 1977. Courtesy of the Mandl Family.

medical school on the continent east of Paris.[32] It was thus a rather appealing destination for medical students. Nevertheless, the important information is that Kun, similar to Fenyő, chose to fashion the story of his choice of destination as a result of coincidences.

Bence Szabolcsi, unlike Fenyő and Kun, did not claim to end up in his place of study coincidentally. It was admittedly a well-informed and premeditated decision on his part to enroll in the University of Leipzig. He was an especially talented disciple of the well-known composer Zoltán Kodály in Budapest. Although there was no musicology training in Hungary at that time, Bence Szabolcsi originally tried to enroll in the faculty of humanities in Budapest and continue his studies with Kodály. Thus, if it was not for the numerus clausus law, he would not have chosen peregrination.

In addition, being the younger brother of Lajos Szabolcsi, the great protector of the Jewish numerus clausus exiles and the conceiver of Központi Zsidó Diáksegítő Bizottság (KZSDB, Central Jewish Student Aid Committee), Bence Szabolcsi must have often heard the exile interpretation of his sojourn in Leipzig. Since there was a big age gap (ten years) between the brothers and both of their parents had died while Bence was a teenager, Lajos filled a fatherly function in Bence's life, both emotionally and in terms of financing him while he studied.[33] The years in Leipzig were formative for Bence in terms of not only studies but also life experience and listening to concerts by acknowledged musicians. Yet he wrote to Kodály "my master, please do not entirely forget me in my exile."[34]

László Farádi looked at his studies in Vienna through an entirely different lens. In his autobiography, he distanced himself from his fellow Hungarian Jews and kept himself out of the category of exiles by using the academic prominence of his alma mater, the Viennese medical school. He claimed, "I was not pushed by the constraint of the numerus clausus, I was only pulled to Vienna by the fame of the Viennese medical school."[35] However, it is worth remembering that he published this autobiography over half a century later in Hungary, during the Kádár regime, in which Farádi held a position of power as a deputy health care minister. Because of his prominent position in the government, it was important for him to emphasize that he had studied in one of the world's best medical schools of the 1920s. This claim could also be an attempt to downplay the significance of his Jewishness; however, he tells the prehistory of his peregrination which highlights the importance of being Jewish in the context of the 1920s and 1930s.

The reader of Farádi's autobiography cannot help but notice the obvious contradiction within his own story. As he himself writes earlier, originally he applied to the universities of Budapest and Pécs, both of which rejected him "because of the numerus clausus."[36] However, he wanted to become a doctor at any cost, so he started daydreaming about studying in Paris until his father told him the only way for him to study was to go to Vienna, where he could move in with an aunt. Thus, he studied in Vienna between 1926 and 1930. Enjoying his medical studies, the city's left-wing political subculture and rich cultural life notwithstanding, he tried to get into a Hungarian university continuously during these years, particularly in Pécs or in Budapest. He reapplied to the Hungarian Royal Erzsébet University (in Pécs) every year and three times to the Hungarian Royal Péter Pázmány University (in Budapest), and as soon as he succeeded at getting into the medical faculty in Pécs, he left Vienna for Pécs.[37]

György Kis, a student of textile engineering seems to have been quite happy to study in Czechoslovakia. The letters he sent to his family from Liberec—referred to by its German name, Reichenberg, by Hungarian Jewish students—are full of enthusiasm both for his studies at the college for textile engineering (Textilschule) and for life in the friendly little Czech town.[38] There were twenty-nine Hungarian students in his cohort,[39] and six of them were close enough to Kis for him to mention them in his family correspondence. A certain

Professor Mitter, who was particularly popular with students, apparently regarded them as one of the best cohorts he taught. Kis continually emphasized to his parents how hard his workload was and how much he studied.[40] Fortunately, there was some time left for dance parties where he and his fellow Hungarian students danced and flirted with local girls.[41]

The highlights of his Liberec experiences according to his letters were the excursions with fellow Hungarian students, a goulash party, and a study field trip in various Czech textile factories in May 1926. The goulash party was hosted by his landlady, Mrs. Pfeiffer, where Kis and his friend (and presumably roommate) "Feri" Burger cooked Hungarian goulash soup and invited the landlady's brother and two fellow Hungarian students, "Pista" Donát and "Bandi" Faragó. They were so satisfied with the result that "all of us felt as if we were back home in Hungary," as Kis wrote to his family.[42] For the study field trip, Kis summarized the significance of the towns visited to textile production and dedicated some additional remarks to a few of them, such as to Karlovy Vary, where "there were many Hungarians and many Jews."[43] This is the only occasion in his letters when he writes about Jews, although most probably all or nearly all of his fellow Hungarian students were Jewish. Even in this context, he writes about Hungarian tourists and Jewish tourists in the famous bath town, not about students.

Miklós Glatter, who would soon become a famous poet with a new last name, Radnóti, enrolled in the same college in Liberec as György Kis, in the academic year following Kis's graduation.[44] Both of them were exiles of the numerus clausus law and both of them would die as victims of the Shoah. Their letters were published in the twenty-first century with the intention of documenting pre-Shoah correspondences for a general public (that is, not only for historians). Kis's letters were published by his son, Ádám Kis, who included in the same volume both the Liberec letters of his father and the letters György Kis sent home one and a half decades later, from the eastern front of Second World War as a Jewish forced laborer in the Hungarian army.[45] In this way, his son, who was deprived of the chance to know his father at all, emphasizes the contrast between Kis's happy youth and his suffering during the Shoah. Radnóti's Liberec letters, on the other hand, are part of a large collection published by the literary scholar Tamás Bíró-Balogh. In the huge corpus of Radnóti letters, the ones sent from Liberec are testimonies of a life experience deemed not very important in the oeuvre by either Radnóti or Bíró-Balogh.[46]

Kis and Radnóti were taught the same subjects by the same professors in the same school, yet Kis immensely enjoyed the study program, while Radnóti detested it. The reason was their different motivation. Kis wanted to work with textiles, and he indeed would work in this profession after his return to Hungary; meanwhile, Radnóti was pressured to enroll by his adoptive father and could not wait to leave the whole textile industry behind to enroll in a faculty of humanities, which he later did in Szeged.

Bence Szabolcsi's letters, judged as worthy of publication by music historians Ferenc Bónis and György Kroó in the 1990s because of Szabolcsi's role in establishing musicology in Hungary between the 1950s and 1970s, reveal an attitude toward the institution he studied at, the University of Leipzig, somewhere between Kis's enthusiasm and Radnóti's indifference. He was passionately interested in his musicology studies; however, the positivist stance of the Leipzig musicology school alienated him.[47] In terms of socializing, Bence Szabolcsi, similarly to György Kis, dedicated most time to meeting with fellow (mostly Jewish) Hungarians. This was also due to necessity: As the brother of Lajos Szabolcsi, he could not escape taking up the role of representing the KZSDB in Leipzig and this rendered him a community leader of the local Hungarian Jewish student colony.[48] As he wrote in a letter in 1922: "I had to take upon myself managing the issues of the Student Action. . . . First it was somewhat hard to explain to them—just like to uncle Déry on the following day—that they are entitled to this stipend . . . and they do not need to kiss the hands of anybody for it. And that in addition this is not a private matter, this is the issue of a generation and so on. . . . These kids are poisoned by liberalism."[49] Mr. Déry was the president of the Leipzig Hungarian Association, a gentleman who by this time had been living out of Hungary for four decades. The KZSDB tried to mobilize philanthropists of Hungarian (and Jewish) background everywhere to financially aid numerus clausus exiles. It seems that Bence Szabolcsi thought Mr. Déry was not generous enough because he made poor students feel inferior for needing his money. The young Szabolcsi interestingly attributed this behavior to the liberal bourgeois background he also came from. His correspondence with both his sister-in-law and Zoltán Kodály indeed shows that in Leipzig he went through a process of detachment from this liberal bourgeois milieu.[50]

Most ego documents by Jewish emigrants match the exile narrative of their peregrination that was dominant in the contemporary Hungarian Jewish media because the students interacted with those who wrote about their plight. At the same time, it is necessary to keep in mind that whose letters and diaries survived until today and who published memoirs and autobiographies influences the sample. In addition, almost all of the available ego documents by exiled students were written after the Shoah and hence concentrate on how the authors survived the genocide and reflect on the time of their peregrination as a prelude to the main events of their lives.

Fig. 2.3 Giorgio Mandl on the rocks, Italy, 1936. Courtesy of the Mandl Family.

Poverty is an equally central topic in narratives by students and by journalists. Bence Szabolcsi, in addition to the widespread problem of housing poverty and malnourishment, witnessed the dramatic 1922 inflation in Weimar Germany. The young Szabolcsi was worried that his brother, not living in Germany, would not believe how quickly the prices rose and desperately emphasized that he only spent money on the most necessary things; he stopped buying books and urged his brother to look at his budget notes.[51] Earlier, before inflation, when life in Leipzig was expensive but prices were not rising by the hour, the young musicologist had a lighter tone when writing about his everyday life with the cousin he shared accommodation with: "Konrád decided to sew his socks by himself and I decided to write the books which I wanted to buy."[52]

Concerning politics, most students who authored ego documents, portrayed interwar Austria and Germany as intellectually stimulating yet stressful environments due to the rise of antisemitism and xenophobia already in the 1920s. Czechoslovakia and Italy, on the contrary, are represented as friendly host

Fig. 2.4 Giorgio Mandl with his Topolino car in Italy in the 1930s. Courtesy of the Mandl Family.

countries despite the vivid antisemitic student mobilization Czechoslovakia saw on several occasions, particularly in 1929 (as described in this part of chapter 1: Religious Outsiders and Ethnic Minorities at Universities). The road of Italian Fascism toward antisemitism was indeed slow and not conspicuous for foreign Jewish students until their expulsion in 1938.[53] Although the politically minded students noticed the strength of the radical right wing in Austria and Germany (most notably Miklós Kun, Bence Szabolcsi, and László Farádi), almost all of them blame themselves retrospectively for not having foreseen the extent of the danger of Nazism.

In conclusion, we may state that stopping Jewish educational mobility was central to the institution of the Jewish quota in Hungary because such mobility was the main avenue of Jews' social integration and assimilation. Jewish community institutions, therefore, intentionally promoted and supported the peregrination of Jewish youth. We must add that noble efforts notwithstanding, they could not counterbalance the impact of the Jewish quota,[54] but they reduced the harm by contributing to the study and living expenses of over five thousand, possibly nearly ten thousand, Jewish quota exiles.

Based on the data from university documents, the upwardly mobile son of a Jewish small-scale merchant from the capital emerges as the "ideal type" of the Jewish numerus clausus exile. (About the few women among them, see chapter 4.) The hypothesis that the large majority of migrant students in the age of the numerus clausus were refugees of antisemitism was confirmed and even its extent (81%) matched the contemporary expectation (80%). Four out of five Hungarian students abroad were Jewish.

At the same time, the hypotheses connected to social mobility were not all confirmed. The empirical study proved that peregrination was an escape route to evade the quota for the less privileged Jewish youth. Jewish exiled students were less likely to come from the middle class or the upper middle class than Jewish students who studied in Hungary. Thus, social capital was indeed an important factor in obtaining a quota spot.

The hypothesis about the geographical aspect of social mobility of Jewish emigrant students was disproved. Over one-third of the students was born in Budapest and less than one-third came from small towns and villages. In terms of regional selection, after Budapest and its suburbs, the western (Transdanubia) and central parts (between the Danube and the Tisza Rivers) of Hungary sent the most students. At the same time, in Hungary half of the Jewry lived in the capital and around it, so the fact that this was not the case among Jewish emigrant students demonstrates the social mobility of provincial Jewry despite the numerus clausus law.

Jewish emigrant students positioning themselves in the matrix of religious, ethnic, and national self-identification were visibly influenced by the realities experienced abroad. In Austria and Czechoslovakia, the category of Jewish nationality existed and almost one-fifth of the sample identified with it in their university documents, even though in Hungary this legal category did not exist. In Vienna, we find Hungarian Jews as active members of both Jewish and Hungarian student associations, so although they may not have rejected Zionism and the concept of a Jewish nation, many held on to their Hungarian national identity. Consistent with this, the surviving ego documents where students related their peregrination mostly echo the negative version of the exile narrative promoted by KZSDB; thus, many saw their peregrination as a true exile from their homeland, Hungary.

THREE

LEFTISTS

"Later on in life I often encountered my fellow students from Brno in different places of the movement, most of them fought here in Hungary, but some participated in the antifascist struggles of other countries, many in the Spanish Civil War."[1] So recalled the Communist Piroska Döme, who studied in Brno in the 1930s, of her fellow students and comrades half a century later.

BESIDES THE RACIAL QUOTA DIRECTED against Jews, Article 3 of the numerus clausus law also defined "loyalty to the nation" and "upstanding moral stance" as prerequisites of university admission.[2] Originally, this meant noninvolvement in the revolution in October 1918—also called Aster Revolution, which led to the establishment of the First Hungarian Republic—and the 1919 Hungarian Republic of Councils. The participants of the former event can be referred to as Octobrists, and many of them disagreed with the establishment of the Republic of Councils and the Red Terror that accompanied it. Logically, as years passed by and new cohorts came of age, university applicants were less and less likely to have participated in either of these events. Yet Communism, more so than other movements, continued to represent a threat for Hungary's right-wing regime. Therefore, from the mid-1920s, "nonloyal" youth referred to students caught participating in Communist activism. In contrast to Jews, who could enroll for new academic years after 1920 if fitting in in the new quota, students known or suspected to have been participants in the revolutions were expelled permanently.

Importantly, radical right-wing student activism played an essential role in the inception and preservation of the numerus clausus law. These students argued that the revolutionary Red Terror had been a result of the rise of a Jewish intellectual proletariat and the law would prevent the repetition of such a tragedy. This student activism had a dual institutional manifestation in the aftermath of the First World War, as presented by Béla Bodó, historian of the White Terror: the traditional university fraternities and the university militias. The fraternities functioned as the civilian public face of the militias, and the militias were the military wings of the fraternities.[3] In 1920, their demonstrations led to a ministerial decree that rendered student screening committees part of the law's enforcement mechanism. These committees examined students' behavior during the Aster Revolution and in the Republic of Councils. They had the right not only to reject new applicants but also to exclude already enrolled fellow students, thereby preventing them from finishing their studies, for being unpatriotic or morally unacceptable.[4]

The establishment of the right-wing antirevolutionary regime under Admiral Miklós Horthy's leadership—in Jewish history symbolized by the numerus clausus—was preceded by the White Terror in 1919–20, when university militias played an active role. One hundred thousand Hungarians escaped the country due to the White Terror, including tens of thousands of workers and peasants, not only students and intellectuals and not only Jews.[5] In order to legitimize his rule and gain the benevolence of the Entente, Horthy eventually broke away from the White militia, although he had approved their actions. Distancing himself from the White Terrorists was necessary to make Western statesmen more sympathetic to him than his opponents and also more sympathetic to Hungary, a state that had been on the losing side in the First World War and was expecting huge territorial losses according to peace plans. Although the worst-case scenario did not materialize, the final result—the Peace Treaty of Trianon signed on June 4, 1920—was nevertheless catastrophic.[6] Hungary lost over two-thirds of its territory and nearly 40 percent of its inhabitants.

Reacting to the catastrophes of the Red Terror and the Treaty of Trianon, numerous Hungarian politicians and public figures called for the defense of "Christian values" in public life with a previously unknown zeal. Public intellectuals of all Christian confessions repeatedly proclaimed the country's identity as a Christian nation. These calls were often little more than coded antisemitic language,[7] with most radical right-wingers meaning "Gentile" when referring to Christian, and Paul Hanebrink warns that we should take the Christianity within Christian nationalist ideology seriously.[8] Christian nationalists demanded a national society in which the public sphere was defined as a Christian space. A new consensus identifying Hungary as a Christian nation was broadly accepted, although vaguely defined. No one described what it meant to establish the "Christian idea" in all aspects of public life, but within higher education, the numerus clausus law was a manifestation of Christian nationalism.[9]

Christian nationalist hostility did not target only Jews. Political Christianity is a value system that seemed to be threatened by subversive elements in society, which is why the numerus clausus also restricted the access of political enemies of the state. In practice, excluding Jewish students was different from excluding students on ideological grounds, since religious affiliation—and by extension Jewish descent—was easily visible in personal documents, while Communist activism was underground. Hence, the exclusion of Communists was not as successful as the restriction of Jewish access.

There were many ways to fail to stand up to the Christian values prescribed by the political system, such as being a Social Democrat, a Communist, or an avant-garde artist.[10] Hence, the new antirevolutionary Hungary became unlivable for not only Jewish Hungarians but also virtually the entirety of *other Hungary*, a term of abuse in the period's right-wing discourse referring to the participants of the postwar Octobrist (1918) and Communist (1919) resurrections as well as residents of Budapest, which was portrayed as the sinful capital city of this other Hungary.[11] To the opponents of the official regime, however, the other Hungary denoted the better, oppressed half of the nation. Remembering Hungary's role as a refuge for Poles after Poland was occupied by Germany and the Soviet Union in 1939, the conservative politician József Antall Jr. noted in 1989 that the Hungarians (including his father József Antall Sr.) who helped the refugees demonstrated what "the other, the eternal Hungary was capable of while the government sided with the Nazi aggressors."[12]

The first major wave consisted of refugees from Béla Kun's Communist takeover in 1919, and the second wave consisted of Communists and their sympathizers persecuted during the antirevolutionary White Terror. Thus, after the fall of the Hungarian Republic of Councils, those Communists joined the Hungarian refugee population of Vienna, from which many liberal and bourgeois Hungarians had previously escaped. It is thus no wonder that the representatives of this diverse other Hungary in emigration could not create a united front against the Christian national regime. According to prominent historian of liberal thought György Litván, in principle all streams of the political emigration agreed in 1919–20 that they should join forces with each other and with democrats who remained in Hungary; however, later their cooperation was important only for the leader of the short-lived republic of 1918, Mihály Károlyi. Moreover, conflicts went beyond theoretical and tactical questions, and the different factions looked at each other as lethal enemies. Each group's prominent figures wrote memoirs to justify their own choices and to discredit the competing groups.[13] With regard to the nonprominent rank-and-file members of the emigration, they tended to return to Hungary during the 1920s as the antirevolutionary system was consolidated under István Bethlen's premiership and violent persecution was no longer part of everyday life.

However, Communists who came of age during the 1920s and 1930s often left Hungary if they pursued higher education, since "any student caught in Communist activity, even the most innocent or minor one, faced expulsion from all high schools and universities in Hungary."[14] They could be put on trial—on the basis of Law III of 1921 popularly called "law of order"—for "participating in a movement or organization aiming at violently subverting or annihilating the lawful order of state and society, especially if aiming at the violent establishment of the exclusive domination by one social class."[15] This is what happened in 1932 when a group of university students and instructors were arrested for distributing Communist leaflets at university campuses in Budapest. It led to the Red Student Affair and the exclusion of a few students who then went on to study in Czechoslovakia.

From their small group a larger emigrant student group emerged that is remembered as the Brno group, whose story is the focus of this chapter. Communist activism and its persecution were also present at the level of gymnasia. A prominent member of the Brno group, Pál Weidlinger, had gotten in trouble already as a gymnasium student for editing and distributing an illegal Communist newspaper called *Vörös Diák* (Red Student).[16] Tibor Seres, the husband of the earlier cited Piroska Döme, was also arrested at a very young age in Hungary as a Communist, and Döme commented about his arrest, "With such a past he could of course not even think of ever graduating from a Hungarian college. This is how he ended up in Brno."[17]

By and large, Vienna and Berlin emerged as centers of Hungarian emigration in 1919–20, and the Soviet Union grew as a hub of Communist emigrants during the 1930s. Nevertheless, with regard to university students who emigrated for political reasons, Czechoslovakia also played a highly significant role. By 1920, Czechoslovakia had become the center of the Octobrist political exiles and their activities. Even Communists had an easier time there than in post-1919 Hungary, where the Communist Party was forced underground and the Social Democratic Party was only allowed to operate in large cities. As a contrast, in Czechoslovakia, Communist groups and publications were accessible even for German- and Hungarian-speaking foreign students, although the situation of foreign Communists was not without challenges. As Piroska Döme remembered, "Czechoslovak authorities never missed an occasion to express their nationalism. This caused a lot of bitterness to us."[18]

Besides a more permissive political atmosphere, Czechoslovakia was attractive because of its large Hungarian minority, which constituted the bulk of the readership of the most well-known newspaper of the Hungarian left-wing emigrant community: *Bécsi Magyar Újság* (The Hungarian Newspaper of Vienna). This minority lived in the current (2025) territory of Slovakia, which was part of Hungary before the Treaty of Trianon (as Upper Hungary) and part of Czechoslovakia thereafter. As a result, many citizens of post–First World War Hungary had been born in Czechoslovak territories or had family ties there and could claim residence, which enabled emigrant students to enroll in universities without having to pay the high tuition fees of foreigners.[19]

Arthur Linksz, who appeared in chapter 2, provides a good example. Although a Jew, he was originally a political refugee of the numerus clausus law. He had been a university student in Hungary before the discriminatory law was introduced and could, in theory, have continued his studies. However, Linksz needed to flee because he had joined the "Lenin boys" (Red soldiers) during the Republic of Councils and was present when a group of Lenin boys shot a priest. Linksz fled Hungary in 1919 and did not dare set foot in the country until 1924.[20] Linksz was not among the culprits in the trial of this murder, so his memoir is the only source about his role in it. In any case, this revolutionary son of a modern Orthodox rabbi rather ironically found refuge in the ultra-Orthodox yeshiva of Bratislava in 1919. Eventually, he made it to the medical faculty of the German University of Prague and later to the University of Kiel in Germany.

From a younger cohort than Linksz, Sándor Strausz was also excluded from Hungarian higher education for his politics rather than his Jewish descent. He obtained a quota spot at the University of Szeged and was later expelled as a Communist, so he continued his studies in Prague. After fighting in the Spanish Civil War, he was interned in southern France, like so many other refugees from Spain. For his Communist activity, he was put on trial in a military court but succeeded in escaping in 1940 to Belgium, where he fought against the Nazi occupiers. He nearly survived the war, but the Nazis caught and executed him in August 1944, just twelve hours before Brussels's liberation.[21] Like Strausz, Károly Perczel was also first able to enroll in a university in Hungary and was then excluded for Communist activism. He was one of the students arrested for participating in the 1932 Communist student action in Budapest.

Writing about this 1932 trial, the Social Democratic daily *Népszava* noted that "the accused are not the offspring of destructive elements. . . . The fathers are all well-known, outstanding people, with high positions."[22] And as Perczel later put it, "among the intellectual sons of bourgeois families, left-wing thinking became very fashionable. . . . We knew that Socialism was a social order where there was no extreme poverty and no extreme wealth—we knew the latter one too. . . . This luxury was in such a contrast with the world of people we saw on the street."[23]

After the trial, Perczel was not allowed to continue his studies in Hungary, so he left for Brno's German Technical College (Deutsche Technische Hochschule, henceforth DTH), where his friend and comrade András Tömpe was studying. As the anecdote goes, Brno, as opposed to Prague, was perceived as a stronghold of Communists. András Tömpe's nephew István Tömpe recalls in his family history that "Károly Perczel promised his father that he would go to study in Prague, and not to the Communist nest, Brno. Needless to say, he used his fresh passport to go to Brno."[24] Another rebellious son, Pál Weidlinger, told his son the same story about his escape to Brno. He claimed that his parents did not even know where he was while he studied at the DTH. Similar to Perczel and Tömpe, Weidlinger had already attracted the attention of the police as a gymnasium student through his involvement in the *Vörös Diák*.[25] Although he was indeed rebellious, his family not only knew about his whereabouts but also visited him in Brno in 1934.[26] Therefore, the way he passed on his story to the next generation demonstrates that choosing Brno has become part of the romantic trope of the rebellious Communist youth breaking away from their parents. This trope existed in an older age cohort too, among those who entered adulthood in the time of the Republic of Councils. Katalin Zalai, a historian of Hungarian women's emigration in the Soviet Union, presents the story of the six Averle sisters in the same vein. All six felt alienated by their wealthy bourgeois father and became Communists. According to Zalai, this was the path of many in their generation.[27]

The political loyalty clause of the numerus clausus law led to the exile of Jewish and non-Jewish young Communists. Nevertheless, having a Jewish background was an aggravating circumstance for culprits in political crimes during the Horthy era, and this potentially led to Jewish subversive youth being more likely to study abroad than their non-Jewish comrades.[28] In addition, due to the antisemitic numerus clausus law, Hungarian Jews of the period grew up in an atmosphere of discrimination and exclusion that politicized some of them to the extent that they wanted to subvert the unfair social order they suffered from. Others originally left Hungary as exiles of the Jewish quota and became political and radical left-wingers during their peregrination.

Such mechanisms can be particularly well demonstrated through the case study of the Brno group. Significantly, the DTH had the second-largest number of Hungarian engineering students after Budapest's Technical University.[29] Such a visible presence was due to the high number of Jewish exiles; most of these students were not part of the Communist movement, but they provided a crowd from where Hungarian Communists tried to pull new sympathizers.

During the Habsburg period, the DTH had only a few students from Hungary. In the academic year 1918–19, when the Austro-Hungarian monarchy collapsed, there were only nine students from the Hungarian lands. The number of Hungarian citizens grew to thirty-six by the summer of 1920 and to forty-one by the 1920–21 academic year. The striking increase in the number of Hungarian citizens had a lot to do with the White Terror sweeping through Hungary and the introduction of the numerus clausus law in September 1920.[30]

However, in 1925 we can see a more significant boost. While 71 Hungarian citizens were enrolled in the summer semester of 1924–25, the number grew to 121 in the following academic year, peaking at 219 in the summer semester of 1927–28.[31] At the same time, the most memorable period of Hungarian students' presence in Brno had not even started in this time, as it came in the early 1930s with their participation in the foreign students' struggle against the worsening of their material and legal circumstances. Communists were at the forefront of the struggle.

From the late 1920s to the late 1930s, a total of thirty-five Hungarian students at the DTH were also members of the underground Hungarian Communist Party's youth organization, Alliance of Communist Young Workers in Hungary (Kommunista Ifjúmunkások Magyarországi Szövetsége, hereafter KIMSZ). As we can learn from a collective (unpublished) memoir written by Hungarian Communists who had studied in Brno in the 1930s, in general only five or six cell members were present in Brno at any given time, with a total of thirty-five cell members over the course of the whole period. The cell regularly held cultural, educational, and leisure activities, which attracted another thirty sympathizers, or circle members, that is, students who regularly attended the events.[32] Cell members observed these students and evaluated their potential to enter KIMSz, which depended on not only ideological suitability but also candidates' trustworthiness and ability to maintain secrecy. Although the Communist movement and party were legal in Czechoslovakia, this legality was not extended to foreigners.

The Brno cell of KIMSz had existed since at least 1928, but its activities intensified after the Red Student Affair in 1932, when a group of friends called "the Gang of Thirteen" (Tizenhármas Társaság) arrived in Brno and maintained close contact with Hungary.[33] At the DTH, more emphasis was placed on exams than on class attendance, which meant that students could spend as much as five months of the year in Hungary.[34] Moreover, in Brno, Hungarian students could avail themselves of the Czechoslovak Hungarian press, including Communist materials.

The Hungarian KIMSz cell operating in Brno was also part of the Komunistická studentská frakce (hereafter Kostufra), the Czechoslovak Communist Party's student faction, which included local and foreign students (although officially it was not allowed to enroll foreigners). Kostufra had Bulgarian, Romanian, and Polish branches as well. The cover organization for the Hungarian faction was a hiking club that also organized a reading circle, debate nights, and lectures (in Hungarian); theater and musical performances; and choir recitals. Hiking was an important costume and community event in the labor movement at the time and is also a popular activity in the Czech lands. One of the Hungarian students in Brno, Endre Merényi, photographed everyday student life (see figs. 3.1 and 3.2), and a significant number of his photos are of hiking students. The Communist hikers were also active members of the DTH's Socialist student association—Arbeitsgemeinschaft Sozialistischer Hochschüler (hereafter ASH)—which operated legally.[35] Most members of the hiking club had regularly attended similar events organized by the Friends of Nature Hiking Association (Természetbarátok Turista Egyesülete, hereafter TTE) back in Hungary. In Hungary, Communists never succeeded in taking over TTE, which attracted workers and intellectuals of diverse left-wing streams, while in Brno, they infiltrated and came to dominate it. In any case, DTH students who continued to participate in TTE's events in Hungary over the summer, particularly in its summer camp in Horány, connected Brno's German student life with Hungarian left-wing culture. It is even assumed that they picked up the word *volé* (volleyball) in Brno and then introduced it into common Hungarian parlance.[36]

In Brno, foreign students, above all, the Hungarian Communists, organized plenty of actions during the 1930s. At the DTH, the Deutsche Studentenschaft (German student association) and the ASH were rivals, but they cooperated with each other when the Czechoslovak state increased tuition fees in the early 1930s and when a special tax, almost equal to the tuition fee, was introduced for foreign citizens.[37] The Brno chapter of the Aktionskomitee der Mittellosen Studenten der Čechoslowakischen Republik (Action Committee of Indigent Students in the Czechoslovak Republic) conducted an awareness raising campaign to convince local German students, who were not foreigners but Czechoslovak citizens, that they should not stand idly by while the foreign students' tax prevented foreign students from enrolling because this would reduce the DTH's student body and possibly lead to its closure. The campaign involved the distribution of leaflets, a successful enrollment boycott (resulting in the rector permitting foreign students to pay the enrollment fee in several installments), and the organization of student

Fig. 3.1 Endre Merényi (middle), Hungarian Jewish student of the Deutsche Technische Hochschule, with fellow students, Brno, Czechoslovakia, 1931. The photograph was taken with a mechanical self-timer. Merényi perished in the Shoah as a forced laborer. Courtesy of Péter Merényi Lengyel.

Fig. 3.2 Endre Merényi (second from the left) with fellow students in a dormitory in Brno, Czechoslovakia, in the early 1930s. Photo by and of Endre Merényi (taken with a mechanical self-timer). Courtesy of Péter Merényi Lengyel.

assemblies.[38] Although the Aktionskomitee was a single-issue organization, the faculty correctly identified it as a project of the Socialist ASH.[39]

On the one hand, student success in the fight against the foreigners' tax was in the professors' interest because the continued existence of the DTH, and the professors' jobs, depended on a large number of students. On the other hand, the faculty was anxious to maintain "Ruhe und Ordnung" (quiet and order) at the college and to keep the Socialist students' activity at bay. Therefore, an assembly on the foreigners' tax organized by the Aktionskomitee on January 20, 1933, was permitted to take place in the geometry lecture hall, though with several security measures. The story can be reconstructed from the perspective of the rector and the student participants.[40]

Only currently enrolled students could participate in the assembly, and they had to submit their enrollment booklets (*Meldungsbuch*) before entering. According to the rector, the assembled students did not keep to the pre-agreed agenda; some spoke without permission and delivered inciting speeches that encouraged a rebellious atmosphere. The rector dispersed the meeting and cleared the lecture hall without returning the enrollment booklets to the 192 participants. On the next day, these students, including the Hungarian Döme, Seres, and Tömpe, gathered in front of the rector's office and loudly requested the return of their booklets, which the rector interpreted as an illegitimate demonstration.

The protest movement against foreigners' special fees was a formative event for Communist students. The Aktionskomitee also succeeded in organizing a solidarity movement. Several Czech and Slovak student associations from all over the country wrote protest letters to the DTH faculty in solidarity with the chastised students.

After numerous hearings, the DTH's disciplinary committee concluded that Socialist students were responsible for the restlessness and agitation of the student body, though they could not decide whether or not a secret Communist faction of foreign students existed.[41] This question became more pressing in the next academic year, due to a new decree by the Czechoslovak Ministry of Education and Culture, which prohibited universities from admitting "foreigners who have caused unrest at the universities, interfered in the internal affairs of the state or disrupted discipline at the university in any other way."[42] The Brno police sent a list of foreign students of the DTH who belonged to this category to the rectorate.[43]

Based on information provided by an informer, Rudolf Nowak, the police identified numerous foreign students as secret Kostufra members and expelled

Fig. 3.3 Jenő Elek (Eckstein when the photograph was taken) sitting at a table in his lodging in Brno, Czechoslovakia, around 1930. He studied engineering beginning in 1928, first in Prague's Deutsche Technische Hochschule; in 1930, he transferred to Brno's Deutsche Technische Hochschule. We see humorous rules for tenants on the wall. He was expelled from Czechoslovakia in 1933 for Communist activism; therefore, he could not graduate and moved back to Hungary, where he lived until his death in 1996 after surviving the Shoah. Courtesy of László Elek.

them from Czechoslovakia. This expulsion is one of the often-mentioned memorable events in accounts of the Brno alumni and their children. The disciplinary proceedings and the records of faculty meetings reveal that about thirty Communists were expelled from the country and, hence, from the Technical College.[44] Piroska Döme remembered 40 to 50,[45] while one of the expelled students, László Czitrom, wrote about 140 when repeating the story in a letter to the Soviet embassy in Mexico City.[46] Many decades later, Döme, Perczel, and László Kádár emphasized the ease with which it was possible to evade expulsion. Kádár stayed for another two years after his expulsion and finished his studies at the DTH.[47] Perczel responded to his interviewer's puzzlement over expelled foreigners continuing to study with no residence permit: "Yes, they still attended [the DTH]! This was sort of a democratic illegality."[48]

Fig. 3.4 Endre Merényi hiking with fellow students in the mountains of Moravia, Czechoslovakia in the early 1930s. Photo by and of Endre Merényi, taken with a mechanical self-timer. @Péter Merényi Lengyel.

The expelled students never found out that Nowak was eventually punished. He may have joined the Communist faction simply to spy on his fellow students, but his record of having once belonged to a Communist group made it later impossible for him to pursue a career in engineering after the Nazi occupation of Czechoslovakia. In 1939, his father, Rudolf Nowak Sr., wrote a desperate letter to the DTH blaming Hungarian Communist students for his son's youthful mistake: "My son may have committed some youthful foolishness, yet it is not possible that his existence is made impossible in the German Lebensraum. . . . Unfortunately, he came into close contact with many Hungarian students of Communist attitude."[49]

By the time Nowak's father lodged his complaint, most of the Hungarian Communist students had returned to Hungary, a few after having fought in the Spanish Civil War. The majority of Brno alumni, however, did not fight in Spain but returned to Hungary after their studies. The majority of the Gang of Thirteen were also in Budapest in the late 1930s, where they habitually met at the Kis-Ilkovics café and pastry shop. They were anxious to find an escape route from the country, especially since the Anschluss of Austria in March 1938, when the Third Reich came to border Hungary. In early 1939, their comrade Sebestyén Endre Bakonyi notified them from Paris that Bolivian visas were available for engineers.[50]

While his friends were preparing to emigrate in Budapest, in Paris Bakonyi convinced Pál Weidlinger to join. Bakonyi, Weidlinger, György Bartos, and János Varga formed the vanguard of the Bolivian emigration. According to Weidlinger's son, they did not think of themselves as refugees because "they had long since adapted to exile as the normal state of affairs."[51] Moreover, they despised nostalgia. During their transatlantic journey on the ship *Oropesa*, the four friends coauthored a humorous travel diary full of sarcasm directed at the European nostalgia of fellow Jewish travelers titled "The Adventurous Journey of the Oropesa."[52]

Other members of the Gang of Thirteen soon followed, including Imre Erdős, whose unpublished memoir is the main source of their life in Bolivia. Another friend from Brno, Pál Zoltán, found another escape route and emigrated with his bride, whom he had met in Brno, through Uruguay to Argentina. Resettling to distant Latin America was, however, a difficult decision to make. Their friend and comrade Gyula Krausz (later Karádi) is a case in point. He and his wife, Jolán Vadas, had initially planned to join the others in Bolivia. They hoped to be able to earn a living anywhere with a patent of his. In the end, however, they did not dare leave their parents behind to face the dramatically deteriorating situation in Hungary.[53]

Latin America turned out to be a favorable place for ambitious engineers. Weidlinger was hired by a flourishing Bolivian company and his friends founded their own company, Alpha. Pál Zoltán designed a new factory building for a profitable firm in Argentina.[54] The engineers of Alpha not only worked together but also lived together in a commune. They sought connections to Bolivians but limited their contacts with fellow Hungarians and other European refugees to political comrades.

They were eager to establish themselves professionally, though this did not entail only engaging in apolitical behavior. In 1941, they founded the Hungarian Democratic Circle of Bolivia, which kept in touch and offered financial support to the left-wing movement of Hungarian emigrants in Argentina, Brazil, Chile, Mexico, and Uruguay by supporting their publications.[55] This was possible thanks to the profitability of Alpha. Alpha's founders also organized a Communist group of recent immigrants in Bolivia (mostly of fellow European refugees) and entered into cooperation with the Bolivian revolutionary left-wing party, Partido de la Izquierda Revolucionaria. Several meetings of foreign and Bolivian Communists were hosted by Ferenc Neuländer (later Talyigás). A military putsch in 1943 placed them in a difficult position, and in 1944, Neuländer was arrested (along with several comrades) and imprisoned at Lake Titicaca for three weeks. He was ultimately set free on the condition that he left Bolivia, which he did.[56]

As soon as the Second World War ended and the hope of building Communism in their home country materialized, most emigrants of the Brno group eagerly sought connections to their friends in Hungary and eventually returned. A letter by Jolán Karádi (née Vadas) to Imre Erdős from 1946 testifies to the interest of Karádi's emigrant friends in the new political atmosphere of Hungary and the opportunities it could offer to engineers: "You ask, Imre, whether in case you returned, you could earn a modest living. Well, only a modest one indeed. Gyuszi [Gyula Karádi] has a great position and influence, but it comes with a meager salary, not proportionate to his achievements."[57]

Karádi was one of many intellectuals who visibly advanced in their careers after 1945 for, among other reasons, being a long-standing Communist. At the same time, numerous non-Communist Jewish intellectuals' careers also blossomed right after 1945, as they could finally start working in their professions in positions they were qualified for. Being a graduate of a foreign university or college, such as the DTH, was now an advantage because it implied having been persecuted in the previous regime. Within a few years, however, it turned into a great disadvantage for two reasons. First, as the Cold War unfolded, having ties to Western countries could make someone vulnerable to suspicions. Second, it was common knowledge that before the war, mainly Jews studied abroad due to the Jewish quota, so a history of studying abroad drew the malice of antisemites, who were present in the Communist movement too, not only among right-wingers.

After 1948, Muscovites—as Communists who returned from exile in the Soviet Union were referred too—dominated the Hungarian Workers' Party (Magyar Dolgozók Pártja, abbreviated as MDP). Many of them viewed others' sojourning in the West in the past as grounds for suspicion and a pretext for persecution. The Muscovites also distrusted the Communists who had been active in Hungary during the Horthy era, when the Communist Party was underground. Communists who had emigrated to the West before or during the Second World War became targets of even more hostility upon their return.

During the Stalinist period, between 1948 and 1953, a criteria system—in fact, a checklist—was proposed (and accepted) within the party for a review of the past of those cadres who were in the most important positions of the party, state, and economy. One of the six factors recommended for checking was whether cadres had lived in the West or had participated in the Spanish Civil War.

These criteria were taken into account when choosing victims for the show trials, starting with the trial of Interior Minister László Rajk in 1949. A satellite trial of the Rajk affair was built around the "Swiss group," leading to the execution of Tibor Szőnyi and Ferenc Vági and the imprisonment of nearly a dozen alumni of the Eidgenössische Technische Hochschule in Zürich. Like the DTH alumni, they had been political and Jewish exiles of the numerus clausus law before the war, and a number of them had been active in the Hungarian underground Communist movement.

Unlike the engineers trained in Brno, however, they had stayed in Switzerland during the Second World War. In the preparatory stage of the Rajk trial, Tibor Szőnyi was even considered the instigator of a fictitious plot in which a group of cosmopolitan, intellectual Jews had allegedly spied for the United States.[58] In May 1949, Szőnyi was arrested on charge of spying and was forced to name Rajk as his spymaster. At this point, the plot of the show trial gravitated from "the West" to Yugoslavia and from Szőnyi to Rajk.[59] This was equally dangerous for comrades who had studied in Brno in the interwar period because Rajk had been the contact person for the Brno KIMSz in the 1930s.

Two Brno graduates, Zoltán Radó and Miklós Szűcs, lost their lives in the show trials, and several others served lengthy prison sentences in the early 1950s. In the end, there was no trial dedicated to the Brno group. Still, as a document of the State Security Office (Államvédelmi Hatóság, hereafter ÁVH) demonstrates, the notion of the Brno group was being constructed behind the scenes. According to Vladimir Farkas, a leading figure at the ÁVH, Mátyás Rákosi, the party leader, considered all Brno alumni in the Hungarian Communist movement to be spies, and during the interrogation of Szűcs, who was charged with Trotskyism and spying for British intelligence, his time in Brno was brought up.[60] It is worth noting that Farkas made this accusation more than three decades after the trials, and he may have attributed this to Rákosi in order to downplay his own role.

Internal tensions between the Muscovites, on the one hand, and the "illegals" and returnees from the West, on the other hand, were only one factor in the Stalinist show trials. Antisemitism also played an important role. Preparations for an anti-Zionist trial in Hungary directed the ÁVH's attention to the technocrats heading various institutions of the economy who had studied in Brno before the war. As a "Note on the Brno group" (an internal memo of the ÁVH, the state security office) summed up:

> Many among the "Brno students" are placed in significant leadership positions in different spheres of the state apparatus and the economy. Most of them are of high bourgeois background who joined the student movement in Brno as a faction and functioned as a separate Hungarian faction for a long time. Upon returning to Hungary, they created similar factionist and Trotskyist

> connections. After the liberation those who were already in Hungary and the returnees achieved significant positions by mutually supporting each other. Several of the Brno students are regarded by the authorities as suspicious for being Trotskyist and potentially guilty of crimes connected to spying, sabotage, and harm. Several of them have been arrested for different issues: Károly Perczel, a head of department in the Ministry of Constructions, radio engineer Miklós Szücs [*sic*], Zoltán Radó who has been executed for spying and was a head of department in the Ministry of Industry.[61]

The ominous wording ("suspicious," "potentially guilty," "crimes connected to") demonstrates that the investigation was about casting for roles in a fictitious plot still missing a core event. Fortunately for the twenty-one engineers, whose short biographies follow the afore-cited introduction, this fictional plot was not developed further and remained stuck at the stage of constructing the Brno group.[62] The investigators connected the listed engineers to three already executed or imprisoned longtime Communists of Jewish origin who had studied in Brno in the age of the numerus clausus law. They allegedly came from upper-class bourgeois families, joined the student movement in Brno, and had Trotskyist connections. Nevertheless, the gravest accusation seems to have been that they continued to mutually help each other.

Stalin died less than three months after this document was created, and the anti-Zionist show trials were dropped. Thanks to this, the "Note on the Brno group" was relegated to the archives. It was not acted on, and several imprisoned DTH alumni were set free in 1954, including László Kozma and Károly Perczel. Kozma was not regarded as a member of the Brno group, by himself or by others. However, he was imprisoned in the same trial against engineers of the Standard Company in which Zoltán Radó was executed in 1950.[63] In addition to Radó, Miklós Szűcs, the leader of the Hungarian Communist cell in Brno in the early 1930s, fell victim. He died in prison due to being tortured during ÁVH interrogations in 1950 and was then buried in an unmarked grave.[64] Only in 1964 was his case reopened; he was declared innocent, and afterward, his body was exhumed and given a proper burial.[65]

It is instructive to compare the 1952 description of the Brno group, which was written from the perspective of hostile outsiders, with the 1972 history of the Brno group, which was written by the Brno graduates themselves (and includes a list of the people *they* considered to be members).[66] Signed by seven Brno graduates, "Recollection about the Hungarian students' Communist movement in Brno, 1928–1938" is a collective memoir, which was written for the Institute of Party History.[67] It was submitted to this institute in late March

1972, though the authors must have started working on it prior to December 15, 1971, when András Tömpe, whose signature is missing, took his life.

Among the ninety-three fellow students and comrades listed, the ÁVH had identified fourteen as Brno group members twenty years earlier. Another half dozen regarded by the ÁVH as part of the group were not mentioned in 1972 when the insiders had an opportunity to define the group's contours. The collective biographical elements they chose to emphasize shed light on their selection criteria: Despite the persecutions in the 1950s, "they nevertheless remained in the Party." Even in 1956, almost without exception, they remained faithful to the party and were among the first to continue their activity in the framework of the Hungarian Socialist Workers' Party (Magyar Szocialista Munkáspárt MSZMP).[68] The memoir, as an expression of loyalty to the party, excluded those who, although comrades in Brno in the 1930s, were no longer Communists. Such was the case of Pál Weidlinger, an exile of the Red Student Affair in 1932 and a member of the Gang of Thirteen who not only settled in the United States in 1943 but also stayed there during the Cold War, thus leaving the fold.

As for András Tömpe, his tragic death is not mentioned, although he may have been the most eminent member of the group. He served as ambassador to East Germany when the Warsaw Pact invaded Czechoslovakia in 1968, and he resigned in protest. After his suicide, caused by "social, political and personal reasons,"[69] he was buried in the mausoleum of the Hungarian labor movement's outstanding heroes in Budapest. Thus, members of the Brno group could have taken pride in him, but they did not because in the last years of his life, he criticized the party.

We may conclude that having been politically exiled caused students during the Horthy era troubles and sorrow even long after the age of the numerus clausus law and long after their youths. Although they struggled for Socialism, some were persecuted under the self-proclaimed Socialist postwar regime, which even took the lives of several long-standing Communists among them. Soviet advisers exported Stalinist purges against Trotskyists and different left-wing movements first to Spain in the 1930s and a decade later to the east-central European countries that were forced to join the Socialist part of the world after the Second World War. Tragically, antisemitism continued to target Jews even after the Shoah and Jews who had originally been exiled by the numerus clausus law for their politics rather than their Jewish descent.

FOUR

WOMEN

IN THE WORDS OF HISTORIAN Katalin Fenyves, "The Numerus Clausus was the symbolic moment when anti-Semitism and sexism met."[1] Until 1920, women were not emancipated in Hungary (they achieved only limited voting rights in 1918), whereas the Jewish minority was; thus, Jewish men could enroll in a university under the same conditions as their non-Jewish peers. Another historian, Katalin Szegvári, dedicated an entire book to the intertwining of sexism and antisemitism in interwar Hungary, particularly in the academic sphere.[2] Meanwhile, Judith Szapor has argued, based on a study of over 160 biographies of Hungarian Jewish women who could not study in the age of the numerus clausus law, that the law altered the course of women's emancipation in important ways.[3]

The idea of the numerus clausus came up at the overcrowded medical faculty at the Hungarian Royal University in Budapest. The theological faculty of the same university contributed with the idea of "proportionality" in the student body. The council of the medical faculty argued that the number of medical students had to be limited so that enrolled students would receive a proper education. The number of students had to match teaching and equipment capacities. The council members suggested seriously cutting down the number of women in this framework. The dean of the same university's theology faculty, Mihály Kmoskó, added the suggestion that much less women and much less Jews should be allowed to enroll [than the number of female and Jewish university students studying at the time]. He justified his proposal with an antisemitic argument: In the last two prewar decades "too many" Jewish students had attained degrees of higher education, leading to the emergence of an intellectual proletariat and the rise of unemployment; these youngsters founded the freethinking Galilei Circle and were responsible for the Aster Revolution. Kmoskó also suggested that faculties should take into account the moral and intellectual merits of the applicants and the proportion between different religious and racial groups in the student body.[4] The latter idea was completed by other professors of the theological faculty who proposed that the proportion between nationalities at the faculties should mirror their proportion within the general population rather than only regulate Jews' share in the student body. It is noteworthy that the legal faculty disagreed, they were eager to exclude women entirely, but were not interested in setting up racial, national or denominational quotas.

Even though a restriction or ban on women's university enrollment necessarily entailed a restriction on Jewish enrollment, due to the high share of Jews among female secondary school graduates, there was more resistance to women's exclusion than to that of Jews. The Christian middle class, whose interests were supposed to be protected, also had daughters with intellectual aspirations, and there were antisemitic intellectual women who lobbied for women's right to study while agreeing with the exclusion of Jews. With the implementation of the Jewish quota, Jewish women's enrollment was further limited.

Consequently, the National Alliance of Hungarian University and College Students (Magyar Egyetemi és Főiskolai Hallgatók Országos Szövetsége, hereafter MEFHOSZ) and MANSZ (the previously referenced National Alliance of Hungarian Women) requested in 1923 that all faculties open their doors to women. The Ministry of Religion and Public Education, which was brought in to resolve the matter, inquired about the faculties' standpoints in the matter. In Budapest most faculties rejected the idea, while the provincial cities' faculties supported it. Andor Ladányi, historian of universities, used the existential interests of the middle class, for whom women's ability to work and support their families was necessary, to explain MEFHOSZ and MANSZ's petition.[5] The postwar inflation and the shrinking of the country due to the Trianon Treaty certainly impoverished the middle class. As intellectuals from the lost territories immigrated to the small country, jobs were a scarce resource. We may add that the faculties also followed their own existential interests when commenting on the petition. In Budapest in the early 1920s, universities still appeared overcrowded, while the provincial universities began facing a lack of students, leading to questions about their legitimacy.

Similar to male antisemitic politicians who advocated a "change of guards" (*őrségváltás*) in economics, referring to taking away positions from Jews, right-wing female public intellectuals pushed out feminists from the public sphere. They were more successful in their change of guard than economic antisemites. Among women's organizations a change of guard effectively took place from Feministák Egyesülete to MANSZ.[6] Meanwhile, some Jewish capitalists cooperated with the emerging interwar political establishment despite its antisemitism because of its anti-Communism and kept their positions in the elite, remaining instrumental for the country's economy.

In the second half of the 1920s, MANSZ even overtook the representation of interests for women university students and graduates.[7] First, they supported the foundation of the International Federation of University Women's (IFUW) Hungarian chapter, the Association of Hungarian University and College Graduate Women (Egyetemet és Főiskolát Végzett Magyar Nők Egyesülete, henceforth EUMANE).[8] The support of MANSZ, however, was half-hearted, as historian Barbara Papp argues. EUMANE was founded in response to a famous attack against women's higher education by professor and cultural politician Gyula Kornis in his 1925 misogynist pamphlet titled "Women at University." Interestingly, it was published in *Napkelet,* a journal edited by MANSZ leader Cécile Tormay;[9] however, Tormay was hesitant to publish a response to Kornis by Marianne Czeke and Emma Ritoók, the first president of EUMANE, in *Napkelet,* and when she did, it was in the Miscellaneous section among small news, not in a prominent column, as the misogynist pamphlet by Kornis had been.[10]

It is noteworthy that Emma Ritoók fell out with the progressive Sunday Circle—an informal but influential and regularly convening intellectual club existing between 1915 and 1918 where philosophy, arts and politics were discussed—she used to be part of, and after the Aster Revolution of October 1918 and the Communist Revolution (or rather takeover) of March 1919, she turned against liberals and Jews.[11] Nevertheless, EUMANE took a different approach to politics than the antisemitic right-wing MANSZ. EUMANE did not exclude Jews; the only entrance criteria were being a woman and a graduate of higher education. Omitting antisemitism was in line with the general stance of the international umbrella organization. This was demonstrated in 1934 at IFUW's congress (held in Budapest), where the following statement was added to its constitution in reaction to the German member organization's new antisemitic policies: "No federation or association shall be admitted or retained as a member of IFUW which debars qualified women from membership by reason of their race, religion or political opinions."[12]

However, EUMANE never achieved the influence MANSZ did. Hence, women's right to higher education in general was not promoted as strongly as Christian women's right to it, particularly those Christian women in the historical middle class, meaning noble or, at least, with a long-standing bourgeoisie family background, even if impoverished. In fact, one female icon of the period, Hungary's first female member of parliament, Margit Schlachta, enthusiastically supported the Jewish quota.[13]

According to a monograph on women intellectuals in the Horthy era by Barbara Papp and Balázs Sipos, the subsequent governments of the interwar period did not follow a consistent sexist policy in higher education but rather passed [the governments] restrictions and concessions curtailing women's rights to education. While the restriction of women's access to higher education was backed by the government in 1920, within five years the Ministry of Religion and Public Education began to pressure Budapest's medical faculty to admit female students, to no avail, and dormitories were established to help female university students.[14] On the whole, though, these measures did little to improve women's higher education opportunities, and the share of female students in Hungarian higher education, after peaking in 1916–17 at 16.1 percent (1,187 female students), never reached 15 percent during the interwar period.[15]

After a relative easing of universities' attitude toward women from the late 1920s, in 1934 Bálint Hóman, minister for religion and public education, restricted women's admission to certain faculties, which he justified by citing the high number of unemployed university graduates.[16] He did so in instructions sent to universities' councils. For instance, he addressed the Hungarian Royal University of Engineering and Economics Palatine József as follows: "I am herewith notifying the honorable Council that—in order to make job-finding easier to the freshly graduated students—I find it necessary to restrict the admission of women to university. Therefore, I rule as follows: within the number of first-year students admissible in the academic year 1934–1935 women be admitted to the Department of Economics and Commerce up to 30 (thirty) % of the total."[17]

With regard to humanities and medicine, he ordered these faculties to restrict the share of women to 30 percent of the student body as well, whereas pharmacy faculties could take up to 50 percent female students. Colleges—which were less prestigious than universities—could admit women without limitation. Humanities faculties had higher numbers of women students, partly because they were historically among the first to admit women and partly because women were pushed out from technical, legal, theological, and, between 1919 and 1926, even medical faculties; hence, the introduction of this quota was particularly painful there. All in all, Hungary ranked in the lowest third among European countries for women's participation in higher education at the time.[18]

A particularly interesting case study is women's access to engineering faculties. Engineering (alongside other STEM disciplines) was and continues to be regarded as a masculine field, and as a result, the Technical University of Budapest was particularly unwelcoming to women.[19] The question of women's access was discussed and rejected by the university council even prior to the First World War. Nevertheless, a few women were studying there, because chemistry students of the Hungarian Royal University in Budapest were allowed to attend the Hungarian Royal University of Engineering and Economics Palatine József's lectures and laboratory seminars. And there were women among these chemistry students, since the chemistry department belonged to the faculty of humanities. In this way, thirty-two women attended classes at the Technical University in 1912–13 and thirty-seven in the following academic year.[20]

Women entered this university as regularly enrolled students rather than guests in 1918 when all faculties were open to them, and they met less hostility in the years to come than in the medical faculty of Pázmány Péter University. In 1927, however, it was prohibited for them to enroll in civil engineering and chemical engineering. The faculty of architecture applied a 5 percent quota on women, and in the faculty of economics, they could enter only if there were fewer applicants than the number of admissible students (which the minister had a right to define under the numerus clausus law).[21] In exceptional cases, women made it into the faculty of their choice thanks to their fathers' influence; one example is Judith Pogány, who was admitted to the Faculty of Chemistry and Chemical Engineering, at the faculty's insistence, because she was the daughter of physicist Béla Pogány, their colleague.[22] Judith Pogány became the university's first female chemical engineering graduate in 1939.

On top of the previously outlined misogynist marginalization and exclusion, Jewish women occasionally even encountered physical violence on Hungarian campuses. Róbert Kerepeszki, an expert on Hungary's radical right-wing student organizations, draws attention to the weakening of the idea of chivalry leading to "acts of violence against the female body previously unprecedented and unaccepted in any social setting."[23]

Due to the animosity Hungarian women encountered in the medical faculty in Budapest and in the only technical university of the country in the interwar period, it is especially worth looking into the population of female students who emigrated to study these disciplines. In addition, studies in these fields provide knowledge and degrees that are relatively easy to make use of in other countries, unlike the legal field, from which women were entirely excluded in Hungary. Thus, it is no surprise that medicine and engineering were the most popular disciplines among interwar Hungarian migrant students.

Fig. 4.1 Close up of Rózsi Meller, a Hungarian Jewish woman who studied in Germany. She was a successful author of dramas and novels. In 1945, she resumed her scientific career in Hungary. Courtesy of András Meller.

In examining the gender aspects of students' emigration from Hungary in the age of the numerus clausus, the same sample is used as in the chapter on Jewish exiled students (chapter 2). My initial research questions were whether the proportion of women among Hungarian students abroad was higher or lower than that among students in Hungary and whether Jews were more overrepresented among migrant female students than among migrant male students. An additional question was whether women were more likely than men to stem from intellectual and middle-class families due to contemporary patriarchal society making social mobility less viable for women. Finally, because urbanization is an important part of describing social background and social mobility, the question of whether women came from more urban environments than their male peers emerges too.

Only 124 students in the sample of 1,131 emigrants were women, a lower proportion than that found among students in Hungary.[24] However, we must remember that in Hungary, women had the largest share of the student body in humanities faculties, which are not represented in my sample.[25] In the sample, women made up 15 percent of medical students and 2 percent of engineering students. Meanwhile, in Hungary in 1931–32, around the middle of the period under examination here, 15.7 percent of medical and 0.3 percent of engineering students were women.[26] Thus, in medicine, the gender proportion was nearly the same among students who studied in Hungary as among those who studied abroad, while that of engineering students is much lower, which aligns with the aforementioned fact that women could study at technical universities only in exceptional cases. In terms of religion, 103 (83%) of the 124 women of the sample concerned were Jewish exiles, which is slightly higher than their share among men (81%).

Since in Hungary female university students were characteristically recruited from higher social layers than male students, it was expected that also among migrant students, women would be more likely to stem from the middle class and the high bourgeoisie than their male peers.[27] Contrary to this hypothesis, however, the class background of female and male emigrant students was very similar: 62 percent of women and 61 percent of men came from the lower middle class, and 21 percent of women and 17 percent of men from the middle class proper. (These classifications are to be understood in the same way as in chapter 2 [see table 4.1].) Thus, the sample disproves what one intuitively assumes about women's social mobility: rather, they had a similar chance for upward social mobility as their male counterparts.

Nevertheless, studying abroad, which was for many Hungarian Jews the only way to go to university in the age of the numerus clausus law, was more difficult for women than for men. According to the social norms of the period, women were supposed to live with their families until marriage. Thus, on the one hand, Jewish families were less happy to send their daughters than their sons abroad; on the other hand, the same families would have been likely to support the same daughters' study ambitions if they could have achieved them in Hungary rather than abroad. More of Hungarian Jewish women who studied in Vienna, Prague, Berlin, and Bologna were unmarried when they emigrated than of East Central European Jewish female students in interwar Belgium. We know the social selection of the latter from Pascale Falek's research.[28] It is noteworthy that Falek's study includes Hungarian Jewish women, but only six of the one thousand female students she examined came from Hungary. Returning to my sample, few individuals among them are identifiable as sisters of other (female or male) migrant students. At the same time, we know of women who studied in different foreign cities and study fields than their brothers and were equally supported by their families in their endeavors; one such example is the Bauhaus architect Zsuzsanna Bánki, the younger sister of the medical student Ödön Bánki.[29]

Table 4.1 Social mobility of female and male migrant students: fathers' occupations

Father's occupation	**Women**		**Men**		**Class background**
Farmer	2 (2%)		11 (2%)		Lower than middle class
Unskilled and skilled worker	3 (3%)	12%	24 (4%)	13%	
Artisan	5 (6%)		44 (7%)		
Retailer	30 (35%)		234 (38%)		Lower middle class
Private clerk	9 (10%)		49 (8%)		
Public clerk	13 (13%)	62%	86 (14%)	61%	
Specialized public employee	3 (3%)		8 (1%)		
Clergy, teacher, employed intellectual in humanities	3 (2%)	21%	20 (3%)	17%	
Elementary school teacher and director	0		6 (1%)		Middle class proper
Doctor, medicine-related intellectual	9 (10%)		35 (6%)		
Other professional intellectual	6 (7%)		42 (7%)		
High bourgeois, entrepreneur	3 (3%)	3%	35 (6%)	6%	Upper middle class
Living from revenues, retired	2 (2%)		25 (4%)		
Whole sample	124		1,000		
Valid cases	86 (100%)		619 (100%)		
Missing data	38		381		

Similar to social selection, the geographical selection of female migrant students was comparable to that of their male peers, albeit with minor differences, as tables 4.2 and 4.3 demonstrate. Over a third of women and men were born in Budapest, and in both cases, the second most common birthplace category was a village or small town. However, over a fifth of women came from a town with

Table 4.2 Types of birth place of female and male migrant students

Type of place of birth	Women (124)	Men (1,000)
Budapest	42 (34%)	347 (35%)
Towns with county rights	13 (10%)	146 (15%)
Towns with settled councils	26 (21%)	26 (16%)
Other localities (villages and small towns)	35 (28%)	315 (32%)
Abroad	5 (4%)	17 (2%)
Whole sample	124	1,000
Valid cases	121 (100%)	988 (100%)
Missing data	3	12

Table 4.3 Regional selection of female and male migrant students

Region of birth	Women (124)	Men (1,000)
Budapest and suburbs	47 (39%)	382 (39%)
Left bank of the Danube	3 (3%)	40 (4%)
Right bank of the Danube (Transdanubia)	16 (13%)	138 (14%)
Between Danube and Tisza	16 (13%)	134 (14%)
Fiume and surroundings	0	1 (0.1%)
Croatia and Slavonia	2 (2%)	2 (0.2%)
Transylvania	0	15 (2%)
Left bank of the Tisza	16 (13%)	107 (11%)
Right bank of the Tisza	13 (11%)	146 (15%)
Crossing of Tisza and Maros	2 (2%)	7 (1%)
Abroad	5 (4%)	17 (2%)
Whole sample	124	1,000
Valid cases	120 (100%)	989 (100%)
Missing data	4	11

a settled council, while only 16 percent of men did. Looking at their regional backgrounds, we find that Budapest and its suburbs sent the largest proportion of students to Vienna, Prague, Berlin, and Bologna: 39 percent of women and of men. For both sexes, the second most common region fell far below Budapest and its suburbs. In men's case, the right bank of the Tisza was the second most common region of origin (15%), while for women an equal percentage (13%) stemmed from Transdanubia (between the Danube and the Tisza Rivers) and from the left bank of the Tisza.

In sum, women emigrant students' backgrounds did not differ from those of men to the expected extent. Notably, the sample data support that over four-fifths of women and men were pushed out from Hungarian higher education by the Jewish quota. Add to this finding the fact that so-called Jewish overschooling was even more characteristic of women than men but that hardly over 10 percent of the emigrant students were women; one sees the double discrimination Jewish women experienced in access to higher education. Therefore, academic misogyny appears to have been an additional push factor for young intellectual women, whose majority was unwanted also because of their Jewishness, to emigrate.

Due to so many of the interwar Hungarian female emigrant students being Jewish, most of the ego documents by and sources about this group also reflect on emigration as connected to antisemitism. The memoir by Lili Fenyő, referred to in chapter 2, is a unique source since, as its title promises, it provides snapshots of Jewish numerus clausus exiles' student life.[30] Furthermore, because the author and her roommates are women, it also necessarily offers insight into the situation of Jewish women among the exiled students. Moreover, as it was published in 1929, immediately after the author graduated in Italy, it is the only memoir thus far found about the topic that occurs within the numerus clausus period.

The term *memoir* means "memory" and is used for one genre within ego documents where the narrator's recollections are organized around one moment or short period rather than an entire lifespan (which is the case in an autobiography);[31] this moment of focus is the memoir's bracketed time. All the known numerus clausus exiles' memoirs except Fenyő's were written after the Shoah, and so in *Pillanatfelvételek a külföldön élő magyar diákság életéből* (Snapshots from the life of Hungarian students abroad, hereafter "Snapshots"), the author's pre-Shoah experience with emigration, even if motivated by Hungarian antisemitism, features as a prelude to the tragedy and not as the main topic.

In "Snapshots," Fenyő claims to be writing a testimony of emigrant students' collective experience. The author and the fellow Hungarian Jewish migrant students (women and men alike) she claims to represent cannot imagine that they would experience more severe, even murderous, antisemitism than what they were then facing in higher education.

Fenyő presents herself as the ideal scholarship holder for the Central Jewish Student Aid Committee: a Neolog Jew who keeps some central Jewish religious traditions and frames her Jewish identity as religious belonging that is compatible with Hungarian patriotism. The story told here is the story of young patriotic Hungarians (Fenyő and her friends) who are unjustly exiled from their homeland by the numerus clausus and yet are willing to use the knowledge gained abroad for the sake of Hungary.

Since the experience Fenyő brings from Hungary is living in an atmosphere where antisemitism is widespread and being Jewish simply "matters" in all walks of life, her main observation about Italy is that being Jewish or not (surprisingly for her) simply does not matter. As a Jew, she finds it easy and pleasant to live in Florence. However, being a female student is more difficult. She describes Italians as kind people but not progressive enough to understand why it is important for a woman to study at university. They make fun of her and her female friends and wonder why they are not married. However, Fenyő and her friends are "serious student girls" who "have no time to deal with such childish questions." They want to be "women who work." She concludes this chain of thought with the observation that "these Italians are kind people, but they do not understand anything. One cannot have a serious conversation with them."[32]

She describes a rich social life where Italian, Hungarian, and other foreign students spend plenty of time together, men and women alike. She does not write about any encounter with men who court her, and she presents an image of herself as a laborious student who does not want to take time from her life for such matters anyway. At the same time, she includes an episode where she helped a (female) friend prepare for a promising date.[33]

The three girls at the center of "Snapshots"—Fenyő and her two roommates, Teri and Margit—seem to have a closer and more confidential relationship with their local Italian landlady than male ego document authors have with theirs. Or, at least, Fenyő found it more important to write about this relationship. The same is true for the relationship among the roommates. They perform several daily rituals together, such as Sunday morning museum visits to escape their heatless room for a while and a Sunday afternoon letter writing routine in which they all write basically the same message to their parents, only with different signatures.[34]

Fenyő also tells her readers about spending the Jewish holidays abroad in more detail and more intimately than most of her fellow male ego document authors. Passover, where the family or community seder dinner plays a central role, makes the exiled students presented by Fenyő particularly sad and lonely. In a complaining tone, she remarks that "here we do not even know when the holiday will be."[35] Her comment is also revealing about her secular background: She needs to be around her community and Jewish information sources to be aware of the major holidays' timing.

A seder dinner invitation by an elderly Florentine Jewish couple diminishes the students' homesickness. Before the dinner, Fenyő and her friends go to the synagogue, and her description of being there as a foreign Jew is a telling testimony of the important role of the "community of fate" as a central aspect of Jewish identity even before the Shoah. Later, Jews' claiming the community of fate as the basis of their Jewish identity came to be known as "Holocaust Jews," those who would not be Jewish if it was not for this communal trauma; however, from Fenyő's account, we see the notion of community of fate preceded the Shoah.[36]

The importance Fenyő attributes to the Jewish community of *fate*, which is at least as high a priority as the aspect of being a community of *faith*, seemingly contradicts the official stance of the interwar Hungarian Neolog (non-Orthodox) Jewish community. The latter identified Jews as "Hungarians of the Israelite faith" whose only particularity among Hungarians is their faith and not their fate or where their loyalties lie. However, the definition of who is Jewish is of course never so simple, and with regard to the Jewish quota at Hungarian universities and other antisemitic measures, Jewish community of fate was acknowledged in the Neolog press. Fenyő relates to this complex nature of Jewish identity during her Florentine Passover in the following lines: "Some kind of community holds us together—our religion, our language, our customs—or maybe our fate, the community of our suffering—and strongest of all: Jewish love. These customs are not strange for us—we speak this language perfectly—these songs are also old, familiar, sad melodies—this love connects us—it also brings Hungary closer where our parents are praying in the temple in the same way."[37]

As is seen from the aforementioned episodes of Fenyő's narrative, the narrator's main concerns are the experience of exile from Hungary, integration in Italy, Hungarian patriotism, and Jewish community of fate and faith. With the exception of courtship, where Fenyő finds tension for a woman who takes her studies and ambition seriously, the reader mostly learns her opinion about spheres of life where gender played little role. Thankfully, Fenyő's narration can be completed based on numerous letters written by other women who were in a similar situation to hers, being Jewish women pushed out from their home country's universities by antisemitism as well as misogyny.

To survey other women's perspectives, one can review the letters by Ida Somló and Erzsébet Kardos, the diary by Dora Klein, the memoirs by Piroska Döme (cited in chapter 3), and readers' letters to journals.[38] Letters by Somló and Kardos are similar to the memoir by Fenyő in that they capture the experience of emigration when the authors were in that situation. Klein wrote her autobiography many decades later as a survivor of Auschwitz, yet her youthful experience was similar to that of Fenyő, since she was a foreign Jewish woman in Fascist Italy, albeit from Poland, not Hungary.[39] In addition, she used diaries she had kept in the 1930s to inform her work. Döme wrote multiple autobiographic texts, and all of them concentrate on her being a political exile as a Communist when she studied.[40] She found this episode of her life important enough to publish it separately and not only within her autobiography.[41]

Letters by Ida Somló deal with topics related to being a woman even less than Fenyő's memoir does. At the same time, she corresponded in a motherly tone. She regularly referred to her (a few years) younger male friend, Ödön Bánki, as "my son" and gave him advice from the position of the more experienced adult, one could even say of the "yidishe mame": "My son, write to your mother more often and take care of yourself. . . . Your mother sends as many kisses as you have sent to her."[42] A collective letter she sent to Bánki and two other friends reveals that she fashioned herself as the emotional caretaker of a whole circle of friends: "My children! Böske, Ilonka, Dönci! It is still very recent that I have left, I am still in the train and abroad, I cannot write to you yet, just to thank you for accompanying me with love on my difficult road, you do not even know how much you helped me, I just want to ask you to stay there and stand by me and love me, because my love is great, true and never-ending."[43]

These letters are unpublished and unedited. I received her letters addressed to Ödön Bánki written in the first half of the 1920s from the addressee's daughter, Esther Bánki. Bánki was himself a refugee of the Jewish quota, a medical student from Győr who peregrinated to Germany and the Netherlands. Somló and Bánki studied together medicine in Würzburg in the early 1920s medicine in Würzburg and kept corresponding for years to come. Thanks to Esther Bánki and Somló's son, the Serbian writer Ivan Ivanji (1929–24), I learned about the lives of both, which helped contextualize the letters.[44]

Ida Somló was possibly a Jewish quota exile in the sense that coming from the Banat and being a Hungarian Jew, she may have wanted to study in a Hungarian university rather than a Serbian one and may have been prevented from doing so by the Hungarian numerus clausus.[45] Her son, however, did not know why his parents chose to study in Würzburg and later in Leipzig. He did know, however, that his parents started dating as teenagers and that Ida followed her husband, Ferenc Iványi, to all the stations of his peregrination and then back home to the Banat. At the same time, Ida was a proud and independent "modern woman," which she expressed not only by pursuing university studies and a medical career but also by wearing her hair short and smoking.[46]

Ilona and Erzsébet Kardos, two sisters addressed by Ida Somló in the previously quoted letter as "Ilonka" and "Böske," are authors of numerous other letters sent to Ödön Bánki in the first half of the 1920s. They left for Germany because of the Jewish quota in Hungary. Erzsébet Kardos wrote to Bánki in a similarly warm tone as Ida Somló, albeit from a position of equality rather than with motherly undertones. In her surviving letters she did not mention specifically gender-related issues, she focused, on the one hand, on practicalities connected to peregrination and, on the other hand, on the alienation she felt. Her perception of having to be itinerant fits the exile narrative of Fenyő and of the Hungarian Jewish media of that period. With the important difference that although she had a few close friends among fellow Hungarian Jewish students, generally she felt irritated by belonging to this group. She complained about a train ride that "from Würzburg I was left alone with the two Hungarian Jews. It was impossible to avoid conversation. In Vienna I escaped, but then I met them again. . . . By the way, on the Viennese station, for my great surprise, I bumped into Bandi Weigl."[47]

In another letter where she complained about losing semesters due to switching between universities, she contemplated that "we have to sacrifice the value of the coming semester and of many years to come together with the possibilities of beauty they could bring, to something bigger that is beyond us, that is nowadays called 'history.'"[48] In this way she echoed Fenyő's opinion that as representatives of a minority, they had to excel as students abroad. And Kardos indeed would excel in psychoanalysis. She is remembered as one of the most talented promising psychoanalysts of the Budapest School of Psychoanalysis whose oeuvre and life was tragically broken when she was murdered in the Shoah.[49] As Fenyő put it (as quoted in this book's introduction), "Sad and great is our destiny. Yet it is fascinating. Since we not only study, but we also feel the responsibility of all our deeds. Hungarian Jewry looks after us. We cannot just pass the exams, we cannot only become doctors, engineers, teachers—we have to become the best doctor, the best engineer, the best teacher. . . . We must prove that the sacrifices were not in vain."[50]

Klein, like Döme and unlike Fenyő, was also politically persecuted since she was a Communist in addition to being pushed out of Polish academia as a Jew and a woman. It is not clear whether she left Poland as a Communist or joined the movement during her studies in Czechoslovakia, but at least according to her narration, she got in trouble in Bratislava because foreign students were not allowed to carry out Communist activism. Although in Italy Communist activity was forbidden even for citizens, she got away with it for quite a few years. She experienced repercussions for her politics only when she wanted to get married in 1936 to an Italian navy officer who could only marry a foreigner with the permission of the Navy Ministry. At this point, Klein was obliged to leave Taranto, a port city where she had lived with her fiancé. Nevertheless, she was not sent back to Poland but could settle anywhere in Italy on the condition that it was not a place of military importance. A few months later, she was informed that the ministry would not permit her fiancé to marry her because she was "subversive." She could then be sure that the authorities knew about her previous activism in Bratislava.[51] Later, the ministry notified her fiancé that his marriage to a foreigner would have been permitted had she not been "of Jewish race."[52] Besides the heartache of not being able to marry the person she loved, Klein would not be able to work as a physician in Italy if she could not marry a citizen. Although she graduated in Bologna, foreign citizens could not join the appropriate professional organization in Italy, which had been a prerequisite for practicing medicine since 1935. As she wrote to her fiancé: "If we do not get married, I will continue to be a stranger in Italy and will not be able to practice my profession."[53]

Klein came from an even more assimilated background than Fenyő: Her parents had abandoned Jewish religious rituals and did not go to synagogue even on Rosh Hashanah or Yom Kippur. Although in greatly emotional moments they spoke Yiddish, with their daughter they always communicated in Polish and discouraged her from using Yiddish.[54] Klein referred to the ghetto benches where Jewish students were forced in many Polish universities as an "apartheid ante litteram" (apartheid before the term was used).[55]

Jolán Weinberger, a Hungarian Jewish woman who became a surgeon in Italy, approached the Hungarian Jewish weekly *Egyenlőség* in a letter in 1938 and drew the editor's attention to Jewish women refugees' particular difficulties. At this time Austrian Jewish refugees of the Anschluss were at the center of attention, and Weinberger made a proposition to help them. Nevertheless, she referred to her own experience as someone forced to wander by the numerus clausus law: "With regard to the current sad circumstances, please do publish my below lines: starting with the wandering of numerus clausus victims (I belong to them), the escape of our German fellow Jews and the influx of Austrian Jews nowadays, the question arises how to host them."[56] As she saw, refugees were often deceived even in supposedly kosher hotels recommended by Jewish communities (she pointed out a case in Milan), and the lack of proper accommodation put women refugees in danger of either prostitution or conversion, for to avoid the former, many looked for a shelter in monasteries.

The author of numerous ego documents, Piroska Döme belonged to all three categories discriminated against in Hungarian universities during the interwar period: woman, Jew, and Communist. She was lucky to have middle-class (albeit not wealthy) parents for whom the education of their daughter, alongside that of their three sons, was important. Moreover, as she remembered, her father valued female emancipation and wanted to make a point by equally educating his daughter.[57] Therefore, Piroska studied in a gymnasium, and thereafter, she was supported financially so that she could study mathematics at the Pázmány Péter University, where she could not enroll as a student but attended lectures by the famous mathematician Lipót Fehér. Besides that, she joined a student group of the Alliance of Communist Young Workers in Hungary (Kommunista Ifjúmunkások Magyarországi Szövetsége, KIMSz).

As a consequence of her involvement in the Communist movement, she became implicated in the 1932 trial against "Red students" and lost all chance to ever obtain a Jewish quota spot at a Hungarian university—even a professor would have pulled strings for her in vain.[58] Hence, her father traveled to Brno to prepare the ground for Piroska's studies in this Moravian city. She informed her father about her plan to pursue an engineering career rather than one in teaching mathematics in the following way: "What would you say if I would like to be an engineer? I have considered it, because there are so many teachers, in addition, this degree is at least not attached to place and language. On the top of it, this is something much more productive, and you know that I prefer practical things."[59]

Unlike Weidlinger and the Tömpe family, who explained their attraction to Brno with the city's fame of being a radical left-wing stronghold (as detailed in chapter 3), the equally Communist Döme did not mention this factor at all, not even when writing recollections for the public in state socialist Hungary. Instead, she emphasized that it was an unexpensive and hence available city for petit bourgeois emigrant students who could not move to more prestigious university towns in Germany, Switzerland, or France.[60] In line with her focus on politics and Communist values, when it comes to women's special situation while studying abroad, the episode she highlights in this respect from her life in Brno is when a comrade, Erzsébet Perczel, was excluded from their party cell for wearing too "feminine and pretty" clothing, which was evaluated as inappropriate for a Communist woman.[61] In interviews conducted by the author with their children, these episodes are often mentioned as examples of the dogmatism of Communist students among former *numerus clausus* exiles.[62]

Döme mentions in her private autobiography that she and Tibor Seres—at the time still Schlesinger—wore conventional clothes on their wedding, she a white dress and he a tailcoat, which triggered their comrades' disapproval.[63]

Döme enrolled in electrical engineering at Brno's German Technical College (Deutsche Technische Hochschule, DTH) but never finished the coursework. She also became a prominent member of the Brno group, presented in chapter 3. According to her retrospective interpretation, she and her husband were simply more committed to Communism than to their studies. In the shadow of Fascism (they got married in April 1933), they thought that the advance of Communism was too urgent to waste time studying and that without this advance, there was no future for them anyway. Hence, they switched to the shorter study program of Brno's famous Textilschule (as opposed to the four-year program of electric engineering at the DTH) so that they had a degree but could return to Hungary to continue their work for the Communist Party in 1934.[64]

This worried Piroska's parents to a great extent; they believed a college degree was key to a successful life. They had a hard time convincing Piroska and Tibor of this. In 1935, Tibor made an attempt to enroll again in Brno and traveled there with Piroska's father. His enrollment was hindered, however, by his conscription into military service in Hungary. By 1937, when he finished the service, the two youngsters again made an attempt. In hindsight, Döme explained this intention with their new conviction that highly educated professionals are also needed for Communism and would play an important role when the working class finally took the power.[65]

However, Döme interpreted her youth in this way four and a half decades later when she published her autobiography in 1983 in state socialist Hungary. Thus, she possibly had in the back of her mind all the conflicts around intellectuals within the party, particularly suspicions raised against Jewish intellectuals in the Rákosi era (1949–56) that were manifested in show trials, internment (even of Tibor Seres), and executions. In the 1980s, however, when she wrote the public autobiography, the topics of Jewishness and antisemitism (particularly Communist antisemitism) were not to be emphasized. At the same time, she did mention that most Hungarians who studied in Brno were there because of the numerus clausus law, possibly a coded way to indicate they were Jewish.[66]

In any case, in 1937 Piroska indeed returned to Brno to prepare for her husband's reenrollment in the DTH and to find a job for herself to support their family, which by this time included a little boy (György Seres, who shared the private autobiography by Piroska Döme, written for her descendants, with me). Her father's enthusiasm for women's education notwithstanding, he convinced Piroska not to continue studying so that at least her husband could become an electrical engineer. Döme does not interpret her decision to not continue her studies as a sacrifice for her husband and child but as a dedication to the Communist cause.[67] In fact, based on knowledge on their whole lives, one can take it that she was indeed even more committed to politics than her husband. However, their plan to resettle in Brno did not work out, and they continued their life in Hungary.

This chapter has shown, through a historical sociological sample of emigrant students, that Jewish women had a harder time studying outside of Hungary than men. Nevertheless, those who made it to a foreign university, did not come from a more privileged social background than their male peers. They used higher education to achieve social mobility as successfully as men. An approach based on testimonies by women led to the conclusion that the exiles of misogyny often happened to be Jewish as well. The three categories discriminated against in interwar Hungarian universities intersected intricately. While the marginalization of Jews and the exclusion of Communists characterized the whole interwar period, misogynist policies varied by faculties and time periods. At the same time, Jews among women met more hostility than non-Jewish women, and academic misogyny was partly triggered by Jewish overschooling being more pronounced among women than men. This made the marginalization or exclusion of women practical for antisemites. However, antisemitic nationalist intellectual women stood up for Christian women's right to education and did not let them be entirely deprived of study possibilities. Women's access to higher education was nevertheless severely restricted when compared to the post–First World War reform by the Károlyi government.

In this study, exile by misogyny had to be exemplified by lives of Jewish women because of the intertwining of antisemitic, sexist, and political exclusionary mechanisms. Similarly, the life trajectories of Hungarian Communist emigrant women who settled in the Soviet Union in the interwar period or during the Second World War also were exemplified by the story of a Jewish family in Katalin Zalai's recent monograph.[68] She hypothesized that the worldview of these radicalized women was shaped by the prejudices they suffered from as women and as Jews.[69]

EPILOGUE

PEREGRINATION WAS ORIGINALLY AN INHERENT part of university studies, first because of the concentration of universities in Italy and western Europe and their scarcity in central and eastern Europe and then because of the tendency of denominational segregation in the aftermath of the Reformation and the Counter-Reformation. Hungarian Protestants were especially eager to support the peregrination of their youth. Peregrination was also considered intellectually essential for studies. During the long nineteenth century, nation-states first supported their citizens' studies abroad and then built up their own higher education to train their intelligentsia. The history of universities in the Russian Empire differed significantly from that in the rest of Europe; in the early phase of the period, they were more open to students whose religion differed from the dominant Orthodox Christianity, but then a somewhat original method of exclusion developed: quotas used to restrict the access of (Roman) Catholics and Jews. The first anti-Jewish measure bearing the name *numerus clausus* was introduced in the Russian Empire in 1887 and led to massive Jewish student emigration toward central and western Europe.

The Hungarian numerus clausus law of 1920 was thus not the first regulation of its kind. However, it was the first piece of antisemitic legislation in twentieth-century Europe (although in practice Hungary was not the only country where Jewish quotas were enforced), preceding Nazi Germany by nearly one and a half decades. Throughout this book, I have put forward the argument that the numerus clausus law was not solely an anti-Jewish law but the fundament of a university admission system that entirely excluded revolutionary left-wingers from higher education and seriously harmed women's access. Therefore, after the historical sociology of the Jewish exiles of the quota system, thus Jewish students who studied abroad in the age of the numerus clausus law (1920–45, but mostly up until 1938), I dedicate separate chapters to students expelled from Hungarian universities for their Communist activism and to women who escaped Hungarian academic misogyny by studying abroad.

The picture that unfolds from the sample of Hungarian migrant students of medicine and engineering in Berlin, Bologna, Prague, and Vienna recalls an observation by the Austrian Jewish writer, Stefan Zweig, himself a refugee from Nazism, who saw a massive drive in Jewish merchants' children to leave commerce behind and become intellectuals in general and liberal professionals in particular. I confirmed the hypothesis that most Hungarian emigrant students in the interwar period were Jewish. Even the proportion of Jews matched the contemporary expectation: Four out of five Hungarian students abroad were Jewish both among women and men. The empirical study also proved a less obvious hypothesis: Peregrination was an escape route to evade the quota for less privileged Jewish youth. Jewish quota exiles were less likely to come from the middle class or the high bourgeoisie than were Jewish students who studied in Hungary. Thus, social capital was an important factor for obtaining a quota spot in Hungary.

At the same time, half of Jewish students within Hungary also hailed from the lower-middle class. Higher education thus continued to function as a means of Jewish social mobility, the grave restriction of Jews' access notwithstanding. Considering this, antisemites' dissatisfaction with the results of the numerus clausus law might have been justified in the short run, even though five to ten thousand Jewish students went abroad, and we do not know how many Jews did give up on university studies.

The political persecution and sexist marginalization intrinsic to the admission system also hit Jews due to authorities' antisemitic bias and to Jewish women making up a larger portion of secondary school graduates than their non-Jewish peers and therefore becoming a larger portion of the women who attended university as well. At the same time, contemporary social norms made it harder for women to spend years abroad studying, and this fact is visible in this study's finding that only every tenth migrant student was a woman.

Migrant students were not necessarily welcomed abroad in the 1920s when overcrowding of the universities and anxiety over intellectuals' unemployment concerned most of the world's war-torn countries more than the possibility of brain drain. The next decade saw growing xenophobia in European countries and the expansion of the Nazi Third Reich. A major destination of Hungarian students, the University of Vienna, was a hotbed of antisemitism from the very beginning of the modern political antisemitic movement in 1879–80 and continued to be after the First World War.

The Viennese Technical College, in fact, even introduced a numerus clausus stipulation in the form of a 10 percent quota on foreign applicants of Jewish *Volksbürgerschaft* (ethnic citizenship) between 1923 and 1933, despite the disapproval of the Austrian Ministry of Education. Nevertheless, the excellent Viennese school of medicine offered various pull factors—for some the vivid Zionist student life, for others the left-wing political milieu of Red Vienna—in addition to its proximity to Hungary. Brno was not much farther either geographically or culturally, and the First Czechoslovak Republic's democratic ethos was attractive for Jews experiencing the opposite in their native Hungary. Nevertheless, as Hungarians, they were not particularly welcomed by Czechoslovak authorities, and as Jews, they encountered hostility mainly from *völkisch* German peers in Brno and Prague as well as sometimes from Czech and Slovak fellow students. Weimar Germany, similar to Austria, provided an ambivalent experience to foreign Jewish students. Although they encountered rampant xenophobia and antisemitism during the great inflation in the early 1920s, as a center of science, Germany became the adoptive homeland of the most well-known Hungarian numerus clausus exiles: János Neumann (John von Neumann), Leó Szilárd, Ede (Edward) Teller, and Jenő (Eugene) Wigner. Because they were first exiled by antisemitism from Hungary in 1933 and then once again by Nazism, Tibor Frank referred to their emigration as "double exile."[1]

It is only at this point when Hungarian Jewish students appear at the Hebrew University of Jerusalem, even though in 1925 it was partially founded with the aim to respond to Jewish students' problem of being pushed out from the universities of east-central Europe. The case of Hungarian Jews with the Hebrew University was similar to their stance toward Zionism. Some of the founding fathers (Theodor Herzl and Max Nordau in the case of Zionism) of both were Hungarian Jews, but they were not followed by masses. A generation of Hungarian Jews born in the 1880s, thus older than the numerus clausus exiles, became some of the founding faculty of the Hebrew University. Andor Fodor filled the very first professorship of the young university and organized its first department, the Institute of Chemistry. Another Hungarian, the mathematician Mihály (Moshe) Fekete served several times as the dean of the faculty for sciences and as the rector in the aftermath of the Second World War. While no Hungarians enrolled in 1928–29 when teaching was launched, forty-one did in 1939–40.[2] The very first doctoral degree of the Hebrew University was conferred in 1936 on a Hungarian, Raphael Patai.

Among the countries treated in this monograph, Italy was by far the friendliest environment for foreign Jewish students. Therefore, when Fascist Italy introduced antisemitic legislation in 1938, the Hungarian Jewish weekly *Egyenlőség* rightfully presented it as the end of the era of "wandering students": "We can only say farewell to this uplifting, beautiful chapter of recent Hungarian Jewish history with some degree of sentimentalism and with the deep conviction that this struggle of ours and of the students has not been in vain."[3] It was noted in the same article that "the Italian universities have been closed to foreign Jews, just as the Viennese [universities] were closed [earlier] this year. And slowly but surely, the strange, interesting Hungarian Jewish life form, which was born during the past two decades—the wandering Jew—is coming to an end."[4]

The author (presumably editor in chief Lajos Szabolcsi) identified this moment as the end of an era because it followed the exclusion of Jews from Austrian universities (March) by a few months. Even though migrant students could still go to Belgium, Czechoslovakia, France, and Switzerland, it was justified to assume that student migration would diminish with the closing down of the most important target countries: Germany already in 1933, Austria and Italy in 1938. The Munich Pact took place one month after this article's publication and its consequences terminated Czechoslovak universities' receptiveness toward foreign and local Jewish students. Belgium and Switzerland were too expensive; thus, they were available for fewer numerus clausus exiles, such as George Hodos, cited in chapter 3. Hence, the disappearance of Germany, Austria, Italy, and soon Czechoslovakia from the options indeed greatly decreased Jewish students' peregrination.

The year 1938 also brought about the introduction of the so-called first (anti-)Jewish law (Law XV of 1938) in Hungary, stipulating that Jews could fill a maximum of 20 percent of liberal professional jobs.[5] The official name of the law recalled the logic of the numerus clausus, disguising discrimination as affirmative action: "law on the more efficient securing of the balance of social and economic life."[6]

Because the Jewish subjects of this study were in early adulthood or in middle age going into the Shoah, I conclude this monograph with a summary of their fates. The watershed years in the collective biography of numerus clausus exiles were the same (1933, 1938), independent from the students' age and time of graduation. This is somewhat counterintuitive, since the age difference between the oldest and the youngest cohort could be over two decades, considering that the cohorts of the early 1920s included veterans of the First World War who had been forced to delay their studies and start later than the age of eighteen or continue them in their late twenties. Opportunities for working and living in the target countries of the numerus clausus–provoked emigration were significantly better in the 1920s than in the 1930s; however, the dramatic changes of the 1930s also concerned those who had graduated earlier and established careers and started families.

On the one hand, quite a few exiles of the numerus clausus became prominent figures in the history of science. This group typically left Hungary in the 1920s for Germany and left Germany for the United States in the 1930s. On the other hand, the majority returned to Hungary in the 1930s because there was increasingly less space for foreign Jews in most European countries, especially after 1938. Before 1938, returning home was not a particularly appealing option due to the difficulty of having foreign university degrees accepted and of finding proper jobs matching migrant students' level of education.

Nevertheless, there were numerus clausus exiles who either stayed where they had studied or succeeded in leaving Hungary during the Second World War. A few dozen Hungarian Jewish alumni of Italian universities, such as Aladár Hábermann and Simon Teich, continued to live and work in Italy, even in the Republic of Salò, and joined the anti-Fascist resistance.[7]

Escape overseas (Argentina, Bolivia, Mexico) was touched on in chapter 3 with regard to the Brno group, most of whom returned to Hungary after 1945 "to build socialism." Their engineering degrees were game changers in their escape; they received visas to Bolivia because engineers were sought after. Another Brno alumnus, Charles Weiss, one of the Communist students expelled from the German Technical College of Brno and from Czechoslovakia in 1933–34 (for which he finished his studies in Florence) found another overseas route. Although failing to disembark in Shanghai, he settled in Singapore until its Japanese occupation in 1942, when he escaped to India and joined the British army. Ultimately, he settled in the United Kingdom.[8] And a central character of the Brno group and its Bolivian subgroup, Pál Weidlinger, settled in the United States during the war for good.

Some descendants perceive the numerus clausus–related emigration as the decisive factor that saved their parents. As Emma Cole put it, "Italy allowed them a route to escape the Holocaust."[9] For some, like András Fenyves, as his daughter Magda Fenyves Sadalla emphasized, it was the Vatican that offered rescue. He was set free from a concentration camp in Italy in 1941 thanks to an intervention by Pope Pius XII for the sake of Catholic (former) Jews.[10]

Within Hungary, after 1938, more and more antisemitic measures restricted professional possibilities for Jews. At the same time, compared to Nazi-occupied Europe, Hungary remained a relatively safe country for Jews between 1939 and 1944, at least for women, elderly people, and children. Tens of thousands of men perished in forced labor service on the front; many subjects of this book, the majority of whom were male and of draft age (eighteen to forty-two years old), experienced this aspect of the war.[11] The genocide of Hungarian Jewry, famously the last but the fastest episode of the Shoah, took the lives of many former numerus clausus exiles as well, yet it is impossible to estimate the proportion of the victims and the survivors among them.[12] Since this book is intentionally a social history of not famous and not highly visible students, this was to be expected.

It can nevertheless be stated that being a physician or an engineer thanks to having studied abroad impacted chances of survival, either detrimentally or beneficially. Depending on when a person was called up for labor service, Jewish doctors may have been sent to the eastern front en masse or redirected to Hungary for public health care. Nevertheless, in each of these cases, they were treated differently from Jewish men who were not doctors and from doctors who were not Jewish.

According to an order of August 23, 1940, Jewish men drafted to the Hungarian army were not allowed to perform armed military service like "reliable citizens" did; they had to perform labor service instead. From 1941, a series of harsh, specifically anti-Jewish measures were introduced in the regulation of labor service. This meant that the labor service battalions were sent to the eastern front (where even properly equipped soldiers fell victim in great numbers) without weapons and with worse clothing and smaller food portions than non-Jewish soldiers. Thus, the labor service was one of the ways for the Hungarian state to jeopardize the lives of its Jewish citizens. By 1942, 50,000 Jewish men (compared to an army of 250,000 soldiers) were drafted in labor service.[13] Jewish intellectuals were particularly singled out to be sent to the front line, as the minutes of a meeting in the Ministry of Defense from November 1942 testify: "The main thing is that the more Jews are sent to territories of military action the better, especially the intellectuals."[14] Among the liberal professions, doctors were an especially endangered group of Jewish intellectuals, as Mária M. Kovács demonstrates in her monograph on professional organizations. Because of the especially harsh antisemitism and proactivity of the radical right-wing professional association Hungarian Doctors' National Association (Magyar Orvosok Nemzeti Egyesülete, MONE), half of Hungarian Jewish doctors (2,500 people) perished during the war. Each labor battalion needed 1 physician per 220 soldiers. However, due to MONE's lobbying, in the winter of 1942 ten to twelve times as many Jewish doctors were on the front. In 1941 the Ministry of Defense agreed with MONE to take over its lists of Jewish doctors and use them when compiling lists of Jews to be called up for labor service. At this time, Minister of Interior Ferenc Keresztes-Fischer intervened and moved all the Jewish physicians who were not needed on the front to public medical establishments in Hungary.[15] In the following two years, (male) doctors were exposed to the dangers of the front to the same extent as other Jewish men.

In March 1944, Jewish doctors and engineers were forbidden to work alike; however, engineers' survival chance depended on the same factors as that of all Jews (residence, gender, age, level of assimilation). In the beginning of the Nazi occupation of Hungary (March 1944), the doctors' situation seemed to be the most protected since a third of them performed civilian labor service in public health care, which meant protection from ghettoization and deportation. The Ministry of Interior insisted on this arrangement because there were not enough Gentile doctors fill in for Jewish ones. At this time, many Jewish doctors had graduated before 1920, when Jewish access to universities was not yet restricted, and their number at times exceeded one-third of medical students. Thus, in 1944 the removal of Jewish physicians would have deprived entire regions of public health care. And yet the Chamber of Doctors (an organization to allegedly promote medical doctors' interests, membership in it was a prerequisite to practice the medical profession, and Jews' access was strongly limited to this organization) and MONE pushed further for ridding the country of their Jewish colleagues. By early May, these institutions' leaders had succeeded in passing regulations that allowed the local offices of the chamber to coordinate with the army in order to relocate Jewish doctors to areas where Jews were already being collected for deportation.[16] In the meantime, the chamber of engineers (an organization to allegedly promote engineers' interests, membership in it was a prerequisite to practice the engineering profession, and Jews' access was strongly limited to this organization) at least protected those Jewish engineers, who had been exempted from the effect of the 1939 antisemitic law (Law IV of 1939),[17] which mostly concerned veterans of the First World War with some special merit, with renewing their membership certificates. In addition, it did not sanction Jewish engineers who continued working illegally after March 1944 and occasionally provided them with certificates that they were authorized by the chamber to perform their work despite being Jewish.[18]

Thus, Jewish male doctors could easily fall victim to the antisemitism especially rampant within the medical profession. At the same time, the dire need for doctors in the Hinterland could save them, especially if they were sent to Budapest. In the end, half of Jewish doctors survived the Shoah in Hungary, while hardly more than a third of all Jews survived.[19] Female Jewish doctors were not sent to the front; however, they were part of the large population deported to concentration camps in the spring and summer of 1944. When it came to ghettoization and deportation, residence became the most important factor to increased survival chances (although this was not obvious at all for contemporaries), since only the ghetto of Budapest was spared from deportation. This of course did not guarantee survival in the horrific circumstances within the ghetto and amid mass murders by Arrow Cross militia. It remains a fact nevertheless that most of the surviving Hungarian Jewry lived in Budapest because the genocide of provincial Jewry was so close to complete.

This fact is important when investigating the fates of the migrant students of the interwar period. Jews with foreign university degrees were very likely to settle in Budapest upon returning to Hungary in the 1930s due to the proximity of technical companies (the Tungsram and Standard being typical workplaces for them) and the famous Jewish Hospital of the Pest Israelite Community on Szabolcs Street, which treated fourteen thousand patients a year and employed many medical professionals.[20] In addition, the community purposefully employed as many Jewish doctors in this hospital (in fact a conglomerate of several clinics) as possible who could not find employment elsewhere, for example, due to their foreign degrees not being accepted in Hungary. In this case, they were employed as underpaid or even unpaid medical assistants or nurses. But still, during the Shoah, working in the capital ended up making a critical difference to one's survival.

From the sample of my historical sociological investigation, 243 students (at least that I could unambiguously identify) appear in the Central Database of Shoah Victim's Names as persecuted Jews. Of them, 139 perished. Unambiguous identification was not always possible by cross-checking other sources because several individuals have very common names and many source types (lists of deportees, labor battalion victims, yizkor books) list only names without other information. However, pages of testimony and postwar press notifications from municipal authorities about diseased persons who had been residents of the locality (published in the official *Hungarian Gazette* in 1945–46) include more ample information on individuals. The *Hungarian Gazette* did not refer to the victims as victims of mass murder. However, the place and time of those persons' disappearance or death make it clear that they were victims of the Judeocide. Such notifications often also mention the names of concentration camps where they had been seen for the last time.

Hardly more than one-third of Hungarian Jewry (191,000 people) survived and over one-fourth of this so-called remnant Jewry left Hungary by 1957 in two major waves: first between 1945 and 1949 and then in 1956–57.[21] During the Stalinist years (1949–56)—or, in the Hungarian context, the dictatorship of Mátyás Rákosi, first secretary of the Hungarian Workers' Party—emigration was nearly impossible. Counterintuitively, former numerus clausus exiles were not very likely to join these migratory movements, their experience of emigration notwithstanding. The reason is sociological rather than political: Employed intellectuals had less interest in leaving than Jews who either owned capital (companies, factories, or apartment buildings) that would be nationalized while the owners would be persecuted as class enemies or Jews who had a hard time adjusting to state Socialism due to their religious lifestyle.

Former numerus clausus exiles, even though most were not Communists, were intellectuals marginalized and persecuted by the previous Horthy and Arrow Cross regimes, so they were perfect fits for jobs where educated employees were needed to substitute the previous, politically unreliable ones. This was the case during the (temporary) democratic transition in 1945–47 as well as after the Communist takeover in 1948–49. Public administration, ministries, health care, and industrial companies absorbed them in great numbers not only to substitute pre-1945 personnel but also for employment at new institutional structures. At the turn of the 1940s and 1950s, however, former Jewish emigrant students even within the Communist elite were easily caught up in Stalinist show trials, as we saw in chapter 3.

Tragically, the historical experience of the numerus clausus law did not end either antisemitism or discrimination. The idea of taking away the possibility of studying from someone—rather than broadening access to it for everyone—seems to have been too attractive for policymakers. While in the interwar period the Hungarian state restricted Jews' access to universities to make place for "Christians," from 1949 to 1963 it excluded "class enemies" (the bourgeoisie and the nobility) in order to destroy "the cultural monopoly of the wealthy classes." There were Jewish families where more than one generation were therefore excluded from higher education, one by the interwar Jewish quota and another as bourgeois in the postwar people's democracy. In both admission systems, applicants' talent and commitment to studies were at best secondary factors in deciding whether they were fit for university studies or not. It is noteworthy that the "popular" (népi) movement worked toward the provision of education to talented youth of peasant background before as well as after the war. They addressed the problem of the large majority of the Hungarian population being excluded from secondary and higher education by poverty. The movement had a right-wing as well as a left-wing component and culminated in the postwar activity of National Association of People's Colleges (Népi Kollégiumok Országos Szövetsége, NÉKOSZ), dissolved by the emerging Stalinist dictatorship in 1949.

This monograph has invited readers to rethink the Hungarian numerus clausus law of 1920, the first antisemitic law of twentieth-century Europe, as a tool to exclude political dissenters as well as to de-emancipate two formerly emancipated minorities: Jews and women, albeit the latter were only emancipated in terms of access to higher education and for a very short time in 1918–19. I have pointed out historical contingencies as well as long-term tendencies in European history. In this vein, my narrative has also provided material for reflections on the historical relationship between the medical profession and minorities.

Medical faculties pioneered in accepting Jews and women as students in the Middle Ages and in the nineteenth century, respectively. At the same time, they had a history of fervent antisemitism: In the twentieth century, in some instances, Jewish students were prohibited from anatomy classes unless Jewish cadavers were provided,[22] and more so than other professional chambers, the Hungarian Chamber of Doctors complied with the Nazis in the deportation of its Jewish members. Budapest's medical faculty also overperformed with regard to the women's quota and applied a numerus nullus in the first half of the 1920s. Both the acceptance and the rejection derive from the profession's nature. There must be a sufficient number of doctors; hence, recruitment from new groups is logical at times. At the same time, physicians' ability to heal the sick represents a potentially threatening power that defenders of oppressive hierarchies do not want members of minorities to acquire.

As a farewell, I wish that those who enjoy(ed) the privilege of studying at a university, and experience(d) intellectual as well as cultural enrichment by peregrination shall remember that peregrination converged with exile in multiple historical instances, and for many, this is the case in our present. It is my hope that this book will enhance scholarly interest in the historical interplays between exclusion, exile, and migration. In addition, I hope to have made the case that individual as well as communal agency matters in resisting oppressive measures taken against students.

NOTES

INTRODUCTION

1. Lili Fenyő, *Pillanatfelvételek a külföldön élő magyar diákság életéből* [Snapshots from the life of Hungarian students abroad] (Jupiter Nyomda, 1929), 75.

2. "1920. évi XXV. törvénycikk a tudományegyetemekre, a műegyetemre, a budapesti egyetemi közgazdaságtudományi karra és a jogakadémiákra való beiratkozás szabályozásáról" [Law 1920: XXV on the regulation of enrollment to university, polytechnics, Faculty of Economics at the University of Budapest and law academies], *Net Jogtár* [Online Legal Collection], accessed November 5, 2024, https://net.jogtar.hu/ezer-ev-torveny?docid=92000025.TV.

3. Béla Bodó, *The White Terror: Antisemitic and Political Violence in Hungary, 1919–1921* (Routledge, 2019), 256.

4. This estimation is based on a document by the Central Jewish Student Aid Committee. They counted approximately 1,450 new enrollments each academic year, which is the number of Hungarian Jews who graduated abroad with the financial support of the Central Jewish Student Aid Committee until 1928. We must take into account that there were other students who did not use this committee's help and therefore are not included in this data. The migratory phenomenon continued on a similar scale between 1928 and 1938; hence, for the whole interwar period, the emigrant Hungarian student number approached 10,000. The source of the data for the 1920s is *Szabolcsi Lajos jelentése a Központi Zsidó Diákbizottság működéséről: Jelentés a Magyarországi Izraeliták Országos Irodájának 1929. évi működéséről* [Report by Lajos Szabolcsi on the Activity of the Central Jewish Student Aid Committee to the Office of Israelites of Hungary: Report on the Activities of the Office of Israelites of Hungary in 1929], 1929, K28

(Department of Nationalities and Minorities), 14/53rd item, Magyar Nemzeti Levéltár [Hungarian National Archives].

5. Guy Miron, *The Waning of Emancipation: Jewish History, Memory, and the Rise of Fascism in Germany, France, and Hungary* (Wayne State University Press, 2011), 157.

6. Mária M. Kovács, *The Beginnings of Anti-Jewish Legislation: The 1920 Numerus Clausus Law in Hungary* (Central European University Press, 2023), 41.

7. Kovács, *Beginnings of Anti-Jewish Legislation*, 183–84.

8. In fact, the city's German Technical College trained the highest number of Hungarian engineers between the two world wars just after Budapest's Technical University.

9. "A. m. kir. vallás- és közoktatásügyi miniszter 1920. évi 123.033. számú rendelete a tudományegyetemekre, a műegyetemre, a budapesti egyetemi közgazdaságtudományi karra és a jogakadémiára való beiratkozás szabályozásáról" [Order No. 123.033 of 1920 by the minister of religion and public education about the regulation of enrollment to university, polytechnics, Faculty of Economics at the University of Budapest and law academies], in *Magyarországi Rendeletek Tára*, Ötvennegyedik folyam [Collection of the Decrees of Hungary, vol. 54] (Magy. Kir. Belügyminisztérium, 1920), 1455–60. The table converting Israelites into a new category of Jewish nationals is on p. 1460.

10. Kovács, *Beginnings of Anti-Jewish Legislation*, 118.

11. István Bibó, "Zsidókérdés Magyarországon 1944" [The Jewish Question in Hungary in 1944], in *Zsidókérdés, asszimiláció, antiszemitizmus: Tanulmányok a zsidókérdésről a huszadik századi Magyarországon* [Jewish question, assimilation, antisemitism: Studies on the Jewish question in twentieth century Hungary], ed. Péter Hanák (Gondolat, 1984), 141.

12. For instance, Lee Congdon, *Exile and Social Thought: Hungarian Intellectuals in Germany and Austria, 1919–1933* (Princeton University Press, 1991); Tibor Frank, *Double Exile: Migrations of Jewish-Hungarian Professionals Through Germany to the United States, 1919–1945* (Peter Lang, 2009); Helmut F. Pfanner, *Exile in New York: German and Austrian Writers After 1933* (Wayne State University Press, 1983); Claus-Dieter Krohn and Rita Kimber, *Intellectuals in Exile: Refugee Scholars and the New School for Social Research* (University of Massachusetts Press, 1993).

1. PEREGRINATION, RELIGIOUS OTHERS, AND WOMEN IN THE LONG HISTORY OF UNIVERSITIES

1. Stefan Zweig, *The World of Yesterday. An Autobiography* (Viking Press, 1943), 95.

2. Hilde de Ridder-Symoens, "Mobility," in *Universities in the Middle Ages*, ed. Hilde de Ridder-Symoens (Cambridge University Press, 1992), 281.

3. Ridder-Symoens, "Mobility," 280.

4. Paolo Nardi, "Relations with Authority," in Ridder-Symoens, *Universities in the Middle Ages*, ed. Hilde de Ridder-Symoens (Cambridge: Cambridge University Press, 1992), 79.

5. Ridder-Symoens, "Mobility," 285.

6. Ridder-Symoens, "Mobility," 287.

7. Nardi, "Relations with Authority," 79.

8. Elemér Balogh, *A salvus conductus és a magyar peregrináció* [Salvus conductus and Hungarian peregrination] (József Attila Tudományegyetem, 1996).

9. András Kubinyi, "Städtische Bürger und Universitätsstudenten in Ungarn am Ende des Mittelalters [Urban citizens and university students in Hungary in the late Middle Ages]," in *Stadt und Universität im Mittelalter und in der früheren Neuzeit* [City and university in the Middle Ages and in the early modern period], ed. Erich Maschke and Jürgen Sydow (Thorbecke, 1977), 161–65.

10. Bratislava was part of Hungary up until 1920.

11. Ridder-Symoens, "Mobility," 293.

12. Between 1517 and 1721, the University of Padua conferred 228 doctorates on Jews ("Universities," *Jewish Virtual Library*, accessed October 14, 2024, https://www.jewishvirtuallibrary.org/universities).

13. László Szögi, "Peregrináció és reformáció: Milyen külföldi egyetemekre jártak tanulni a 16–18. századi magyar diákok?" [Peregrination and reformation: Which foreign universities did Hungarian students go to study in the sixteenth–eighteenth centuries?], *Rubicon* 28, no. 12 (2017): 57.

14. Sándor Kovács, "A magyar unitárius peregrinatio academica vázlatos története 1848 után" [Outline of Hungarian Unitarians' peregrination academica after 1848], *Keresztény Magvető* 115, no. 4. (2009): 561.

15. Viktória Molnár Tamusné, "Peregrinatio academica: Külföldi egyetemjárás a Debreceni Református Kollégiumban a 16–17. században" [Peregrinatio academica: Studies abroad and the Calvinist collegium of Debrecen in the sixteenth–seventeenth centuries], *Módszertani közlemények* 47, no. 5. (2007): 239–42.

16. Szögi, "Peregrináció és reformáció."

17. "Historical" Hungary refers to the much larger territory of the country before its borders drastically changed after the First World War.

18. The results are published in a book series: *Magyarországi diákok egyetemjárása az újkorban* [Peregrination of students from Hungary in the Modern era], ed. László Szögi (Budapest, 1994–).

19. László Szögi, "A külföldi egyetemjárás tömegessé válása a 19. század második felében" [The proliferation of external peregrination in the second half of the nineteenth century], in *Pedagógia, Oktatás, Könyvtár. Ünnepi tanulmányok F. Dárdai Ágnes tiszteletére* [Pedagogy, education, library. Festschrift honoring Ágnes Dárdai F.], ed. Helga Csóka-Jaksa et al. (Pécsi Egyetemi Könyvtár és Tudásközpont, 2014), 114.

20. Victor Karády, "Jewish Over-Schooling Revisited: The Case of Hungarian Secondary Education in the Old Regime (1900–1941)," *Yearbook of the Jewish Studies Programme (CEU)*, 1999, 75–91.

21. László Szögi, "Magyarországi zsidó egyetemi hallgatók a német nyelvterület egyetemein és főiskoláin, 1789–1919" [Jewish students from Hungary at universities and colleges in the German-speaking territories, 1789–1919], *ELTE Egyetemi Könyvtár Évkönyvei* 10, no. 1 (2011): 109.

22. Szögi, "A külföldi egyetemjárás," 113.

23. Szögi, "Magyarországi zsidó egyetemi hallgatók," 118.

24. Out of the 2.5 million Jews who fled eastern Europe between 1880 and 1914, 2 million settled in North America, 350,000 in western Europe and 300,000 in other overseas territories (including Palestine) (Haim Hillel Ben-Sasson, ed., *A History of the Jewish People* [Harvard University Press, 1985]).

25. Irina Manitz, "Die akademische 'Ausländerfrage' in russischsprachigen Periodika in Deutschland vor dem 1. Weltkrieg" [The 'Ausländerfrage' in Russian press in Germany before the First World War], in *Universitäten als Brücken in Europa: Studien zur Geschichte der studentischen Migration* [Universities as bridges in Europe: Studies on the history of student migration], ed. Hartmut Rüdiger Peter and Natalia Tikhonov (Peter Lang, 2003), 218–19.

26. Jack Wertheimer, "The 'Unwanted Element': East European Jews in Imperial Germany," *Leo Baeck Institute Yearbook* 26, no. 1 (1981): 23–46. France and Switzerland were the other typical choices.

27. "1920. évi XXV. törvénycikk a tudományegyetemekre, a műegyetemre, a budapesti egyetemi közgazdaságtudományi karra és a jogakadémiákra való beiratkozás szabályozásáról" [Law 1920: XXV on the regulation of enrollment to university, polytechnics, Faculty of Economics at the University of Budapest and law academies], *Net Jogtár* [Online Legal Collection], accessed November 5, 2024, https://net.jogtar.hu/ezer-ev-torveny?docid=92000025.TV.

28. Gyula Gábor, *A numerus clausus és a zsidó egyetem* [The numerus clausus and the Jewish university] (Fráter Nyomda, 1924).

29. For Romanian universities, see Lucian Nastasă, *Antisemitismul universitar în România (1919–1939): Mărturii documentare* [Academic antisemitism in Romania, 1919–1939: Documentary testimonies] (Cluj-Napoca, Editura Institutului pentru Studierea Problemelor Minorităţilor Naţi-Kriterion, 2011); Andrei-Dan Sorescu and Raul Cârstocea, "The (Great) Numbers Game. Demographic Anxieties and Quotas in Nineteenth- and Twentieth-Century Romania and the Global Antisemitic Imaginary," in *Quotas: The "Jewish Question" and Higher Education in Central Europe, 1880–1945*, ed. Michael L. Miller and Judith Szapor (Berghahn, 2024), 113. For Polish universities, see Harry Rabinowicz, "The Battle of the Ghetto Benches," *Jewish Quarterly Review* 552 (1964): 151–59; Grzegorz Krzywiec, "Anti-Jewish Quotas in Interwar Poland: Toward a Reconsideration of the Appeal of Fascism in East Central Europe," in Miller and Szapor, *Quotas*, 345–66.

30. Elisa Signori, "Una 'peregrinatio academica' in età contemporanea: Gli studenti ebrei stranieri nelle Università italiane tra le due guerre" [A 'Peregrinatio Academica' in the contemporary age: The foreign Jewish students at the Italian universities between the two wars], *Annali di storia delle università italiane* 4, no. 1 (2000): 1000–1024.

31. Márta Schneider, "Magyar ösztöndíjasok külföldön" [Hungarian stipendees abroad], in *Régi és új peregrináció: Magyarok külföldön, külföldiek Magyarországon* [Old and new peregrination: Hungarians abroad, foreigners in Hungary], ed. Imre Békési et al., vol. 2, *A peregrináció a magyar irodalom- és művelődéstörténet különböző periódusaiban* [Peregrination in different periods of the history of Hungarian literature and culture] (Nemzetközi Magyar Filológiai Társaság, 1993), 879.

32. Ignác Romsics, *Hungary in the Twentieth Century* (Osiris, 1999), 152.

33. Michael L. Miller, "A Foreign Policy Fiasco? Reactions to the Hungarian Numerus Clausus in Weimar Germany," in Miller and Szapor, *Quotas*, 467–68.

34. For further reading on high-profile emigrants, see Tibor Frank, *Double Exile: Migrations of Jewish-Hungarian Professionals Through Germany to the United States, 1919–1945* (Peter Lang, 2009) and István Hargittai, *The Martians of Science. Five Physicists Who Changed the Twentieth Century* (Oxford University Press, 2006).

35. Mária M. Kovács, *The Beginnings of Anti-Jewish Legislation: The 1920 Numerus Clausus Law in Hungary* (Central European University Press, 2023), 147; *Szabolcsi Lajos jelentése a Központi Zsidó Diákbizottság működéséről. Jelentés a Magyarországi Izraeliták Országos Irodájának 1929. évi működéséről* [Report by Lajos Szabolcsi on the activity of the Central Jewish Student Aid Committee to the Office of Israelites of Hungary: Report on the activities of the Office of Israelites of Hungary in 1929], K28 (Department of Nationalities and Minorities), 14/53rd item, Magyar Nemzeti Levéltár [Hungarian National Archives]. Importantly, KZSDB was called "Central" because there were a number of local student aid committees across the country."

36. Referred to by Joseph Shatzmiller, *Jews, Medicine, and Medieval Society* (University of California Press, 1996), 29. Shatzmiller refers to the manuscript preserved at the Bibliotéque Nationale Paris, ms.héb.1053, fols. 39v, 42r, and 44r. *Introduction to the Practice* (*Practica summaria* in Latin) by Bernard Gordon (1260–ca. 1318) is derived from his voluminous *Lilium Medicine* as a vade mecum for medical students. Bernard Gordon was one of the pioneering pre-Renaissance medical experimentalists who challenged the medical tradition of Hippocrates and Galen. (He is even referenced in the *Canterbury Tales* by Geoffrey Chaucer.) He taught at the University of Montpellier in the second half of the thirteenth and beginning of the fourteenth century.

37. Referred to in Shatzmiller, *Jews, Medicine, and Medieval Society*, 30, where reference is made to a published version of the manuscript in the Bibliotéque Nationale Paris: Luis García-Ballester, Lola Ferre, and Eduard Feliu, "Jewish

Appreciation of Fourteenth-Century Scholastic Medicine," *Osiris*, 2nd ser., 6 (1990): 107–17. *Kitāb al-Manṣūrī* was dedicated to Manṣūr ibn Isḥaq, ruler of the Iranian city Rayy, as indicated by its title. The book's author, Razes (ca. 854–925 or 935), physician, philosopher, and alchemist, is also known as al-Razi and was famous for serving as the chief physician of Baghdad and for differentiating smallpox from measles. He was a proponent of experimental medicine. In his medical treatises, he combined knowledge from ancient texts with his observations from his medical practice. The commentator Gerard de Solo (died ca. 1360) taught in Montpellier in the first half of the fourteenth century.

38. Shatzmiller, *Jews, Medicine, and Medieval Society*, 30.

39. The *Theodosian Code* was compiled under Eastern Roman Emperor Theodosius II and published in 438.

40. Anna Esposito and Micaela Procaccia, "'Iudei de Urbe': La testimonianza di un inventario" ['Iudei de Urbe'? The testimony of an inventory], in *Un pontificato ed una città: Sisto IV (1471–1484). Atti del convegno Roma 3–7 dicembre 1984* [A pontificate and a city: Sixtus IV (1471–1484). Acts of the conference in Rome December 3–7, 1984], ed. Concetta Ranieri et al. (Scuola Vaticana di paleografia, diplomatica e archivistica, 1986), 269–71.

41. Ladislao Münster, "Laurea in medicina conferita dallo studio ferrarese ad un ebreo nel 1426" [A medical degree conferred by the University of Ferrara on a Jew in 1426], *Ferrara viva: Rivista storica e di attualità* 3, nos. 7–8 (1961): 63.

42. Shatzmiller, *Jews, Medicine, and Medieval Society*, 31.

43. See for instance Natalia Aleksiun, "Christian Corpses for Christians!: Dissecting the Anti-Semitism Behind the Cadaver Affair of the Second Polish Republic," *East European Politics and Societies* 25, no. 3 (2011): 393–409.

44. Shatzmiller, *Jews, Medicine, and Medieval Society*, 90–93.

45. Shatzmiller, *Jews, Medicine, and Medieval Society*, 1–3.

46. Shatzmiller, *Jews, Medicine, and Medieval Society*, 1.

47. Mordechai Breuer, *Ha-Yeshivah ha-Ashkenazit* [The Ashkenazic academy] (Faculty of Humanities–Department of the History of the Jewish People, 1962), 14–16. Referred to by Ephraim Kanarfogel, *Jewish Education and Society in the High Middle Ages* (Wayne State University Press, 1992), 51–52.

48. Jacob Katz, *Tradition and Crisis: Jewish Society at the End of the Middle Ages* (New York University Press, 1993), 164–66.

49. Shatzmiller, *Jews, Medicine, and Medieval Society*, 13.

50. David Ruderman and Giuseppe Veltri, eds., *Cultural Intermediaries: Jewish Intellectuals in Early Modern Italy* (University of Pennsylvania Press, 2004).

51. Erika Rummel, "Humanists, Jews and Judaism," in *Jews, Judaism, and the Reformation in Sixteenth-Century Germany*, ed. Dean Phillip Bell and Stephen G. Burnett (Brill, 2006), 3–31.

52. "Levita, Elijah," *Jewish Encyclopedia,* accessed November 6, 2024, https://www.jewishencyclopedia.com/articles/9864-levita-elijah.

53. Ariel Toaff, *Il vino e la carne: Una comunità ebraica nel medioevo* [The wine and the meat: A Jewish community in the Middle Ages] (Il Mulino, 1989), 266–67; Stanislao Majarelli und Ugolino Nicolini, *Il monte dei poveri di Perugia: Periodo delle origini (1462–1474)* [The credit bank of Perugia: The beginnings (1462–1474)] (Banca del Monte di credito, 1962), 75.

54. Ladislao Münster, "Fu Jacob Mantino lettore effettivo dello studio di Bologna?" [Was Jacob Mantino actually a lecturer at the University of Bologna?], *Rassegna mensile di Israel* 20 (1954): 310–21; Shatzmiller, *Jews, Medicine, and Medieval Society,* 34.

55. "Saxony," *Jewish Encyclopedia,* accessed October 15, 2024, https://www.jewishencyclopedia.com/articles/13241-saxony. Such regulation remained in force until 1682.

56. Timothy J. Wengert, "Philip Melanchthon and the Jews: A Reappraisal," in Bell and Burnett, *Jews, Judaism, and the Reformation in Sixteenth-Century Germany,* 112.

57. Michael T. Walton, *Anthonius Margaritha and the Jewish Faith: Jewish Life and Conversion in Sixteenth-Century Germany* (Wayne State University Press, 2012).

58. "Vienna," *Jewish Encyclopedia,* accessed October 15, 2024, https://jewishencyclopedia.com/articles/14699-vienna.

59. Maria Diemling, "Anthonius Margaritha and His 'Der Gantz Jüdisch Glaub,'" in Bell and Burnett, *Jews, Judaism, and the Reformation in Sixteenth-Century Germany,* 305–7.

60. Nathaniel Katzburg, *Fejezetek az újkori zsidó történelemből Magyarországon* [Chapters from the early modern history of Jews in Hungary] (Osiris, 1999), 30–31.

61. Victor Karády, "Jews in the Hungarian Medical Profession, 1782–1947: A Sociohistorical Report," in Miller and Szapor, *Quotas,* 167. Before 1850, no Jewish students at the Polytechnic University of Vienna studied architecture, while 65 percent chose commercial studies.

62. Karády, "Jews in the Hungarian Medical Profession, 1782–1947," 167.

63. Benjamin Nathans, *Beyond the Pale: The Jewish Encounter with Late Imperial Russia* (University of California Press, 2002), 204–5.

64. Jews were otherwise allowed to reside only in the Pale of Settlement; they needed special permission or special status to achieve a residence permit in any other place. The Pale included all of today's (2026) Belarus, Lithuania, and Moldova; much of Ukraine and east-central Poland; and relatively small parts of Latvia and the Western Russian Federation.

65. Nathans, *Beyond the Pale,* 215.

66. Nathans, *Beyond the Pale*, 203.

67. Zsuzsa Hetényi, *In a Mealstrom: The History of Russian—Jewish Prose, 1860–1940* (Central European University Press, 2008), 94.

68. Nathans, *Beyond the Pale*, 218.

69. Darius Staliūnas, "Affirmative Action in the Western Borderlands of the Late Russian Empire?," *Slavic Review* 77, no. 3 (2018): 990.

70. Simon Dubnow, *History of the Jews in Poland and Russia from the Earliest Times Until the Present Day [1915]* (Jewish Publication Society of America, 1918; republished, Avotaynu, 2000).

71. Michael Aronson, *Troubled Waters: The Origins of the 1881 Anti-Jewish Pogroms in Russia*. (University of Pittsburgh Press, 1990); John Klier, *Russians, Jews, and the Pogroms of 1881–1882* (Cambridge University Press, 2011).

72. See a literary elaboration on this topic in a short story by Semyon Yushkevich, one of the most popular Russian Jewish authors of his time: "Disintegration" written in 1895–97 and published in 1902.

73. Paulus Ebner and Juliane Mikoletzky, *Vom Studentencomité zur HTU: Zur Geschichte der Studierenden an der Technischen Universität Wien und ihren Vorgängerinstitutionen* [From students' committee to student union: A history of the students of the Viennese Technical University and its predecessors] (Universitätsarchiv der Technischen Universität Wien, 2006), 25. In Vienna, the exclusion of Jewish members started in 1882 from several fraternities.

74. Werner Hanak-Lettner, ed., *Die Universität als Kampfzone—The University: A Battle Ground* (Jüdisches Museum Wien, 2015), 65.

75. Hanak-Lettner, *Die Universität als Kampfzone*, 70.

76. Arthur Koestler, *Arrow in the Blue. The First Volume of an Autobiography: 1905–1931* (Vintage, 2005), 107–10.

77. Jacob Katz, *From Prejudice to Destruction: Anti-Semitism, 1700–1933* (Harvard University Press, 1980), 274.

78. Miklós Szabó, *Az újkonzervativizmus és a jobboldali radikalizmus története (1867–1918)* [The history of new conservativism and the radical right wing (1867–1918)] (Új Mandátum, 2003), 181.

79. Miklós Konrád, "The Prehistory of the Hungarian Numerus Clausus Law: Political Antisemitism in Hungary, 1895–1914," in Miller and Szapor, *Quotas*, 137.

80. Miklós Szabó, "Az 1901-es egyetemi 'kereszt-mozgalom' (Adalék a magyarországi szélsőjobboldal történetéhez)" [The 'cross-movement' of 1901 (Remarks on the history of the radical right wing in Hungary)], *Történelmi Szemle* 13, no. 4 (1970): 484.

81. Szabó, "Az 1901-es egyetemi 'kereszt-mozgalom,'" 486.

82. Szabó, "Az 1901-es egyetemi 'kereszt-mozgalom,'" 512.

83. Szabó, "Az 1901-es egyetemi 'kereszt-mozgalom,'" 514.

84. For the detailed history of the Galilei Circle, see Péter Csunderlik, *Radikálisok, szabadgondolkodók, ateisták: A Galilei Kör története, 1908–1919* [Radicals, free-thinkers, athesits: The history of the Galilei Circle, 1908–1919] (Napvilág, 2020).

85. Csunderlik, *Radikálisok, szabadgondolkodók, ateisták*, 93–103.

86. The Aster Revolution of 1918 was definitely a revolution, whereas the Communist takeover of March 1919 is better considered a putsch, though it did lead to revolutionary changes. While counterrevolutionaries treated the participants of the Aster Revolution as Communists or at least Communist allies, in fact, it was a democratic revolution with many liberal politicians involved who escaped after the Communist putsch.

87. Nationality was determined by the native tongue in the evaluations of censuses.

88. David Sorkin, "Enlightenment and Emancipation: German Jewry's Formative Age in Comparative Perspective," in *Comparing Jewish Societies*, ed. T. M. Endelman (University of Michigan Press, 1997), 89–112.

89. Kati Vörös, "A Unique Contract: Interpretations of Modern Hungarian Jewish History," in *CEU Jewish Studies Yearbook III*, ed. András Kovács and Eszter Andor (CEU Jewish Studies Program, 2003), 229–55.

90. Viktor Karády, *Zsidóság, modernizáció, polgárosodás* [Jewishness, modernization, embourgeoisement] (Cserépfalvi, 1997).

91. László Marjanucz, "Zsidó identitás és asszimiláció Magyarországon. Interjú" [Jewish identity and assimilation in Hungary. Interview with Viktor Karády], in Karády, *Zsidóság, modernizáció, polgárosodás*, 19.

92. Péter Hanák, "Problems of Jewish Assimilation in Austria-Hungary in the Nineteenth and Twentieth Centuries," in *The Power of the Past: Essays for Eric Hobsbawm*, ed. Pat Thane et al. (Cambridge University Press, 1984), 235–50.

93. Gábor Gyáni, "Polgárosodás mint zsidó identitás" [Embourgeoisement as Jewish identity], in *BUKSZ* 9, no. 3 (1997): 266–76.

94. Erdei never published this famous essay written in 1943–44. It was found in Erdei's bequest and published in two stages five years after the author's death: Ferenc Erdei, "A magyar társadalom a két háború között I" [Hungarian society between the wars I], *Valóság* 19, no. 4 (1976): 22–53, and Ferenc Erdei, "A magyar társadalom a két háború között II" [Hungarian society between the wars II], *Valóság* 19, no. 5 (1976): 36–58.

95. Vörös, "A Unique Contract: Interpretations of Modern Hungarian Jewish History," 230–35.

96. See more in Béla Bodó, *The White Terror. Antisemitic and Political Violence in Hungary, 1919–1921* (Routledge, 2019).

97. Konrád, "Prehistory of the Hungarian Numerus Clausus Law," 148.

98. "A. m. kir. vallás- és közoktatásügyi miniszter 1920. évi 123.033. számú rendelete a tudományegyetemekre, a műegyetemre, a budapesti egyetemi közgazdaságtudományi karra és a jogakadémiára való beiratkozás szabályozásáról" [Order No. 123.033 of 1920 by the minister of religion and public education about the regulation of enrollment to university, polytechnics, Faculty of Economics at the University of Budapest and law academies], in *Magyarországi Rendeletek Tára, Ötvennegyedik folyam* [Collection of the Decrees of Hungary, vol. 54] (Magy. Kir. Belügyminisztérium, 1920), 1455–60.

99. Andor Ladányi, *Az egyetemi ifjúság az ellenforradalom első éveiben, 1919–1921* [The university youth in the first years of the counterrevolution, 1919–1921] (Akadémiai Kiadó, 1979).

100. Victor Karády, "Jewish Over-Schooling Revisited: The Case of Hungarian Secondary Education in the Old Regime (1900–1941)," *Yearbook of the Jewish Studies Programme (CEU)*, 1999, 75–91.

101. This shift occurred across the European continent, not only in the Russian Empire and Hungary. Andrei-Dan Sorescu and Raul Cârstocea established this with regard to Romania. Andrei-Dan Sorescu and Raul Cârstocea, "The (Great) Numbers Game: Demographic Anxieties and Quotas in Nineteenth- and Twentieth-Century Romania and the Global Antisemitic Imaginary," in Miller and Szapor, *Quotas*, 92.

102. *Az 1906.évi május hó 19-ére hirdetett országgyűlés képviselőházi naplója* [The protocols of the Lower House of the Parliament announced for May 19, 1906], vol. 5 (Athenaeum, 1907), 196.

103. Előpataki [pen name], *Aforizmák a zsidókról: Társadalomtudományi eredmények alapján* [Aphorisms about the Jews: Based on social scientific investigations] (Buzárovits Gusztáv, 1911), 22–23.

104. Konrád, "Prehistory of the Hungarian Numerus Clausus Law," 147.

105. Horthy as a governor was the head of state between 1920 and 1944, in lack of a king, since Hungary was still a kingdom.

106. István I. Mocsy, *The Effects of World War I: The Uprooted; Hungarian Refugees and Their Impact on Hungary's Domestic Politics 1918–1921* (Social Science Monographs, 1983), 10–12.

107. Lajos Szabolcsi, *Két emberöltő: Az Egyenlőség évtizedei (1881–1931)* [Two generations: The decades of "Egyenlőség," 1881–1931] (MTA Judaisztikai Kutatócsoport, 1993), 327.

108. Péter Ujvári, ed., *Zsidó lexikon* [Jewish lexicon] (Edition of the Jewish Lexicon, 1929), 554. According to the census of 1920, in post-Trianon Hungary, 46 percent of Jews (215,512 out of 473,310) lived in the capital and the majority of these were affiliated with the Pest side's community.

109. "1928. évi XIV. törvénycikk a tudományegyetemekre, a műegyetemre, a budapesti egyetemi közgazdaságtudományi karra és a jogakadémiákra való

beiratkozás szabályozásáról szóló 1920. évi XXV. törvénycikk módosításáról" [Law 1928: XIV amending Law 1920: XXV on the regulation of enrollment to university, polytechnics, Faculty of Economics at the University of Budapest and law academies], *Net Jogtár* [Online Legal Collection], accessed November 5, 2024, https://net.jogtar.hu/ezer-ev-torveny?docid=92800014.TV&searchUrl=/ezer-ev-torvenyei?keyword%3D1928:XIV.

110. MTI Hírkiadás [News by the Hungarian Telegraphic Agency], November 18, 1927, 13, cited in Kovács, *Beginnings of Anti-Jewish Legislation*, 178.

111. Kovács, *Beginnings of Anti-Jewish Legislation*, 189.

112. Róbert Kerepeszki, "A numerus clausus 1928. évi módosításának hatása Debrecenben" [The impact of the 1928 amendment of the numerus clausus in Debrecen], *Múltunk* 50, no. 4. (2005): 49.

113. For the Easter Jew beatings, it is worth remembering that pogroms tended to occur around Easter in the Middle Ages and early modernity. Thus, there was a very long tradition of violently expressing anti-Jewish hostility during this Christian holiday because of the ancient accusation of Jews having murdered Jesus Christ.

114. Bernard Klein, "Hungarian Politics and the Jewish Question in the Inter-War Period," *Jewish Social Studies* 28, no. 2 (1966): 84–85.

115. Miloslav Szabó, "'Troublesome Foreigners': The Protests Against Jewish Students at Universities in Vienna, Bratislava and Brno, and the Dispute over Quotas in Czechoslovakia, 1929–32," in Miller and Szapor, *Quotas*, 368.

116. Szabó, "'Troublesome Foreigners,'" 372.

117. David de la Croix and Mara Vitale, "Women in European Academia Before 1800—Religion, Marriage, and Human Capital," *European Review of Economic History* 27, no. 3 (2023): 510.

118. Cristina Cammarano, "Women Writers and Education," in *A History of Western Philosophy of Education in the Middle Ages and Renaissance*, vol. 2, ed. Kevin Hary (Bloomsbury, 2021), 149.

119. Ágnes Jobst, "Az emancipáció eszméjének érvényesülése: Hugonnai Vilma élete" [The realization of the idea of emancipation: The life of Vilma Hugonnai], in *Asszonysorsok a 20. században* [Women's lives in the twentieth century], ed. Margit Balogh and Katalin Nagy S. (BME Kommunikáció és Szociológia Tanszék, 2000), 36.

120. Lioudmila Clot, "When Swiss Universities Led the Way in Gender Equity," *Swissinfo*, accessed November 5, 2024, https://www.swissinfo.ch/eng/when-swiss-universities-led-the-way-in-gender-equity/47493416. However, from Swiss women they required entrance exams for their lack of high school attendance, so they needed to take expensive private courses, putting them at a great disadvantage when compared to Swiss men as well as foreign women.

121. Judith Szapor, *The Hungarian Pocahontas: The Life and Times of Laura Polanyi Stricker, 1882–1959* (East European Monographs, 2005), 53.

122. Harriet Pass Freidenreich, *Female, Jewish, and Educated: The Lives of Central European University Women* (Indiana University Press, 2002), 14. The first German girls' gymnasium was established in 1893 in Karlsruhe.

123. Kurt Kempler, "Századvági küzdelem a nők egyetemi felvételéért Magyarországon" [Struggle for women's admission to university in Hungary on the turn of the century], *Orvosi Hetilap* 115, no. 30 (1974): 1776.

124. Katalin N. Szegvári, *Numerus clausus rendelkezések az ellenforradalmi Magyarországon: A zsidó és nőhallgatók főiskolai felvételéről* [Numerus clausus regulations in counterrevolutionary Hungary: On the admission of female and Jewish students to higher education] (Akadémiai Kiadó, 1988), 59.

125. See more about the international network of Hungarian feminists in Dóra Fedeles-Czeferner, *Nőmozgalom, nemzetköziség, önreprezentáció: Feministák az Osztrák-Magyar Monarchia alkonyán* [Women's movement, internationality, self-representation: Feminists at the dusk of the Austro-Hungarian Monarchy] (Kronosz, 2023).

126. Szegvári, *Numerus clausus rendelkezések az ellenforradalmi Magyarországon*, 57.

127. László Szögi, "A nők egyetemi tanulmányainak kérdése a Budapesti orvostudományi karon" [The question of women's university studies in the medical faculty of the University of Budapest], *Orvostörténeti Közlemények* 32, nos. 3–4 (1986): 139–42.

128. Judith Szapor, *Hungarian Women's Activism in the Wake of the First World War: From Rights to Revanche* (Bloomsbury, 2017), 147.

129. Barbara Papp and Balázs Sipos, *Modern, diplomás nő a Horthy-korban* [Modern, intellectual woman in the Horthy era] (Napvilág, 2017), 33–34.

130. Cécile Tormay, "Beköszöntő," in *MANSZ Almanach az 1920-as évre* [The National Alliance of Hungarian Women's almanac for the year 1920] (Szt. István Társulat, 1919), 17. Szamuely's name is in fact spelled with one *l*. Hyphenating Jews' Hungarian last names with their original Jewish-sounding names was a common practice in antisemitic journalism.

131. Andor Ladányi, "Két évforduló: A nők felsőfokú tanulmányainak száz éve" [Two anniversaries: A century of women's higher education], *Educatio* 5, no. 3 (1996): 379.

132. Viktor Karády, "A társadalmi egyenlőtlenségek Magyarországon a nők felsőbb iskoláztatásának korai fázisában" [Social inequalities in the early phases of women's higher learning in Hungary], in *Férfiuralom: Írások nőkről, férfiakról, feminizmusról* [Patriarchy: Writings about women, men, feminism], ed. Miklós Hadas (Replika Kör, 1994), 191.

133. Anna Borgos, "'Put a Stop to the Excessive Influx': The Rhetoric of Restriction Regarding Female and Jewish Students at Budapest University, 1900–1930," *Hungarian Studies Review* 48, no. 1 (2021): 48–78.

134. Michaela Raggam-Blesch, "Zwischen Antisemitismus und Antifeminismus: Jüdische Frauen an der Wiener Universität" [Between antisemitism and antifeminism: Jewish women at the University of Vienna], in *Alma Mater Antisemitica: Akademisches Milieu, Juden und Antisemitismus an den Universitäten Europas zwischen 1918 und 1939* [Alma Mater Antisemitica: Academic Milieu, Jews and antisemitism at Europe's universities between 1918 and 1939], ed. Regina Fritz et al. (New Academic Press, 2016), 259.

135. Harriet Pass Freidenreich, "Gender, Identity and Community: Jewish University Women in Germany and Austria," in *In Search of Jewish Community: Jewish Identities in Germany and Austria, 1918–1933*, ed. Michael Brenner and Derek J. Penslar (Indiana University Press, 1998), 155.

136. Viktor Karády, "Nők a modern iskolázás korai fázisában" [Women in the early phase of modern schooling], in *Felekezeti viszonyok és iskolázási egyenlőtlenségek Magyarországon, 1867–1945* [Denominational relations and educational inequalities in Hungary, 1867–1945] (Replika Kör, 1997), 59.

2. JEWS

1. Stefan Zweig, *The World of Yesterday: An Autobiography* (Viking Press, 1943), 10.

2. Mária M. Kovács, *The Beginnings of Anti-Jewish Legislation. The 1920 Numerus Clausus Law in Hungary* (Central European University Press, 2023), 148.

3. Victor Karády, "Jewish Over-Schooling Revisited: The Case of Hungarian Secondary Education in the Old Regime (1900–1941)," *Yearbook of the Jewish Studies Programme (CEU)* 1, no. 1 (1996–99): 75–91.

4. Andor Ladányi, "On the Amendment to the Hungarian Numerus Clausus Act," in *Studies on the First Anti-Jewish Law and Academic Anti-Semitism in Modern Central Europe*, ed. Victor Karády and Péter Tibor Nagy (Pasts Inc. Centre for Historical Research, History Department of the Central European University, 2012), 70.

5. Péter Tibor Nagy, "The Numerus Clausus Law in Inter-War Hungary: Pioneering European Antisemitism," *East European Jewish Affairs* 35, no. 1 (2005): 13–22.

6. Ernő Ballagi, "Harc a numerus clausus ellen" [Struggle against the numerus clausus], *Egyenlőség*, November 26, 1927, 15.

7. For instance, Miklós Szabolcsi was admitted to the faculty of humanities in Budapest in 1938 despite his merely "good" secondary school diploma because

his father asked the historian Gyula Szekfű to help, drawing on their former professional cooperation. Another example is László Farádi's admission in the medical faculty in Pécs in 1930 because he was on a list of "Jewish students to be admitted." Yet another example is Miklós Kun's being admitted in medicine in Szeged in 1932 because his uncle had good acquaintances among medical professors (Miklós Szabolcsi, "Apámról és emlékiratairól" [About my father and his memoirs], in Lajos Szabolcsi, *Két emberöltő: Az Egyenlőség évtizedei, 1881–1931* [Two generations: The decades of "Egyenlőség" Jewish weekly newspaper, 1881–1931] [MTA Judaisztikai Kutatócsoport, 1993], 15; László Farádi, *Diagnózis az életemről* [A diagnosis of my life] [Gondolat, 1983], 123; Miklós Kun, *Kedves Hilda: Egy elmeorvos az elmebeteg huszadik században* [Dear Hilda: A psychiatrist in the insane twentieth century] [Medicina, 2004], 32).

8. Out of those 1,965 Jewish students, 781 came from families that worked in commerce and banking, 347 from families involved in mines and industry, and 628 in intellectual professions (Bernard Klein, "Hungarian Politics and the Jewish Question in the Inter-War Period," *Jewish Social Studies* 28, no. 2 [1966]: 84).

9. Agnes Katalin Kelemen, "The Exiles of the Numerus Clausus in Italy," *Judaica Olomucensia* 2, nos. 1–2 (2014): 84–86.

10. The numerus clausus law was promulgated in 1920, so 1921–22 was the first academic year when the quota had a full impact on university itineraries. Then, every fifth year of the period was used to gain snapshots of the history of Hungarian students' presence in the cities concerned, which were the most popular target cities based on the contemporary statistics on Hungarian students abroad published for each academic year in the *Hungarian Statistical Yearbooks* (Magyar Statisztikai Évkönyvek) of the 1920s and 1930s.

11. For example, Fascicolo degli studenti, Facoltà di Medicina a Chirurgia 6625 Fischer Julie [Students' files no. 6625, Faculty of Medicine and Chirurgy, Fischer, Julie], Archivio Storico dell'Università di Bologna (Historical Archives of the University of Bologna, henceforth ASUB); Fascicolo degli studenti, Medicina e Chirurgia 11856 Borgida Veronika [Students' files no. 11856, Faculty of Medicine and Chirurgy, Borgida, Veronika], ASUB.

12. One cannot know if anyone else among the non-Jewish (by religion) individuals in this data set were converts. However, they are less than one-fifth of the examined group, and it seems realistic that there were that many non-Jews among Hungarian students abroad.

13. József Technical University was named after Palatine Joseph Habsburg in 1846 and became a university in 1871.

14. William Lanouette and Bela Silard, *Genius in the Shadows: A Biography of Leo Szilard—The Man Behind the Bomb* (University of Chicago Press, 1992), 48–49.

15. Alajos Kovács, "Magyarországi zsidó hallgatók a hazai és külföldi főiskolákon" [Hungarian Jewish students at Hungarian and foreign universities],

Magyar Statisztikai Szemle 16, no. 9 (1938): 898. Those who went to study abroad with a stipend from the Hungarian state were unlikely to be Jewish due to antisemitic policies, so Kovács did not count them in this estimation.

16. See an overview of the research project and its findings here: Victor Karady and Peter Tibor Nagy, "Culturally Composite Elites, Regime Changes and Social Crises in Multi-Ethnic and Multi-Confessional Eastern Europe (The Carpathian Basin and the Baltics in Comparison, cc. 1900–1950)," European Research Council, accessed November 6, 2024, http://elites08.uni.hu. I am thankful for Professors Karády and Nagy for sharing even the nonpublic data sets with me.

17. Karady and Nagy, "Culturally Composite Elites, Regime Changes and Social Crises in Multi-Ethnic and Multi-Confessional Eastern Europe."

18. Judith Szapor, "'You Can Become Anything, Except a Pediatrician': Exploring the General Impact of Hungary's Numerus Clausus Law," in *Quotas: The "Jewish Question" and Higher Education in Central Europe, 1880–1945*, ed. Michael L. Miller and Judith Szapor (Berghahn, 2024), 450.

19. I compared the data sets of the following research with mine: "Processed prosopographical databases (sets of statistical tables for multivariate data analyses) related to students and educated elites in Hungarian institutions of higher education (cc. 1867–1949)/ II. Medical doctors, pharmacists, veterinaries/ i. Graduates of Medicine at the Medical Faculty of the University of Budapest (1770–1950)" and "Processed prosopographical databases (sets of statistical tables for multivariate data analyses) related to students and educated elites in Hungarian institutions of higher education (cc. 1867–1949)/ VIII. Students of technological training," in Karady and Nagy, "Culturally Composite Elites."

20. Kovács, *The Beginnings of Anti-Jewish Legislation*, 126–30.

21. Farádi, *Diagnózis*, 119–22.

22. Jacques Presser, *Memoires als geschiedbron* [Memoirs as historical sources], vol. 8 (Winkler Prins Encyclopedie, 1958), 208–10, cited in Kaspar von Greyerz, "Ego-Documents: The Last Word?," *German History* 28, no. 3 (2010): 277.

23. Andreas Huber, "Antisemitic Pacts: Student Fraternities and the Exclusion of Jews at Austrian Universities in the Interwar Period," in Miller and Szapor, *Quotas*, 295.

24. Éva Kovács, *Felemás asszimiláció: A kassai zsidóság a két világháború között (1918–1938)* [Ambivalent assimilation: The Jewry of Košice between the two world wars, 1918–1938] (Fórum Kisebbségkutató Intézet, 2004); Attila Gidó, *Két évtized: A kolozsvári zsidóság a két világháború között* [Two decades: The Jewry of Cluj between the two world wars] (Erdélyi Múzeum-Egyesület, 2016).

25. Arthur Koestler, *Arrow in the Blue: The First Volume of an Autobiography 1905–1931* (Vintage, 2005), 107–9.

26. "Mitgliederliste des akademischen Vereines jüdischer Mediziner aufgenommen am 5. November 1927" [List of members of the Jewish Medics' Association on November 5, 1927], S164.120, Archives of the University of Vienna (Archiv der Universität Wien, henceforth AUW); "Statuten des Vereines ungarisch sprechender Wiener Hochschüler 6.XII.1929" [Statutes of the Hungarian Speaking Viennese Students, December 6, 1929], S164.201, AUW.

27. Looking at the whole membership, not only at medical students (who were the majority with 92 students out of 148), we find that 17 out of 20 students who were in the leading committee of the association, were Jewish.

28. Ágnes Katalin Kelemen, "Peregrination in the Age of the Numerus Clausus: Hungarian Jewish Students in Interwar Europe" (PhD diss., Central European University, 2019), 36–54.

29. Lili Fenyő, *Pillanatfelvételek a külföldön élő magyar diákság életéből* [Snapshots from the life of Hungarian students abroad] (Jupiter Nyomda, 1929), 5.

30. Miklós Kun, *Kedves Hilda: Egy elmeorvos az elmebeteg huszadik században* [Dear Hilda: A psychiatrist in the insane twentieth century] (Medicina, 2004), 27.

31. Kun, *Kedves Hilda*, 26.

32. Victor Karády, "Funktionswandel der österreichischen Hochschulen in der Ausbildung der ungarischen Fachintelligenz vor und nach dem Ersten Weltkrieg" [The changing function of Austrian colleges and universities in the training of Hungarian professional intelligentsia before and after the First World War], in *Bildungswesen und Sozialstruktur in Mitteleuropa im 19. und 20. Jahrhundert. Education and Social Structure in Central Europe in the 19th and 20th Centuries*, ed. Victor Karády and Wolfgang Mitter (Böhlau, 1990), 179.

33. György Kroó, *Szabolcsi Bence*, vol. 1 (Liszt Ferenc Zeneművészeti Főiskola, 1994), 124.

34. Letter by Bence Szabolcsi to Zoltán Kodály, November 4, 1921, in *Szabolcsi Bence lipcsei levelei Kodályhoz* [Bence Szabolcsi's letters to Kodály from Leipzig], ed. Ferenc Bónis (Kodály Intézet, 1994), 255.

35. Farádi, *Diagnózis*, 86.

36. Farádi, *Diagnózis*, 50.

37. Farádi, *Diagnózis*, 119–23.

38. The college for textile engineering is now part of the Technical University of Liberec as its Faculty for Textile Engineering.

39. Letter by György Kis to his family, February 21, 1926, in *Apám levelei: Legendák, emlékek; 1942, Oroszország–1926, Csehszlovákia* [My father's letters: Legends, memories; 1942, Russia–1926, Czechoslovakia], ed. Ádám Kis and Balázs Kis (SZAK Kiadó, 2015), 100.

40. Letter by György Kis to his parents, February 21, 1926, in Kis and Kis, *Apám levelei*, 95–96.

41. Letter by György Kis to his family, February 21, 1926, in Kis and Kis, *Apám levelei*, 97.

42. Letter by György Kis to his family, February 21, 1926, in Kis and Kis, *Apám levelei*, 99.

43. He referred to Karlovy Vary with its German name, Karlsbad (letter by György Kis to his family, May 9, 1926, in Kis and Kis, *Apám levelei*, 111).

44. At this time Radnóti in some documents referred to himself as Radnóti-Glatter, but in the college, he still enrolled as Nikolaus Glatter (Szonja T. Egriné, "Radnóti Miklós egy éve Liberecben" [One year of Miklós Radnóti in Liberec], *Forrás* 43, no. 9 [2011]: 41–52).

45. Kis and Kis, *Apám levelei*.

46. Tamás Bíró-Balogh, ed., *Különben magyar költő vagyok: Radnóti Miklós levelezése* [Otherwise I am a Hungarian poet: The correspondence of Miklós Radnóti], vol. 1 (Jaffa, 2017).

47. Kroó, *Szabolcsi Bence*, vol. 1, 168.

48. Kroó, *Szabolcsi Bence*, 205.

49. Letter by Bence Szabolcsi to his sister-in-law, Erzsébet Mészáros, November 15, 1922. in Kroó, *Szabolcsi Bence*, 176.

50. György Kroó's already cited monograph on Bence Szabolcsi quotes numerous letters Bence Szabolcsi sent to his sister-in-law, Erzsébet Mészáros. In addition, Ferenc Bónis published Szabolcsi's letters to Zoltán Kodály from the Leipzig period: Ferenc Bónis, ed., *Szabolcsi Bence lipcsei levelei Kodályhoz* [Bence Szabolcsi's letters to Kodály from Leipzig] (Kodály Intézet, 1994).

51. Letter by Bence Szabolcsi to Lajos Szabolcsi, December 22, 1922, in Kroó, *Szabolcsi Bence*, 206.

52. Kroó, *Szabolcsi Bence*, 155.

53. For details on the antisemitic development of Fascism, see Michele Sarfatti, *The Jews in Mussolini's Italy: From Equality to Persecution* (University of Wisconsin Press, 2006). For details on the life trajectories of Hungarian Jewish students of Italian universities after 1938, see Ágnes Katalin Kelemen, "The Exiles of the Numerus Clausus in Italy," *Judaica Olomucensia* 2, nos. 1–2 (2014): 56–103.

54. For instance, in 1923 only 49 percent of Hungarian Jewish secondary school graduates went to university, even counting those studying abroad, in contrast to 85 percent in 1910 (Viktor Karády, *Iskolarendszer és felekezeti egyenlőtlenségek Magyarországon, 1867–1945* [Educational system and denominational inequalities in Hungary, 1867–1945] [Replika Kör, 1997], 251).

3. LEFTISTS

1. Piroska Döme, *Fény és árnyék* [Light and shadow] (Kossuth, 1983), 91.

2. "1920. évi XXV. törvénycikk a tudományegyetemekre, a műegyetemre, a budapesti egyetemi közgazdaságtudományi karra és a jogakadémiákra való beiratkozás szabályozásáról" [Law 1920: XXV on the regulation of enrollment to university, polytechnics, Faculty of Economics at the University of Budapest and

Law Academies], *Net Jogtár* [Online Legal Collection], accessed November 11, 2024, https://net.jogtar.hu/ezer-ev-torveny?docid=92000025.TV.

3. Béla Bodó, *The White Terror: Antisemitic and Political Violence in Hungary, 1919–1921* (Routledge, 2019), 251.

4. Bodó, *White Terror*, 256.

5. György Litván, "Irányzatok és viták a bécsi magyar emigrációban" [Streams and debates in the Viennese Hungarian emigration], in *Magyar gondolat—szabad gondolat* [Hungarian thought—Free thought], György Litván (Osiris, 2008), 227.

6. Romania gained 103,000 square meters of land from Hungary; Czechoslovakia, 62,000; the Serbo-Croatian-Slovenian Kingdom, 21,000; and Austria, 4,000. More excessive demands by the neighboring states, however, included a "Slavic corridor" between Bratislava and Zagreb and some territories south of former "Upper Hungary" (Felvidék). See details in Ignác Romsics, *Hungary in the Twentieth Century* (Osiris, 1999); Balázs Ablonczy, *Trianon-legendák* [Legends of Trianon] (Jaffa, 2015).

7. For instance, Lee Congdon interprets the self-description of the Hungarian political elite as "national" and "Christian" to distinguish themselves in opposition to "Jewish" and "alien" (*Exile and Social Thought* [Princeton University Press, 1991], 304).

8. Paul Hanebrink, *In Defense of Christian Hungary* (Cornell University Press, 2006), 2–4.

9. Hanebrink, *In Defense of Christian Hungary*, 83.

10. Congdon, *Exile and Social Thought.*

11. Hanebrink, *In Defense of Christian Hungary*, 76.

12. Ágnes Katalin Kelemen, "Refugees and the 'Other Hungary': The Historiography of the Reception of Refugees in Twentieth-Century Hungary," *Zeitschrift für Ostmitteleuropa-Forschung/Journal of East Central European Studies* 71, no. 4 (2022): 492.

13. Litván, "Irányzatok és viták a bécsi magyar emigrációban," 253–54.

14. Judith Szapor, "'You Can Become Anything, Except a Pediatrician': Exploring the Gendered Impact of Hungary's Numerus Clausus Law," in *Quotas: The "Jewish Question" and Higher Education in Central Europe, 1880–1945*, ed. Michael L. Miller and Judith Szapor (Berghahn, 2024), 450.

15. "1921. évi III. törvénycikk az állami és társadalmi rend hatályosabb védelméről" [Law 1921: III on the more effective protection of the order of state and society], *Net Jogtár* [Online Legal Collection], accessed November 11, 2024, https://net.jogtar.hu/ezer-ev-torveny?docid=92100003.TV&searchUrl=/ezer-ev-torvenyei%3Fpagenum%3D38.

16. Zsolt K. Horváth, "Szubkultúrák forrásvidékén: Népi kultúra, munkáskultúra és baloldali közösségiség Vajda Lajos életműve körül" [The

sources of subcultures: Popular culture, workers' culture and leftist communality around the oeuvre of Lajos Vajda], *Fordulat* 7, no. 3 (Winter 2009): 47–64.

17. Piroska Döme, "Diákévek és hazatérés" [Student years and return], *Valóság* 25, no. 6 (1982): 86.

18. Döme, "Diákévek és hazatérés," 87.

19. See more details about the intricacies of true and false residence claims in Czechoslovakia by Hungarian students of Czechoslovak universities in Ágnes Katalin Kelemen, "Migration and Exile: Hungarian Medical Students in Vienna and Prague, 1920–1938," in *At the Crossroads of Human Fate and History—Studies in Honour of Tibor Frank on His Seventieth Birthday*, ed. János Kenyeres et al. (Eötvös Loránd University, School of English and American Studies, 2018), 222–41.

20. Arthur Linksz, *Harc a harmadik halállal. Ifjúságom Magyarországon* [Fighting the third death: My youth in Hungary] (Magvető, 1990), 328.

21. *Magyar Életrajzi Lexikon* [Hungarian Biographical Lexicon], vol. 2, L–Z (Akadémiai, 1982), 662.

22. "A kommunistasággal vádolt tanárok és egyetemi hallgatók pöre" [The trial of university students and instructors accused with Communism], *Népszava*, October 4, 1932, 7.

23. Károly Perczel, interview by Ilona Dér Szabóné, 1986, interview no. 44, Veritas Oral History Archívum (Oral History Archive of the Veritas Research Institute for History, henceforth Veritas-OHA).

24. István Tömpe, *Az elitek árulása* [The betrayal by the elites] (Noran Libro, 2015), 81.

25. Horváth, "Szubkultúrák forrásvidékén," 47–64.

26. Tom Weidlinger, *The Restless Hungarian: Modernism, Madness, and The American Dream* (SparkPress, 2019), 51.

27. Katalin Zalai, *"Idegenbe szakadt hazánk lányai": Magyar nők szovjet emigrációban a két világháború között* ["Our homeland's daughters far away": Hungarian women in Soviet emigration between the two world wars] (Napvilág, 2022), 239.

28. András Kristóf Kósa-Grimm, "Schmidt, a rendőrspicli? Stolte István és az 1932-es kommunista szervezkedés a Pázmány Péter Tudományegyetemen" [Schmidt, the spy of the police? István Stolte and the 1932 Communist organization at the Pázmány Péter University], *Múltunk* 64, no. 1 (2019): 141–42.

29. Ágnes Katalin Kelemen, "Next year in Brno? Brno's Significance for Hungarian Jews in the Age of the Numerus Clausus and Beyond," in Miller and Szapor, *Quotas*, 359–84.

30. At the same time, the increase in the number of Hungarian nationals also grew due to the fact that Slovakia became part of Czechoslovakia and a

significant Hungarian population came with it. Thanks to the separate statistics on students' nationality and citizenship in the German Technical College's administration, however, it is easy to separate the number of Hungarians from Slovakia and of Hungarians from Hungary.

31. "Ausweis über die an der technischen Hochschule in Brünn inskribierten Hörer ungarischer Staatsangehörigkeit," B34 Německá technika Brno/ Fascikl 424 Sign. 8./Statistika zapsaných 1917–1929, Moravský zemský archiv v Brně (Brno Moravian Provincial Archives, henceforth MZA). This table was attached to the rector's letter to the Hungarian Central Statistical Office sent on June 11, 1926.

32. One circle included five to six members; they were taught ideology by a more senior member of the movement: *Visszaemlékezés a magyar diákok kommunista mozgalmára Brünnben 1928–1938* [Recollection about the Communist movement of Hungarian students in Brno, 1928–1938], March 28, 1972, 867.f.1/b-325, Politikatörténeti és Szakszervezeti Levéltár (Archives of Political History and the Trade Unions, henceforth PSZL).

33. It could be translated as the Society of Thirteen, but I follow Tom Weidlinger's translation (*The Restless Hungarian: Modernism, Madness, and the American Dream* [Spark Press, 2019], ebook).

34. Perczel, interview.

35. *Visszaemlékezés.*

36. Judit Csatlós, ed., *Vízizrí: Munkáskultúra a Duna partján* [Water fun: Workers' culture on the bank of the Danube], Exhibition catalog (Kassák Museum, 2016), 34.

37. The Deutsche Studentenschaft in fact represented only "Aryan" Germans and a "völkisch" worldview; therefore, Jewish and left-wing German students joined the ASH or Jewish student clubs.

38. One such leaflet is preserved in B34 Německá technika Brno/Fascik. 526 Sign. 79a Discipl. zál. studentů 1932–1945, MZA.

39. Verhandlungsschrift Nro. XII vom 16. Juni 1933 Punkt IV.d., B34 Německá technika Brno/Fascikl. 526 Sign. 79a Discipl. zál. studentů 1932–1945, MZA.

40. B34 Německá technika Brno/Fascikl. 526 Sign. 79a Discipl. zál. studentů 1932–1945, MZA; Döme, "Diákévek és hazatérés," 88–89. Károly Perczel, although not yet in Brno in January 1933, also talked about these actions with enthusiasm, as an example of successful popular front politics (Perczel, interview).

41. Verhandlungsschrift No. XII vom 16. Juni 1933 Punkt IV.d., MZA.

42. Decree Nr.Z.93.145. by the Czechoslovak Ministry of Education and Culture published on September 21, 1933, referred to in the minutes of the faculty council at the German Technical College of Brno. Sitzung No. I. 5. Oktober 1933, B34 Německá technika Brno/Kniha 201 Protokoly sezení profesorského sbor 1933–34, MZA.

43. Sitzung No. I. 5. Oktober 1933, B34 Německá technika Brno/Kniha 201 Protokoly sezení profesorského sbor 1933–34, MZA.

44. Protokoly sezení profesorského sbor 1933–34, MZA; Discipl. zál. studentů 1932–1945, B34 Německá technika Brno/Fascik. 526 Sign. 79a, MZA.

45. Döme, "Diákévek és hazatérés," 90.

46. Veronica Czitrom, Steven Czitrom, and Paul Czitrom, *Carolyn and Laszlo: What a Life!; The Baus, Feuerstein, Czitrom and Lusztig Families* [*Carolyn y Laszlo: Qué vida!; Las familias Baus, Feuerstein, Czitrom y Lusztig*] (Veronica, Steven, and Paul Czitrom Baus, 2001), 175–79.

47. László Kádár, *Visszaemlékezéseim a kommunista mozgalomban való, felszabadulás előtti tevékenységemről* [My memories about my activity in the pre-liberation Communist movement], September 1, 1961, 867.2/k-235 B, PSZL.

48. Perczel, interview.

49. "Brief von Rudolf Nowak in Angelegenheit des Sohnes Ing. Rudolf Nowak wegen Ausfertigung einer Bestätigung an das Rektorat der deutschen technischen Hochschule in Brünn," January 18, 1939, B34 Německá technika Brno /Fascikl. 526 Sign. 79a Discipl. zál. studentů 1932–1945, MZA.

50. Weidlinger, *Restless Hungarian.*

51. Weidlinger, *Restless Hungarian,* 110.

52. "The Adventurous Journey of the Oropesa," family document, courtesy of Éva Karádi.

53. Conversation with their daughter, Éva Karádi, February 8, 2020.

54. Interview with Tamás Zoltán by Ágnes Katalin Kelemen, March 17, 2021.

55. "Kik voltak az ellenség ügynökei a délamerikai szabad magyar mozgalomban, vagy kikről feltehető, hogy azok voltak?" [Who were the enemy's agents in the South American Hungarian movement or who can be assumed to be?], Folder No. 2.1, I/54-b (V-142731/2), folder's topic: Ádám György, Állambiztonsági Szolgálatok Történeti Levéltára (Historical Archives of the State Security Services, henceforth ÁBTL).

56. Interview with Katalin Talyigás and András Talyigás by Ágnes Katalin Kelemen, March 15, 2021.

57. Jolán Vadas, letter to Imre Erdős, October 4, 1946, private collection of Éva Karádi.

58. Tibor Hajdu, "A Rajk-per háttere és fázisai" [The background and phases of the Rajk-trial], *Társadalmi Szemle* 47, no. 11 (1992): 19.

59. One of the imprisoned members of the Swiss group, György H. Hódos, eventually told his story and provided an analysis of the show trials in general (*Show Trials: Stalinist Purges in Eastern Europe 1948–1954* [Praeger, 1987]).

60. Vladimir Farkas, interview by Péter Borenich, 1985–1988, interview no. 200, Veritas-OHA. Farkas only mentioned the Textilschule of Brno in this context, but in fact, many more Hungarians studied at the DTH.

61. Á.V.H. Vizsgálati dosszié Jacobson 101890/6/A. VII/13-g/Feljegyzések a cionistákkal kapcsolatban / Feljegyzés a "brünniek csoportjáról" [State Protection Authority investigative file "Jacobson" 101890/6/A. VII/13-g/(Notes on the Zionists / Notes on the "Brno Group")], 3 December 1952, 53, ÁBTL.

62. One member of the list is in fact mistakenly included as a graduate of Brno's DTH.

63. László Kozma was rehabilitated, thus the unfair judgment was annulled in November 1989 (six years after his death).

64. "Boncolási jegyzőkönyv" [Autopsy report], November 23, 1950, folder "Miklós Szűcs" No. 2.1, I/98 (V-142821), ÁBTL.

65. "Határozat az exhumálás elrendeléséről" [Decision on ordering exhumation], April 6, 1964, Folder "Miklós Szűcs" No. 2.1, I/98 (V-142821), ÁBTL.

66. According to László Kádár, one of the insiders, he and several comrades (Gyula Karádi, István Bartos, Sebestyén Endre Bakonyi, Ferenc Talyigás, and Pál Takács) submitted a collective memoir about their years in Brno to the Institute of Party History as early as 1954. See L. Kádár, *Visszaemlékezéseim*. Regrettably, however, this is not to be found in PSZL that preserves the documents of this institution.

67. *Visszaemlékezés*, 13.

68. MSZMPwas the name of the reorganized Communist Party after the 1956 revolution.

69. Árpád Pünkösti, "Merni meghalni? Merni élni?" [Daring to die? Daring to live?], *Új Tükör* 25, no. 47 (1988): 8.

4. WOMEN

1. Katalin Fenyves, "When Sexism Meets Racism: The 1920 Numerus Clausus Law in Hungary," *Hungarian Cultural Studies* 4, no. 4 (2011): 87.

2. Katalin N. Szegvári, *Numerus clausus rendelkezések az ellenforradalmi Magyarországon: A zsidó és nőhallgatók főiskolai felvételéről* [Numerus clausus regulations in counter-revolutionary Hungary: On the admission of female and Jewish students to higher education] (Akadémiai Kiadó, 1988).

3. Judith Szapor, "'You Can Become Anything, Except a Pediatrician': Exploring the Gendered Impact of Hungary's Numerus Clausus Law," in *Quotas: The "Jewish Question" and Higher Education in Central Europe, 1880–1945*, ed. Michael L. Miller and Judith Szapor (Berghahn, 2024), 432. Judith Szapor collected the biographies with the help of Éva Karádi (referred to in chapter 3 as a donor of documents and informer of my research) in a project where I also participated, Academic Antisemitism, Women's Emancipation, and Jewish Assimilation, funded by the Canadian Social Sciences and Humanities Research Council Insight Grant.

4. Szegvári, *Numerus clausus rendelkezések az ellenforradalmi Magyarországon*, 96–97.

5. Andor Ladányi, "Két évforduló: A nők felsőfokú tanulmányainak száz éve" [Two anniversaries: A century of women's higher education], *Educatio* 5, no. 3 (1996): 379.

6. Judith Szapor, *Hungarian Women's Activism in the Wake of the First World War: From Rights to Revanche* (Bloomsbury, 2017), 6.

7. Szegvári, *Numerus clausus rendelkezések az ellenforradalmi Magyarországon*, 85.

8. IFUW took a new name in 2015: Graduate Women International.

9. Gyula Kornis, "Nők az egyetemen" [Women at university], *Napkelet* 3, no. 1 (1925): 60–69.

10. Marianne Czeke and Emma Ritoók, "Nők az egyetemen" [Women at university], *Napkelet* 3, no. 5 (1925): 496–504.

11. Szapor, *Hungarian Women's Activism in the Wake of the First World War*, 115–31.

12. Christine von Oertzen, "Whose World? Internationalism, Nationalism and the Struggle over the 'Language Question' in the International Federation of University Women, 1919–1932," *Contemporary European History* 25, no. 1 (2016): 290.

13. It is still noteworthy that during the Shoah, she rescued Jews (Szapor, *Hungarian Women's Activism in the Wake of the First World War*, 144).

14. Barbara Papp and Balázs Sipos, *Modern, diplomás nő a Horthy-korban* [Modern, intellectual woman in the Horthy era] (Napvilág, 2017), 33.

15. Fenyves, "When Sexism Meets Racism," 98.

16. Barbara Papp, "Nőoktatás és 'képzett nők' a két világháború között" [Women's education and "educated women" between the two world wars], in *Zsombékok: Középosztályok és iskoláztatás Magyarországon a 19. század elejétől a 20. század közepéig* [Hills: Middle classes and education in Hungary from the early nineteenth to the mid-twentieth century], ed. György Kövér (Századvég, 2006), 717.

17. Éva Katalin Vámos, "Women's Opportunities of Studying and Practising Engineering in Hungary from 1895 to 1968," *Technikatörténeti Szemle* 23, no. 1 (1997–98): 107.

18. Papp, "Nőoktatás és 'képzett nők' a két világháború között," 739.

19. According to technology historian Éva Katalin Vámos, this institution was the first technical college in the world to be named a university. It has been referred to as a university since the 1860s and officially named as such in 1871. In 1934, its name was again changed to Royal Hungarian University of Engineering and Economics Palatine József (Vámos, "Women's Opportunities of Studying and Practising Engineering in Hungary from 1895 to 1968," 102).

20. Mária Palasik, "A magy nők a műszaki felsőoktatásban, a mérnöki pályán és a műszaki tudományokban a XX. században" [Hungarian women in technical higher education, in the engineering profession and in technical sciences during the twentieth century], *Múltunk* 48, no. 3 (2003): 134.

21. Vámos, "Women's Opportunities of Studying and Practising Engineering in Hungary from 1895 to 1968," 106.

22. Vámos, "Women's Opportunities of Studying and Practising Engineering in Hungary from 1895 to 1968," 107.

23. Róbert Kerepeszki, "Nationalist Masculinity and Right-Wing Radical Student Movements in Interwar Hungary," *Hungarian Studies Review* 41, nos. 1–2 (2014): 66.

24. In seven cases, the gender of the student could not be decided because the name was illegible on their enrollment forms.

25. Followed by pharmacy and medical schools (Papp and Sipos, *Modern, diplomás nő a Horthy-korban*, 118). Unfortunately, we do not know the number of Hungarian women in foreign universities, because the *Hungarian Statistical Yearbooks* contained only the total number of Hungarian students, female and male, abroad.

26. Viktor Karády, "Nők a modern iskolázás korai fázisában" [Women in the early phase of modern schooling], in *Felekezeti viszonyok és iskolázási egyenlőtlenségek Magyarországon, 1867–1945* [Denominational relations and educational inequalities in Hungary, 1867–1945] (Replika Kör, 1997), 59.

27. Karády, "Nők a modern iskolázás korai fázisában," 61.

28. Pascale Falek, "A Precarious Life: East European Female Jewish Students in Interwar Belgium" (PhD diss., European University Institute, 2011), 92.

29. Esther Bánki, "'Denn Du denkst doch nicht etwa, dass eine Frau ein Haus bauen kann': Das Leben der Architektin Zsuzsanna Bánki 1912–1944," in *Entfernt: Frauen des Bauhauses während der NS-Zeit—Verfolgung und Exil* [Removed: The women of the Bauhaus during National Socialism—Persecution and exile], ed. Inge Hansen-Schaberg, Wolfgang Thöner, and Adriane Feustel (Edition Text + Kritik, 2012), 159–74. Esther Bánki, "Ein mutiger Weg in schwierigen Zeiten—Das Leben der Bauhäuslerin Zsuzsanna Bánki [A courageous road in difficult times—The life of Bauhaus architect Zsuzsanna Bánki]," in *100 éves a Bauhaus* [The Bauhaus is 100 years old], ed. András Veöreös and Tamás Horváth (Győr-Moson-Sopron Megyei Építész Kamara, 2019).

30. Lili Fenyő, *Pillanatfelvételek a külföldön élő magyar diákság életéből* [Snapshots from the life of Hungarian students abroad] (Jupiter Nyomda, 1929).

31. Sidonie Smith and Julia Watson, *Reading Autobiography: A Guide for Interpreting Life Narratives* (University of Minnesota Press, 2010), 1.

32. Fenyő, *Pillanatfelvételek*, 28.

33. Fenyő, *Pillanatfelvételek*, 67–69.

34. Fenyő, *Pillanatfelvételek*, 62.

35. Fenyő, *Pillanatfelvételek*, 70–71.

36. Also very importantly, the phrase *community of fate* preceded the use of the German equivalent, *Schicksalsgemeinschaft*, by Hitler to refer to Aryan Germans in one of his first speeches to the Reichstag.

37. Fenyő, *Pillanatfelvételek*, 72. *Temple* in this context refers to a synagogue.

38. Letters from Ida Somló and Erzsébet Kardos to Ödön Bánki are parts of the private collection of Esther Bánki (Ödön's daughter), to whom I am grateful for sharing.

39. Dora Klein, *Vivere e sopravvivere: Diario 1936–1945* [To live and to survive: Diary 1936–1945] (Mursia, 2001).

40. Piroska Döme, *Fény és árnyék* [Light and shadow] (Kossuth, 1983); *Juranics Antalné Döme Piroska visszamelékezései* [Recollections by Piroska Döme/Mrs. Antal Juranics] I, March 1967, 867-d-2, PSZL. In addition, she wrote a family history for her own grandchildren and great grandchildren at the age of eighty in 1992. Her son, György Seres, kindly shared a completed version of it with me that was finished in 2002 when Piroska turned ninety: Piroska Döme, *Családtörténet* [Family history], private document, 2002, private collection of György Seres.

41. Piroska Döme, "Diákévek és hazatérés" [Student years and return], *Valóság* 25, no. 6 (1982): 86–101.

42. Letter from Ida Somló to Ödön Bánki without date and place, private collection of Esther Bánki. The date and place of other letters show that the bulk of the Somló–Bánki correspondence was written between 1921 and 1925 in Würzburg, Leipzig, Sülzhayn, and Bečkerek.

43. Letter from Ida Somló without date and place, private collection of Esther Bánki. Dönci is a nickname for Ödön.

44. Interview with Esther Bánki and Ivan Ivanji by Ágnes Katalin Kelemen on April 30, 2019.

45. The Banat region was divided in 1920 between Hungary, Romania, and the Kingdom of Serbs, Croats, and Slovenes. Its Jewish population was largely Hungarian speaking.

46. Interview with Bánki and Ivanji.

47. Letter by Erzsébet Kardos to Ödön Bánki, around 1925, private collection of Esther Bánki.

48. Letter by Erzsébet Kardos to Ödön Bánki, first half of the 1920s, private collection of Esther Bánki.

49. After her studies in Würzburg between 1921 and 1923, Erzsébet Kardos managed to get in the Jewish quota in Hungary at the University of Pécs and eventually graduated in 1927. Thereafter she worked as a medical doctor and pediatrician in Germany, Columbia, and Hungary. Anna Borgos, "A magyar

pszichoanalízis ígérete: Kardos Erzsébet [A promise of Hungarian psychoanalysis: Erzsébet Kardos]," *Imágó* 10, no. 3 (2021): 3347.

50. Fenyő, *Pillanatfelvételek*, 75.
51. Klein, *Vivere e sopravvivere*, 34–44.
52. Klein, *Vivere e sopravvivere*, 65.
53. Klein, *Vivere e sopravvivere*, 22.
54. Klein, *Vivere e sopravvivere*, 30.
55. Klein, *Vivere e sopravvivere*, 30.
56. Jolán Weinberger, "Levél Genovából: Otthont a bolygó zsidóknak!" [Letter from Genova: Shelter for the wandering Jews!], *Egyenlőség*, April 7, 1938, 17.
57. Döme, *Fény és árnyék*, 5.
58. *Juranics Antalné Döme Piroska visszamelékezései.*
59. *Juranics Antalné Döme Piroska visszamelékezései.*
60. Döme, *Fény és árnyék*, 47.
61. Döme, *Fény és árnyék*, 54. Erzsébet Perczel was the wife of Károly Perczel, who appeared in chapter 3.
62. See details on the "Brno children" in Ágnes Katalin Kelemen, "Next Year in Brno? Brno's Significance for Hungarian Jews in the Age of the Numerus Clausus and Beyond," in Miller and Szapor, *Quotas*, 359–84.
63. Döme, *Családtörténet*, 170.
64. Döme, "Diákévek és hazatérés," 90.
65. Döme, *Fény és árnyék*, 80.
66. Döme, *Fény és árnyék*, 47.
67. Döme, *Családtörténet*, 173–74.
68. See the fifth chapter, titled "Az Arvale lányok" [The Arvale girls], in *"Idegenbe szakadt hazánk lányai": Magyar nők szovjet emigrációban a két világháború között* ["Our daughters in exile": Hungarian women in Soviet emigration between the two world wars], by Katalin Zalai (Napvilág, 2022), 225–99.
69. Zalai, *"Idegenbe szakadt hazánk lányai,"* 239.

EPILOGUE

1. Tibor Frank, *Double Exile: Migrations of Jewish-Hungarian Professionals Through Germany to the United States, 1919–1945* (Peter Lang, 2009).
2. *Yearbook of the Hebrew University of Jerusalem* (Hebrew University of Jerusalem, 1957), 166.
3. "Nincs többé bujdosó diák . . . [No more wandering students...]," *Egyenlőség*, August 25, 1938, 3–4.
4. This paragraph was already published in English translation by Michael L. Miller, so I quote it from his translation: "From White Terror to Red Vienna: Hungarian Jewish Students in Interwar Austria," in *Wien und die Jüdische*

Erfahrung 1900–1938: Akkulturation—Antisemitismus—Zionismus [Vienna and the Jewish Experience 1900–1938. Acculturation—Antisemitism—Zionism], ed. Barbara Eichinger and Frank Stern (Böhlau, 2009), 323.

5. I refer to it as a so-called first anti-Jewish law, because the numerus clausus was an anti-Jewish law too and preceded this one by eighteen years.

6. "1938. évi XV. törvénycikk a társadalmi és a gazdasági élet egyensúlyának hatályosabb biztosításáról" [Law 1938: XV on the more effective securing of the balance of social and economic life], *Net Jogtár* [Online Legal Collection], accessed November 14, 2024, https://net.jogtar.hu/ezer-ev-torveny?docid=93800015.TV.

7. Anna Maria Hábermann, *Labirinto di carta* [The labyrinth of papers] (Proedi Editore, 2010); Simone Teich Alasia, *Un medico della Resistenza: I luoghi, gli incontri, le scelte* [A physician of the resistance: The places, the encounters, the choices] (SEB27, 2010); Ágnes Katalin Kelemen, "The Exiles of the Numerus Clausus in Italy," *Judaica Olomucensia* 2, nos. 1–2 (2014): 56–103.

8. Personal correspondence between his daughter Emma Cole and me on July 20, 2023.

9. Personal correspondence between Emma Cole and me on July 20, 2023.

10. Domenico Stranieri, "La storia del Dott. Fenyves [The story of Dr. Fenyves]," personal blog, August 11, 2014, http://domenicostranieri.blogspot.com/2013/09/la-storia-del-dott-fenyves.html?m=1.

11. Forced labor service also concerned Jewish women, particularly in the age cohort between eighteen and thirty years old, but on a smaller scale than men, and because women were not taken to the Eastern front, the victims of forced labor service were usually men. The forced labor service of women was used for reconstructions and cleaning up destruction caused by the war within Hungary.

12. Randolph L. Braham and Scott Miller, eds., *The Nazis' Last Victims: The Holocaust in Hungary* (Wayne State University Press, 1998).

13. Mária M. Kovács, *Liberal Professions and Illiberal Politics: Hungary from the Habsburgs to the Holocaust* (Woodrow Wilson Center Press, 1994), 126.

14. Quoted by Elek Karsai, ed., *"Fegyvertelen álltak az aknamezőkön . . ." Dokumentumok a munkaszolgálat történetéhez Magyarországon* ["They were standing there unarmed on the minefields . . ." Documents pertaining to the history of the labor service in Hungary] (Magyarországi Izraeliták Országos Képviselete, 1962), vol. 2, 155–74.

15. Kovács, *Liberal Professions and Illiberal Politics*, 127.

16. Kovács, *Liberal Professions and Illiberal Politics*, 131.

17. "1939. évi IV. törvénycikk a zsidók közéleti és gazdasági térfoglalásának korlátozásáról" [Law 1939: IV about the limitation of Jews' takeover of public life and the economy], *Net Jogtár* [Online Legal Collection], accessed November 14, 2024, https://net.jogtar.hu/ezer-ev-torveny?docid=93900004.TV&searchUrl=/ezer-ev-torvenyei%3Fkeyword%3D1939.%2520%25C3%25A9vi%2520IV.

18. Kovács, *Liberal Professions and Illiberal Politics*, 132.

19. Viktor Karády, "A soá mérlege az orvosi kamarák tagságában" [The Shoah's balance sheet in the membership of the doctors' chambers], in *A holokauszt Magyarországon hetven év múltán*, ed. Randolph L. Braham and András Kovács (Múlt és jövő, 2015), 171.

20. Kinga Frojimovics, "Jewish Refugees from Austria in the Hospitals of the Jewish Community of Pest After the 'Anschluß,'" *S.I.M.O.N.—Shoah: Intervention. Methods. Documentation* 5, no. 2 (2018): 97.

21. Viktor Karády, *Túlélők és újrakezdők: Fejezetek a magyar zsidóság szociológiájából 1945 után* [Survivors and re-starters: Chapters from the sociology of post-1945 Hungarian Jewry] (Múlt és jövő, 2002), 68–69.

22. Natalia Aleksiun, "Christian Corpses for Christians!: Dissecting the Anti-Semitism Behind the Cadaver Affair of the Second Polish Republic," *East European Politics and Societies* 25, no. 3 (2011): 393–409.

BIBLIOGRAPHY

ABBREVIATIONS

ÁBTL	Állambiztonsági Szolgálatok Történeti Levéltára (Historical Archives of the State Security Services)
ASUB	Archivio Storico dell'Università di Bologna (Historical Archives of the University of Bologna)
AUW	Archiv der Universität Wien (Archives of the University of Vienna)
MNL	Magyar Nemzeti Levéltár (Hungarian National Archives)
MZA	Moravský zemský archiv v Brně (Brno Moravian Provincial Archives)
PSZL	Politikatörténeti és Szakszervezeti Levéltár (Archives of Political History and the Trade Unions)
Veritas-OHA	Veritas Oral History Archívum (Oral History Archive of the Veritas Research Institute for History)

PRIMARY SOURCES

Legal Documents

"1920. évi XXV. törvénycikk a tudományegyetemekre, a műegyetemre, a budapesti egyetemi közgazdaságtudományi karra és a jogakadémiákra való beiratkozás szabályozásáról" [Law 1920: XXV on the regulation of enrollment to university, polytechnics, Faculty of Economics at the University of Budapest and law academies]. Net Jogtár [Online Legal Collection]. Accessed November 5, 2022. https://net.jogtar.hu/ezer-ev-torveny?docid=92000025.TV.

"1921. évi III. törvénycikk az állami és társadalmi rend hatályosabb védelméről" [Law 1921: III on the more effective protection of the order of state and society]. Net Jogtár [Online Legal Collection]. Accessed November 11, 2024. https://net.jogtar.hu/ezer-ev-torveny?docid=92100003.TV&searchUrl=/ezer-ev-torvenyei%3Fpagenum%3D38.

"1928. évi XIV. törvénycikk a tudományegyetemekre, a műegyetemre, a budapesti egyetemi közgazdaságtudományi karra és a jogakadémiákra való beiratkozás szabályozásáról szóló 1920. évi XXV. törvénycikk módosításáról" [Law 1928: XIV amending Law 1920: XXV on the regulation of enrollment to university, polytechnics, Faculty of Economics at the University of Budapest and law academies]. Net Jogtár [Online Legal Collection]. Accessed November 5, 2024, https://net.jogtar.hu/ezer-ev-torveny?docid=92800014.TV&searchUrl=/ezer-ev-torvenyei?keyword%3D1928:XIV.

"1938. évi XV. törvénycikk a társadalmi és a gazdasági élet egyensúlyának hatályosabb biztosításáról" [Law 1938: XV on the more effective securing of the balance of social and economic life]. Net Jogtár [Online Legal Collection]. Accessed November 14, 2024. https://net.jogtar.hu/ezer-ev-torveny?docid=93800015.TV.

"1939. évi IV. törvénycikk a zsidók közéleti és gazdasági térfoglalásának korlátozásáról" [Law 1939: IV about the limitation of Jews' takeover of public life and the economy]. *Net Jogtár* [Online Legal Collection]. Accessed November 14, 2024. https://net.jogtar.hu/ezer-ev-torveny?docid=93900004.TV&searchUrl=/ezer-ev-torvenyei%3Fkeyword%3D1939.%2520%25C3%25A9vi%2520IV.

"A. m. kir. vallás- és közoktatásügyi miniszter 1920. évi 123.033. számú rendelete a tudományegyetemekre, a műegyetemre, a budapesti egyetemi közgazdaságtudományi karra és a jogakadémiára való beiratkozás szabályozásáról" [Order No. 123.033 of 1920 by the minister of religion and public education about the regulation of enrollment to university, polytechnics, Faculty of Economics at the University of Budapest and law academies]. In *Magyarországi Rendeletek Tára*, Ötvennegyedik folyam [Collection of the Orders of Hungary, vol. 54]. Magy. Kir. Belügyminisztérium, 1920.

Az 1906.évi május hó 19-ére hirdetett országgyűlés képviselőházi naplója [The protocols of the Lower House of the Parliament announced for May 19, 1906]. Vol. 5. Athenaeum, 1907.

Előpataki [pen name]. *Aforizmák a zsidókról: Társadalomtudományi eredmények alapján* [Aphorisms about the Jews: Based on social scientific investigations]. Buzárovits Gusztáv, 1911.

Archival Sources

"Ausweis über die an der technischen Hochschule in Brünn inskribierten Hörer ungarischer Staatsangehörigkeit." B34 Německá technika Brno/Fascikl 424 Sign. 8./Statistika zapsaných 1917–29, MZA.

"Boncolási jegyzőkönyv" [Autopsy report], November 23, 1950. Folder "Miklós Szűcs" No. 2.1, I/98 (V-142821), ÁBTL.
"Brief von Rudolf Nowak in Angelegenheit des Sohnes Ing. Rudolf Nowak wegen Ausfertigung einer Bestätigung an das Rektorat der deutschen technischen Hochschule in Brünn." January 18, 1939/B34 Německá technika Brno/Fascikl. 526 Sign. 79a Discipl. zál. studentů 1932–45, MZA.
"Határozat az exhumálás elrendeléséről" [Decision on ordering exhumation]. April 6, 1964. Folder "Miklós Szűcs" No. 2.1, I/98 (V-142821), ÁBTL.
"Kik voltak az ellenség ügynökei a délamerikai szabad magyar mozgalomban, vagy kikről feltehető, hogy azok voltak?" [Who were the enemy's agents in the South American Hungarian movement or who can be assumed to be?]. Folder No. 2.1. I/54-b (V-142731/2), folder's topic: Ádám György, ÁBTL.
"Mitgliederliste des akademischen Vereines jüdischer Mediziner aufgenommen am 5. November 1927" [List of members of the Jewish Medics' Association on November 5, 1927]. S164.120, AUW.
"Statuten des Vereines ungarisch sprechender Wiener Hochschüler 6.XII.1929" [Statutes of the Hungarian Speaking Viennese Students, December 6, 1929]. S164.201, AUW.
Á.V.H. Vizsgálati dosszié Jacobson 101890/6/A. VII/13-g/Feljegyzések a cionistákkal kapcsolatban / Feljegyzés a "brünniek csoportjáról" [State Protection Authority investigative file "Jacobson" 101890/6/A. VII/13-g/Notes on the Zionists / Notes on the "Brno Group"], December 3, 1952, ÁBTL.
Farkas, Vladimir. Interview by Péter Borenich, 1985–88, interview no. 200. Veritas-OHA.
Fascicolo degli studenti, Facoltà di Medicina a Chirurgia 6625 Fischer Julie [Students' files no. 6625, Faculty of Medicine and Chirurgy, Fischer, Julie], ASUB.
Fascicolo degli studenti, Medicina e Chirurgia 11856 Borgida Veronika [Students' files no. 11856, Faculty of Medicine and Chirurgy, Borgida, Veronika], ASUB.
Juranics, Antalné Döme Piroska visszamelékezései [Recollections by Piroska Döme/ Mrs. Antal Juranics], I. March 1967. 867.f.d-2, PSZL.
Kádár, László. *Visszaemlékezéseim a kommunista mozgalomban való, felszabadulás előtti tevékenységemről* [My memories about my activity in the pre-liberation Communist movement]. September 1, 1961. 867.2/k-235 B, PSZL.
Perczel, Károly. Interview by Ilona Dér Szabóné, 1986, interview no. 44, Veritas-OHA.
Sitzung No. I. 5. Oktober 1933/Německá technika Brno/Kniha 201 Protokoly sezení profesorského sbor 1933–34, MZA.
Szabolcsi Lajos jelentése a Központi Zsidó Diákbizottság működéséről. Jelentés a Magyarországi Izraeliták Országos Irodájának 1929. évi működéséről [Report by Lajos Szabolcsi on the activity of the Central Jewish Student Aid Committee to the Office of Israelites of Hungary. Report on the activities of the Office of

Israelites of Hungary in 1929]. K28 (Department of Nationalities and Minorities), 14/53rd item, MNL.

Verhandlungsschrift No. XII vom 16. Juni 1933 Punkt IV.d./B34 Německá technika Brno/Fascikl. 526 Sign. 79a Discipl. zál. studentů 1932–45, MZA.

Visszaemlékezés a magyar diákok kommunista mozgalmára Brünnben 1928–1938 [Recollection about the Communist movement of Hungarian students in Brno, 1928–1938], March 28, 1972, 867.f.1/b-325, PSZL.

Newspaper and Journal Articles

Ballagi, Ernő. "Harc a numerus clausus ellen" [Struggle against the numerus clausus]. *Egyenlőség*, November 26, 1927, 15.

Czeke, Marianne, and Emma Ritoók. "Nők az egyetemen" [Women at university]. *Napkelet* 3, no. 5 (1925): 496–504.

Egyenlőség. "Nincs többé bujdosó diák . . . [No more wandering students...]" August 25, 1938, 3–4.

Kornis, Gyula. "Nők az egyetemen" [Women at university]. *Napkelet* 3, no. 1 (1925): 60–69.

Kovács, Alajos. "Magyarországi zsidó hallgatók a hazai és külföldi főiskolákon" [Hungarian Jewish students at Hungarian and foreign universities]. *Magyar Statisztikai Szemle* 16, no. 9. (1938): 897–902.

Népszava. "A kommunistasággal vádolt tanárok és egyetemi hallgatók pöre" [The trial of university students and instructors accused with Communism]. October 4, 1932, 7–8.

Pünkösti, Árpád. "Merni meghalni? Merni élni?" [Daring to die? Daring to live?]. *Új Tükör* 25, no. 47 (1988): 6–8.

Tormay, Cécile. "Beköszöntő." In *MANSZ Almanach az 1920-as évre* [The National Alliance of Hungarian Women's almanac for the year 1920]. Szt. István Társulat, 1919.

Weinberger, Jolán. "Levél Genovából: Otthont a bolygó zsidóknak!" [Letter form Genova: Shelter for the wandering Jews!]. *Egyenlőség*, April 7, 1938, 17.

Yearbook of the Hebrew University of Jerusalem. Hebrew University of Jerusalem, 1957.

Private Unpublished Sources

"The Adventurous Journey of the Oropesa." Family document. Courtesy of Éva Karádi.

Bánki, Esther, and Ivan Ivanji. Interview by Ágnes Katalin Kelemen, April 30, 2019.

Döme, Piroska. *Családtörténet* [Family history]. Private document, 2002. Private collection of György Seres.

Kardos, Erzsébet. Letter to Ödön Bánki, around 1925. Private collection of Esther Bánki.
Kardos, Erzsébet. Letter to Ödön Bánki, first half of the 1920s. Private collection of Esther Bánki.
Somló, Ida. Letter to Ödön Bánki without date and place. Private collection of Esther Bánki.
Somló, Ida. Letter without date and place. Private collection of Esther Bánki.
Talyigás, Katalin, and András Talyigás. Interview by Ágnes Katalin Kelemen, March 15, 2021.
Vadas, Jolán. Letter to Imre Erdős, October 4, 1946. Private collection of Éva Karádi.
Zoltán, Tamás. Interview by Ágnes Katalin Kelemen, March 17, 2021.

Published Ego Documents (Letters, Autobiographies, Memoirs, Diaries)

Bíró-Balogh, Tamás, ed. *Különben magyar költő vagyok. Radnóti Miklós levelezése* [Otherwise I am a Hungarian poet: The correspondence of Miklós Radnóti]. Vol. 1. Jaffa, 2017.
Bónis, Ferenc, ed. *Szabolcsi Bence lipcsei levelei Kodályhoz* [Bence Szabolcsi's letters to Kodály from Leipzig]. Kodály Intézet, 1994.
Czitrom, Veronica, Steven Czitrom, and Paul Czitrom. *Carolyn and Laszlo: What a Life!; The Baus, Feuerstein, Czitrom and Lusztig Families.* Published in Spanish as *Carolyn y Laszlo: Qué vida!; Las familias Baus, Feuerstein, Czitrom y Lusztig.* Veronica, Steven, and Paul Czitrom Baus, 2001.
Döme, Piroska. "Diákévek és hazatérés" [Student years and return]. *Valóság* 25, no. 6 (1982): 86–101.
Döme, Piroska. *Fény és árnyék* [Light and shadow]. Kossuth, 1983.
Farádi, László. *Diagnózis az életemről* [A diagnosis of my life]. Gondolat, 1983.
Fenyő, Lili. *Pillanatfelvételek a külföldön élő magyar diákság életéből* [Snapshots from the life of Hungarian students abroad]. Jupiter Nyomda, 1929.
Hábermann, Anna Maria. *Labirinto di carta* [The labyrinth of papers]. Proedi Editore, 2010.
Kis, Ádám, and Balázs Kis, eds. *Apám levelei: Legendák, emlékek; 1942, Oroszország–1926, Csehszlovákia* [My father's letters: Legends, memories; 1942, Russia–1926, Czechoslovakia]. SZAK Kiadó, 2015.
Kis, György. Letter to his family, February 21, 1926, in Kis and Kis, *Apám levelei.*
Kis, György. Letter to his family, May 9, 1926, in Kis and Kis, *Apám levelei.*
Klein, Dora. *Vivere e sopravvivere. Diario 1936–1945* [To live and to survive: Diary 1936–1945]. Mursia, 2001.
Koestler, Arthur. *Arrow in the Blue: The First Volume of an Autobiography; 1905–1931.* Vintage, 2005.

Kun, Miklós. *Kedves Hilda: Egy elmeorvos az elmebeteg huszadik században* [Dear Hilda: A psychiatrist in the insane twentieth century]. Medicina, 2004.

Linksz, Arthur. *Harc a harmadik halállal: Ifjúságom Magyarországon* [Fighting the third death: My youth in Hungary]. Magvető, 1990.

Szabolcsi, Bence. Letter to His Sister-in-Law, Erzsébet Mészáros, November 15, 1922, in György Kroó, *Szabolcsi Bence*, vol.1. Liszt Ferenc Zeneművészeti Főiskola, 1994.

Szabolcsi, Bence. Letter to Lajos Szabolcsi, December 22, 1922, in *Szabolcsi Bence*, by György Kroó. Liszt Ferenc Zeneművészeti Főiskola, 1994.

Szabolcsi, Bence. Letter to Zoltán Kodály, November 4, 1921, in *Szabolcsi Bence lipcsei levelei Kodályhoz* [Bence Szabolcsi's letters to Kodály from Leipzig], edited by Ferenc Bónis. Kodály Intézet, 1994.

Szabolcsi, Lajos. *Két emberöltő: Az Egyenlőség évtizedei (1881–1931)* [Two generations: The decades of "Egyenlőség" (1881–1931)]. MTA Judaisztikai Kutatócsoport, 1993.

Szabolcsi, Miklós. "Apámról és emlékiratairól" [About my father and his memoirs]. In L. Szabolcsi, *Két emberöltő*.

Teich Alasia, Simone. *Un medico della Resistenza: I luoghi, gli incontri, le scelte* [A physician of the resistance: The places, the encounters, the choices]. SEB27, 2010.

Tömpe, István. *Az elitek árulása* [The betrayal by the elites]. Noran Libro, 2015.

Weidlinger, Tom. *The Restless Hungarian: Modernism, Madness, and the American Dream* SparkPress, 2019.

Zweig, Stefan. *The World of Yesterday: An Autobiography*. Viking Press, 1943.

SECONDARY LITERATURE

Ablonczy, Balázs. *Trianon-legendák* [Legends of Trianon]. Jaffa, 2015.

Aleksiun, Natalia. "Christian Corpses for Christians!: Dissecting the Anti-Semitism Behind the Cadaver Affair of the Second Polish Republic." *East European Politics and Societies* 25, no. 3 (2011): 393–409.

Aronson, Michael. *Troubled Waters: The Origins of the 1881 Anti-Jewish Pogroms in Russia*. University of Pittsburgh Press, 1990.

Balogh, Elemér. *A salvus conductus és a magyar peregrináció* [Salvus conductus and Hungarian peregrination]. József Attila Tudományegyetem, 1996.

Bánki, Esther. "'Denn Du denkst doch nicht etwa, dass eine Frau ein Haus bauen kann': Das Leben der Architektin Zsuzsanna Bánki 1912–1944." In *Entfernt: Frauen des Bauhauses während der NS-Zeit—Verfolgung und Exil* [Removed: The women of the Bauhaus during National Socialism—Persecution and Exile], edited by Inge Hansen-Schaberg, Wolfgang Thöner, and Adriane Feustel. Edition Text + Kritik, 2012.

Ben-Sasson, Haim Hillel, ed. *A History of the Jewish People*. Harvard University Press, 1985.

Bibó, István. "Zsidókérdés Magyarországon 1944" [The Jewish Question in Hungary in 1944]. In *Zsidókérdés, asszimiláció, antiszemitizmus: Tanulmányok a zsidókérdésről a huszadik századi Magyarországon* [Jewish question, assimilation, antisemitism: Studies on the Jewish question in twentieth century Hungary], edited by Péter Hanák. Gondolat, 1984.

Bodó, Béla. *The White Terror: Antisemitic and Political Violence in Hungary, 1919–1921*. Routledge, 2019.

Borgos, Anna. "A magyar pszichoanalízis ígérete: Kardos Erzsébet [A promise of Hungarian psychoanalysis: Erzsébet Kardos]." *Imágó* 10, no. 3 (2021): 33–47.

Borgos, Anna. "'Put a Stop to the Excessive Influx': The Rhetoric of Restriction Regarding Female and Jewish Students at Budapest University, 1900–1930." *Hungarian Studies Review* 48, no. 1 (2021): 48–78.

Braham, Randolph L., and Scott Miller, eds. *The Nazis' Last Victims: The Holocaust in Hungary*. Wayne State University Press, 1998.

Breuer, Mordechai. *Ha-Yeshivah ha-Ashkenazit* [The Ashkenazic academy]. Faculty of Humanities–Department of the History of the Jewish People, 1962.

Cammarano, Cristina. "Women Writers and Education." In *A History of Western Philosophy of Education in the Middle Ages and Renaissance*, vol. 2, edited by Kevin Gary. Bloomsbury, 2021.

Clot, Lioudmila. "When Swiss Universities Led the Way in Gender Equity." *Swissinfo*, May 7, 2022. https://www.swissinfo.ch/eng/when-swiss-universities-led-the-way-in-gender-equity/47493416.

Congdon, Lee. *Exile and Social Thought*. Princeton University Press, 1991.

Csatlós, Judit, ed. *Vízizrí: Munkáskultúra a Duna partján* [Water fun: Workers' culture on the bank of the Danube]. Exhibition catalog. Kassák Museum, 2016.

Csunderlik, Péter. *Radikálisok, szabadgondolkodók, ateisták: A Galilei Kör története, 1908–1919* [Radicals, free-thinkers, athesits: The history of the Galilei Circle, 1908–1919]. Napvilág, 2020.

De La Croix, David, and Mara Vitale. "Women in European Academia Before 1800—Religion, Marriage, and Human Capital." *European Review of Economic History* 27, no. 3 (2023): 506–32.

Diemling, Maria. "Anthonius Margaritha and His 'Der Gantz Jüdisch Glaub.'" In *Jews, Judaism, and the Reformation in Sixteenth-Century Germany*, edited by Dean Phillip Bell and Stephen G. Burnett. Brill, 2006.

Dubnow, Simon. *History of the Jews in Poland and Russia from the Earliest Times Until the Present Day* [1915]. Jewish Publication Society of America, 1918. Republished, Avotaynu, 2000.

Ebner, Paulus, and Juliane Mikoletzky, *Vom Studentencomité zur HTU: Zur Geschichte der Studierenden an der Technischen Universität Wien und ihren Vorgängerinstitutionen* [From students' committee to student union: A history of the students of the Viennese Technical University and its predecessors]. Universitätsarchiv der Technischen Universität Wien, 2006.

Egriné, Szonja T. "Radnóti Miklós egy éve Liberecben" [One year of Miklós Radnóti in Liberec]. *Forrás* 43, no. 9 (2011): 41–52.

"Ein mutiger Weg in schwierigen Zeiten—Das Leben der Bauhäuslerin Zsuzsanna Bánki [A courageous road in difficult times—The life of Bauhaus architect Zsuzsanna Bánki]." In *100 éves a Bauhaus* [The Bauhaus is 100 years old], edited by András Veöreös and Tamás Horváth. Győr-Moson-Sopron Megyei Építész Kamara, 2019.

Erdei, Ferenc. "A magyar társadalom a két háború között I" [Hungarian society between the wars I]. *Valóság* 19, no. 4 (1976): 22–53.

Erdei, Ferenc. "A magyar társadalom a két háború között II" [Hungarian society between the wars II]. *Valóság* 19, no. 5 (1976): 36–58.

Esposito, Anna, and Micaela Procaccia. "'Iudei de Urbe': La testimonianza di un inventario" ['Iudei de Urbe': The testimony of an inventory]. In *Un pontificato ed una città: Sisto IV* (1471–1484); *Atti del convegno Roma 3–7 dicembre 1984* [A pontificate and a city: Sixtus IV (1471–1484); Acts of the conference in Rome December 3–7, 1984], edited by Concetta Ranieri, Diego Quaglioni, Francesca Niutta, and Massimo Miglio. Scuola Vaticana di paleografia, diplomatica e archivistica, 1986.

Falek, Pascale. "A Precarious Life: East European Female Jewish Students in Interwar Belgium." PhD diss., European University Institute, 2011.

Fedeles-Czeferner, Dóra. *Nőmozgalom, nemzetköziség, önreprezentáció. Feministák az Osztrák-Magyar Monarchia alkonyán* [Women's movement, internationality, self-representation. Feminists at the dusk of the Austro-Hungarian Monarchy]. Kronosz, 2023.

Fenyves, Katalin. "When Sexism Meets Racism: The 1920 Numerus Clausus Law in Hungary." *Hungarian Cultural Studies* 4, no. 4 (2011): 87–102.

Frank, Tibor. *Double Exile: Migrations of Jewish-Hungarian Professionals Through Germany to the United States, 1919–1945*. Peter Lang, 2009.

Freidenreich, Harriet Pass. *Female, Jewish, and Educated: The Lives of Central European University Women*. Indiana University Press, 2002.

Freidenreich, Harriet Pass. "Gender, Identity and Community: Jewish University Women in Germany and Austria." In *In Search of Jewish Community: Jewish Identities in Germany and Austria, 1918–1933*, edited by Michael Brenner and Derek J. Penslar. Indiana University Press, 1998.

Frojimovics, Kinga. "Jewish Refugees from Austria in the Hospitals of the Jewish Community of Pest After the 'Anschluß.'" *S.I.M.O.N.—Shoah: Intervention, Methods, Documentation* 5, no. 2 (2018): 95–103.

Gábor, Gyula. *A numerus clausus és a zsidó egyetem* [The *numerus clausus* and the Jewish university]. Fráter Nyomda, 1924.

García-Ballester, Luis, Lola Ferre, and Eduard Feliu. "Jewish Appreciation of Fourteenth-Century Scholastic Medicine." *Osiris*, 2nd ser., 6 (1990): 85–117.

Gidó, Attila. *Két évtized: A kolozsvári zsidóság a két világháború között* [Two decades: The Jewry of Cluj between the two world wars]. Erdélyi Múzeum-Egyesület, 2016.

Greyerz, Kaspar von. "Ego-Documents: The Last Word?" *German History* 28, no. 3 (2010): 273–82.

Gyáni, Gábor. "Polgárosodás mint zsidó identitás" [Embourgeoisement as Jewish identity]. *BUKSZ* 9, no. 3 (1997): 266–76.

Hajdu, Tibor. "A Rajk-per háttere és fázisai" [The background and phases of the Rajk-trial]. *Társadalmi Szemle* 47, no. 11 (1992): 17–36.

Hanák, Péter. "Problems of Jewish Assimilation in Austria-Hungary in the Nineteenth and Twentieth Centuries." In *The Power of the Past: Essays for Eric Hobsbawm*, edited by Pat Thane, Geoffrey Crossick, and Roderick Floud. Cambridge University Press, 1984.

Hanak-Lettner, Werner, ed. *Die Universität als Kampfzone—The University: A Battle Ground*. Jüdisches Museum Wien, 2015.

Hanebrink, Paul. *In Defense of Christian Hungary*. Cornell University Press, 2006.

Hargittai, István. *The Martians of Science: Five Physicists Who Changed the Twentieth Century*. Oxford University Press, 2006.

Hetényi, Zsuzsa. *In a Maelstrom: The History of Russian-Jewish Prose, 1860–1940*. Central European University Press, 2008.

Hodos, George H. *Show Trials. Stalinist Purges in Eastern Europe 1948–1954*. Praeger, 1987.

Horváth, Zsolt K. "Szubkultúrák forrásvidékén. Népi kultúra, munkáskultúra és baloldali közösségiség Vajda Lajos életműve körül" [The sources of subcultures. Popular culture, workers' culture and leftist communality around the oeuvre of Lajos Vajda]. *Fordulat* 7, no. 3 (Winter 2009): 47–64.

Huber, Andreas. "Antisemitic Pacts: Student Fraternities and the Exclusion of Jews at Austrian Universities in the Interwar Period." In Miller and Szapor, *Quotas*.

Jewish Encyclopedia. "Levita, Elijah." Accessed November 6, 2024. https://www.jewishencyclopedia.com/articles/9864-levita-elijah.

Jewish Encyclopedia. "Saxony." Accessed October 15, 2024. https://www.jewishencyclopedia.com/articles/13241-saxony.

Jewish Encyclopedia. "Vienna." Accessed October 15, 2024. https://jewishencyclopedia.com/articles/14699-vienna.

Jewish Virtual Library. "Universities." Accessed October 14, 2024. https://www.jewishvirtuallibrary.org/universities.

Jobst, Ágnes. "Az emancipáció eszméjének érvényesülése: Hugonnai Vilma élete" [The realization of the idea of emancipation: The life of Vilma Hugonnai]. In *Asszonysorsok a 20. században* [Women's lives in the twentieth century], edited by Margit Balogh and Katalin S. Nagy. BME Kommunikáció és Szociológia Tanszék, 2000.

Kanarfogel, Ephraim. *Jewish Education and Society in the High Middle Ages*. Wayne State University Press, 1992.

Karády, Victor. "Funktionswandel der österreichischen Hochschulen in der Ausbildung der ungarischen Fachintelligenz vor und nach dem Ersten Weltkrieg" [The changing function of Austrian colleges and universities in the training of Hungarian professional intelligentsia before and after the First World War]. In *Bildungswesen und Sozialstruktur in Mitteleuropa im 19. und 20. Jahrhundert. Education and Social Structure in Central Europe in the 19th and 20th Centuries*, edited by Victor Karády and Wolfgang Mitter. Böhlau, 1990.

Karády, Victor. "Jewish Over-Schooling Revisited: The Case of Hungarian Secondary Education in the Old Regime (1900–1941)." *Yearbook of the Jewish Studies Programme (CEU)*, 1999, 75–91.

Karády, Victor. "Jews in the Hungarian Medical Profession, 1782–1947. A Sociohistorical Report." In Miller and Szapor, *Quotas*.

Karady, Victor, and Peter Tibor Nagy. "Culturally Composite Elites, Regime Changes and Social Crises in Multi-Ethnic and Multi-Confessional Eastern Europe (The Carpathian Basin and the Baltics in Comparison, cc. 1900–1950)." Accessed November 6, 2024, http://elites08.uni.hu.

Karády, Viktor. *Felekezeti viszonyok és iskolázási egyenlőtlenségek Magyarországon, 1867–1945* [Denominational relations and educational inequalities in Hungary, 1867–1945]. Réplika Kör, 1997.

Karády, Viktor. "Nők a modern iskolázás korai fázisában" [Women in the early phase of modern schooling]. In *Felekezeti viszonyok és iskolázási egyenlőtlenségek Magyarországon, 1867–1945* [Denominational relations and educational inequalities in Hungary, 1867–1945], edited by Viktor Karády. Replika Kör, 1997.

Karády, Viktor. "A soá mérlege az orvosi kamarák tagságában" [The Shoah's balance sheet in the membership of the doctors' chambers]. In *A holokauszt Magyarországon hetven év múltán*, edited by Randolph L. Braham and András Kovács. Múlt és jövő, 2015.

Karády, Viktor. "A társadalmi egyenlőtlenségek Magyarországon a nők felsőbb iskoláztatásának korai fázisában" [Social inequalities in the early phases of women's higher learning in Hungary]. In *Férfiuralom: Írások nőkről, férfiakról, feminizmusról* [Patriarchy: Writings about women, men, feminism], edited by Miklós Hadas. Replika Kör, 1994.

Karády, Viktor. *Túlélők és újrakezdők: Fejezetek a magyar zsidóság szociológiájából 1945 után* [Survivors and Re-Starters: Chapters from the sociology of post-1945 Hungarian Jewry]. Múlt és jövő, 2002.

Karády, Viktor. *Zsidóság, modernizáció, polgárosodás* [Jewishness, modernization, embourgeoisement]. Cserépfalvi, 1997.

Karsai, Elek, ed. *"Fegyvertelen álltak az aknamezőkön . . .": Dokumentumok a munkaszolgálat történetéhez Magyarországon*. 2. köt. ["They were standing there unarmed on the minefields . . .": Documents pertaining to the history of the labor service in Hungary. Vol. 2]. Magyarországi Izraeliták Országos Képviselete, 1962.

Katz, Jacob. *From Prejudice to Destruction: Anti-Semitism, 1700–1933*. Harvard University Press, 1980.

Katz, Jacob. *Tradition and Crisis: Jewish Society at the End of the Middle Ages*. New York University Press, 1993.

Katzburg, Nathaniel. *Fejezetek az újkori zsidó történelemből Magyarországon* [Chapters from the Early Modern history of Jews in Hungary]. Osiris, 1999.

Kelemen, Ágnes Katalin. "The Exiles of the Numerus Clausus in Italy." *Judaica Olomucensia* 2, nos. 1–2 (2014): 56–103.

Kelemen, Ágnes Katalin. "Migration and Exile: Hungarian Medical Students in Vienna and Prague, 1920–1938." In *At the Crossroads of Human Fate and History: Studies in Honour of Tibor Frank on His 70th Birthday*, edited by János Kenyeres et al. Eötvös Loránd University, School of English and American Studies, 2018.

Kelemen, Ágnes Katalin. "Next Year in Brno? Brno's Significance for Hungarian Jews in the Age of the Numerus Clausus and Beyond." In Miller and Szapor, *Quotas*.

Kelemen, Ágnes Katalin. "Peregrination in the Age of the Numerus Clausus: Hungarian Jewish Students in Interwar Europe." PhD diss., Central European University, 2019.

Kelemen, Ágnes Katalin. "Refugees and the 'Other Hungary': The Historiography of the Reception of Refugees in Twentieth-Century Hungary." *Zeitschrift für Ostmitteleuropa-Forschung/Journal of East Central European Studies* 71, no. 4 (2022): 491–514.

Kempler, Kurt. "Századvági küzdelem a nők egyetemi felvételéért Magyarországon" [Struggle for women's admission to university in Hungary on the turn of the century]. *Orvosi Hetilap* 115, no. 30 (1974): 1775–77.

Kerepeszki, Róbert. "Nationalist Masculinity and Right-Wing Radical Student Movements in Interwar Hungary." *Hungarian Studies Review* 41, nos. 1–2 (2014): 61–88.

Kerepeszki, Róbert. "A numerus clausus 1928. évi módosításának hatása Debrecenben" [The impact of the 1928 amendment of the numerus clausus in Debrecen]. *Múltunk* 50, no. 4. (2005): 42–75.

Klein, Bernard. "Hungarian Politics and the Jewish Question in the Inter-War Period." *Jewish Social Studies* 28, no. 2 (1966): 79–98.

Klier, John. *Russians, Jews, and the Pogroms of 1881–1882*. Cambridge University Press, 2011.

Konrád, Miklós. "The Prehistory of the Hungarian Numerus Clausus Law: Political Antisemitism in Hungary, 1895–1914." In Miller and Szapor, *Quotas*.

Kósa-Grimm, András Kristóf. "Schmidt, a rendőrspicli? Stolte István és az 1932-es kommunista szervezkedés a Pázmány Péter Tudományegyetemen" [Schmidt, the spy of the police? István Stolte and the 1932 Communist organization at the Pázmány Péter University]. *Múltunk* 64, no. 1 (2019): 120–50.

Kovács, Éva. *Felemás asszimiláció: A kassai zsidóság a két világháború között (1918–1938)* [Ambivalent assimilation: The Jewry of Košice between the two world wars, 1918–1938]. Fórum Kisebbségkutató Intézet, 2004.

Kovács, Mária M. *The Beginnings of Anti-Jewish Legislation. The 1920 Numerus Clausus Law in Hungary.* Central European University Press, 2023.

Kovács, Mária M. *Liberal Professions and Illiberal Politics: Hungary from the Habsburgs to the Holocaust.* Woodrow Wilson Center Press, 1994.

Kovács, Sándor. "A magyar unitárius peregrinatio academica vázlatos története 1848 után" [Outline of Hungarian Unitarians' peregrination academica after 1848]. *Keresztény Magvető* 115, no. 4 (2009): 561–87.

Krohn, Claus-Dieter, and Rita Kimber. *Intellectuals in Exile: Refugee Scholars and the New School for Social Research.* University of Massachusetts Press, 1993.

Kroó, György. *Szabolcsi Bence.* Vol. 1. Liszt Ferenc Zeneművészeti Főiskola, 1994.

Krzywiec, Grzegorz. "Anti-Jewish Quotas in Interwar Poland: Toward a Reconsideration of the Appeal of Fascism in East Central Europe." In Miller and Szapor, *Quotas.*

Kubinyi, András. "Städtische Bürger und Universitätsstudenten in Ungarn am Ende des Mittelalters" [Urban citizens and university students in Hungary in the late Middle Ages]. In *Stadt und Universität im Mittelalter und in der früheren Neuzeit* [City and university in the Middle Ages and in the Early Modern Period], edited by Erich Maschke and Jürgen Sydow. Thorbecke, 1977.

Ladányi, Andor. *Az egyetemi ifjúság az ellenforradalom első éveiben, 1919–1921* [The university youth in the first years of the Counter-Revolution, 1919–1921]. Akadémiai Kiadó, 1979.

Ladányi, Andor. "Két évforduló. A nők felsőfokú tanulmányainak száz éve" [Two anniversaries. A century of women's higher education]. *Educatio* 5, no. 3 (1996): 379–89.

Ladányi, Andor. "On the Amendment to the Hungarian Numerus Clausus Act." In *Studies on the First Anti-Jewish Law and Academic Anti-Semitism in Modern Central Europe,* edited by Victor Karády and Péter Tibor Nagy. Pasts Inc. Centre for Historical Research, History Department of the Central European University, 2012.

Lanouette, William, and Bela Silard. *Genius in the Shadows: A Biography of Leo Szilard—The Man Behind the Bomb.* University of Chicago Press, 1992.

Litván, György. "Irányzatok és viták a bécsi magyar emigrációban" [Streams and debates in the Viennese Hungarian emigration]. In *Magyar gondolat–szabad gondolat* [Hungarian thought–Free thought]. Osiris, 2008.

Magyar Életrajzi Lexikon [Hungarian Biographical Lexicon]. Vol. 2, L–Z. Akadémiai kiadó, 1982.

Majarelli, Stanislao, und Ugolino Nicolini. *Il monte dei poveri di Perugia: Periodo delle origini* (1462–1474) [The credit bank of Perugia: The beginnings (1462–1474)]. Banca del Monte di credito, 1962.

Manitz, Irina. "Die akademische 'Ausländerfrage' in russischsprachigen Periodika in Deutschland vor dem 1. Weltkrieg" [The 'Ausländerfrage' in Russian press in Germany before the First World War]. In *Universitäten als Brücken in Europa: Studien zur Geschichte der studentischen Migration* [Universities as Bridges in Europe: Studies on the History of Student Migration], edited by Hartmut Rüdiger Peter and Natalia Tikhonov. Peter Lang, 2003.

Marjanucz, László. "Zsidó identitás és asszimiláció Magyarországon. Interjú" [Jewish identity and assimilation in Hungary. Interview with Viktor Karády]. In *Zsidóság, modernizáció, polgárosodás* [Jewry, modernization, embourgeoisement], by Viktor Karády. Cserépfalvi, 1997.

Miller, Michael L. "A Foreign Policy Fiasco? Reactions to the Hungarian Numerus Clausus in Weimar Germany." In Miller and Szapor, *Quotas*.

Miller, Michael L. "From White Terror to Red Vienna: Hungarian Jewish Students in Interwar Austria." In *Wien und die Jüdische Erfahrung 1900–1938: Akkulturation—Antisemitismus—Zionismus* [Vienna and the Jewish Experience 1900–1938: Acculturation—Antisemitism—Zionism], edited by Barbara Eichinger and Frank Stern. Böhlau, 2009.

Miller, Michael L., and Judith Szapor, eds. *Quotas: The "Jewish Question" and Higher Education in Central Europe, 1880–1945*. Berghahn, 2024.

Miron, Guy. *The Waning of Emancipation: Jewish History, Memory, and the Rise of Fascism in Germany, France, and Hungary*. Wayne University Press, 2011.

Mocsy, István I. *The Effects of World War I: The Uprooted; Hungarian Refugees and Their Impact on Hungary's Domestic Politics 1918–1921*. Social Science Monographs, 1983.

Münster, Ladislao. "Fu Jacob Mantino lettore effettivo dello studio di Bologna?" [Was Jacob Mantino actually a lecturer at the University of Bologna?]. *Rassegna mensile di Israel* 20, no. 8 (1954): 310–21.

Münster, Ladislao. "Laurea in medicina conferita dallo studio ferrarese ad un ebreo nel 1426" [A medical degree conferred by the University of Ferrara upon a Jew in 1426]. *Ferrara viva: Rivista storica e di attualità* 3, nos. 7–8 (1961): 63–72.

Nagy, Péter Tibor. "The Numerus Clausus Law in Inter-War Hungary: Pioneering European Antisemitism." *East European Jewish Affairs* 35, no. 1 (2005): 13–22.

Nardi, Paolo. "Relations with Authority." In *Universities in the Middle Ages*, edited by Hilde de Ridder-Symoens. Cambridge University Press, 1992.

Nastasă, Lucian. *Antisemitismul universitar în România (1919–1939): Mărturii documentare* [Academic antisemitism in Romania, 1919–1939: Documentary testimonies]. Editura Institutului pentru Studierea Problemelor Minorităţilor Naţi-Kriterion, 2011.

Nathans, Benjamin. *Beyond the Pale: The Jewish Encounter with Late Imperial Russia.* University of California Press, 2002.

Oertzen, Christine von. "Whose World? Internationalism, Nationalism and the Struggle over the 'Language Question' in the International Federation of University Women, 1919–1932." *Contemporary European History* 25, no. 1 (2016): 275–90.

Palasik, Mária. "A magy nők a műszaki felsőoktatásban, a mérnöki pályán és a műszaki tudományokban a XX. században" [Hungarian women in technical higher education, in the engineering profession and in technical sciences during the twentieth century]. *Múltunk* 48, no. 3 (2003): 132–58.

Papp, Barbara. "Nőoktatás és 'képzett nők' a két világháború között" [Women's education and 'educated women' between the two world wars]. In *Zsombékok: Középosztályok és iskoláztatás Magyarországon a 19. század elejétől a 20. század közepéig* [Hills: Middle classes and education in Hungary from the early nineteenth to the mid-twentieth century], edited by György Kövér. Századvég, 2006.

Papp, Barbara, and Balázs Sipos. *Modern, diplomás nő a Horthy-korban* [Modern, intellectual women in the Horthy era]. Napvilág, 2017.

Pelini, Francesca, and Ilaria Pavan. *La doppia epurazione: L'Università di Pisa e le leggi razziali tra guerra e dopoguerra* [The double purge: The University of Pisa and the racial laws between war and post-war period]. Il Mulino, 2009.

Pfanner, Helmut F. *Exile in New York: German and Austrian Writers After 1933.* Wayne State University Press, 1983.

Raggam-Blesch, Michaela. "Zwischen Antisemitismus und Antifeminismus. Jüdische Frauen an der Wiener Universität" [Between antisemitism and antifeminism: Jewish women at the University of Vienna]. In *Alma Mater Antisemitica: Akademisches Milieu, Juden und Antisemitismus an den Universitäten Europas zwischen 1918 und 1939* [Alma Mater Antisemitica: Academic Milieu, Jews and antisemitism at Europe's universities between 1918 and 1939], edited by Regina Fritz, Grzegorz Rossolínski-Liebe, and Jana Starek. New Academic Press, 2016.

Ridder-Symoens, Hilde de. "Mobility." In *Universities in the Middle Ages.* Cambridge University Press, 1992.

Ridder-Symoens, Hilde de, ed. *Universities in the Middle Ages.* Cambridge University Press, 1992.

Romsics, Ignác. *Hungary in the Twentieth Century.* Osiris, 1999.

Ruderman, David, and Giuseppe Veltri, eds. *Cultural Intermediaries: Jewish Intellectuals in Early Modern Italy.* University of Pennsylvania Press, 2004:

Rummel, Erika. "Humanists, Jews and Judaism." In *Jews, Judaism, and the Reformation in Sixteenth-Century Germany,* edited by Dean Phillip Bell and Stephen G. Burnett. Brill, 2006.

Sarfatti, Michele. *The Jews in Mussolini's Italy: From Equality to Persecution*. University of Wisconsin Press, 2006.

Schneider, Márta. "Magyar ösztöndíjasok külföldön" [Hungarian stipendees abroad]. In *Régi és új peregrináció: Magyarok külföldön, külföldiek Magyarországon* [Old and new peregrination: Hungarians abroad, foreigners in Hungary], edited by Imre Békési, József Jankovics, László Kósa, and Judit Nyerges, vol. 2, *A peregrináció a magyar irodalom- és művelődéstörténet különböző periódusaiban* [Peregrination in different periods of the history of Hungarian literature and culture]. Nemzetközi Magyar Filológiai Társaság, 1993.

Shatzmiller, Joseph. *Jews, Medicine, and Medieval Society*. University of California Press, 1996.

Signori, Elisa. "Una 'peregrinatio academica' in età contemporanea: Gli studenti ebrei stranieri nelle Università italiane tra le due guerre" [A "Peregrinatio Academica" in the contemporary age: The foreign Jewish students at the Italian universities between the two wars]. *Annali di storia delle università italiane* 4, no. 1 (2000): 1000–1024.

Smith, Sidonie, and Julia Watson. *Reading Autobiography: A Guide for Interpreting Life Narratives*. University of Minnesota Press, 2010.

Sorescu, Andrei-Dan, and Raul Cârstocea. "The (Great) Numbers Game: Demographic Anxieties and Quotas in Nineteenth- and Twentieth-Century Romania and the Global Antisemitic Imaginary." In Miller and Szapor, *Quotas*.

Sorkin, David. "Enlightenment and Emancipation: German Jewry's Formative Age in Comparative Perspective." In *Comparing Jewish Societies*, edited by T. M. Endelman. University of Michigan Press, 1997.

Staliūnas, Darius. "Affirmative Action in the Western Borderlands of the Late Russian Empire?" *Slavic Review* 77, no. 3 (2018): 978–97.

Stranieri, Domenico. "La storia del Dott. Fenyves" [The story of Dr. Fenyves]. Personal blog, August 11, 2013. http://domenicostranieri.blogspot.com/2013/09/la-storia-del-dott-fenyves.html?m=1.

Szabó, Miklós. *Az újkonzervativizmus és a jobboldali radikalizmus története (1867–1918)* [The history of new conservativism and the radical right wing (1867–1918)]. Új Mandátum, 2003.

Szabó, Miklós. "Az 1901-es 'kereszt-mozgalom' (Adalék a magyarországi szélsőjobboldal történetéhez) [The 'cross-movement' of 1901. (Remarks on the history of the radical right wing in Hungary)]." *Történelmi Szemle* 13, no. 4 (1970): 483–516.

Szabó, Miloslav. "'Troublesome Foreigners': The Protests Against Jewish Students at Universities in Vienna, Bratislava and Brno, and the Dispute over Quotas in Czechoslovakia, 1929–32." In Miller and Szapor, *Quotas*.

Szapor, Judith. *The Hungarian Pocahontas: The Life and Times of Laura Polanyi Stricker, 1882–1959*. East European Monographs, 2005.

Szapor, Judith. *Hungarian Women's Activism in the Wake of the First World War: From Rights to Revanche*. Bloomsbury, 2017.

Szapor, Judith. "'You Can Become Anything, Except a Pediatrician': Exploring the Gendered Impact of Hungary's Numerus Clausus Law." In Miller and Szapor, *Quotas*.

Szegvári, Katalin N. *Numerus clausus rendelkezések az ellenforradalmi Magyarországon: a zsidó és nőhallgatók főiskolai felvételéről* [Numerus clausus regulations in counter-revolutionary Hungary: On the admission of female and Jewish students to higher education]. Akadémiai kiadó, 1988.

Szögi, László. "A külföldi egyetemjárás tömegessé válása a 19. század második felében" [The proliferation of external peregrination in the second half of the nineteenth century]. In *Pedagógia, Oktatás, Könyvtár: Ünnepi tanulmányok F. Dárdai Ágnes tiszteletére* [Pedagogy, education, library: Festschrift honoring Ágnes Dárdai F.], edited by Helga Csóka-Jaksa, Éva Schmelzer-Pohánka, and Gábor Szeberényi. Pécsi Egyetemi Könyvtár és Tudásközpont, 2014.

Szögi, László. "Magyarországi zsidó egyetemi hallgatók a német nyelvterület egyetemein és főiskoláin, 1789–1919" [Jewish students from Hungary at universities and colleges in the German-speaking territories, 1789–1919]. *ELTE Egyetemi Könyvtár Évkönyvei* 10, no.1. (2011): 107–18.

Szögi, László. "A nők egyetemi tanulmányainak kérdése a Budapesti orvostudományi karon" [The question of women's university studies in the medical faculty of the University of Budapest]. *Orvostörténeti Közlemények* 32, nos. 3–4 (1986): 139–42.

Szögi, László. "Peregrináció és reformáció: Milyen külföldi egyetemekre jártak tanulni a 16–18. századi magyar diákok?" [Peregrination and reformation: Which foreign universities did Hungarian students go to study in the sixteenth–eighteenth centuries?]. *Rubicon* 28, no. 12 (2017): 50–57.

Tamusné, Molnár Viktória. "Peregrinatio academica: külföldi egyetemjárás a Debreceni Református Kollégiumban a 16–17. században" [Peregrinatio academica: Studies abroad and the Calvinist collegium of Debrecen in the sixteenth–seventeenth centuries]. *Módszertani közlemények* 47, no. 5 (2007): 239–42.

Toaff, Ariel. *Il vino e la carne: Una comunità ebraica nel medioevo* [The wine and the meat: A Jewish community in the Middle Ages]. Il Mulino, 1989.

Ujvári, Péter, ed. *Zsidó lexikon* [Jewish lexicon]. Edition of the Jewish Lexicon, 1929.

Vámos, Éva Katalin. "Women's opportunities of studying and practising engineering in Hungary from 1895 to 1968." *Technikatörténeti Szemle* 23, no. 1 (1997–98): 101–31.

Vörös, Kati. "A Unique Contract: Interpretations of Modern Hungarian Jewish History." In *CEU Jewish Studies Yearbook III*, edited by András Kovács and Eszter Andor. CEU Jewish Studies Program, 2003.

Walton, Michael T. *Anthonius Margaritha and the Jewish Faith: Jewish Life and Conversion in Sixteenth-Century Germany.* Wayne State University Press, 2012.

Wengert, Timothy J. "Philip Melanchthon and the Jews: A Reappraisal." In *Jews, Judaism, and the Reformation in Sixteenth–Century Germany,* edited by Dean Phillip Bell and Stephen G. Burnett. Brill, 2006.

Wertheimer, Jack. "The 'Unwanted Element': East European Jews in Imperial Germany." *Leo Baeck Institute Yearbook* 26, no. 1 (1981): 23–46.

Zalai, Katalin. *"Idegenbe szakadt hazánk lányai": Magyar nők szovjet emigrációban a két világháború között* ["Our daughters in exile": Hungarian women in Soviet emigration between the two world wars]. Napvilág, 2022.

INDEX